About the Author

Samuel A Malone is a self-employed training consultant, lecturer, moderator, examiner and author. He is the author of 20 books published in Ireland, the UK and worldwide on learning, personal development, study skills and business management. Many of his books have been translated into foreign languages and gone into second editions. His most recent book (2014) is titled *Awaken the Genius Within – A Guide to Lifelong Learning Skills* (Glasnevin Publishing, Dublin). He has a M.Ed with distinction (in training and development) from the University of Sheffield and is a qualified Chartered Management Accountant (ACMA), Chartered Global Management Accountant (CGMA) and a Chartered Secretary (ACIS). He is a Fellow of the Irish Institute of Training and Development (FIITD). Previous books published by the author include *Why Some People Succeed and Others Fail* (Glasnevin Publishing, Dublin), *Learning about Learning* (CIPD, London), *A Practical Guide to Learning in the Workplace* (The Liffey Press, Dublin), *Better Exam Results* (Elsevier/CIMA, London) and *How To Set Up and Manage A Corporate Learning Centre* (Gower, Aldershot, UK). All of these books are available online from Amazon.co.uk.

Dedication

To my wife Veronica, my children Caroline, Sandra and David
and my three grandchildren Shane, Kate and Rachel.

Samuel A. Malone

CREATIVITY

(ALL YOU'LL EVER NEED TO KNOW
ABOUT BEING CREATIVE)

AUSTIN MACAULEY
PUBLISHERS LTD.

A CIP catalogue record for this title is available from the British Library.

ISBN 978 1 78455 416 3

www.austinmacauley.com

First Published (2015)
Austin Macauley Publishers Ltd.
25 Canada Square
Canary Wharf
London
E14 5LB

Printed and bound in Great Britain

Acknowledgements

I would like to thank Austin Macauley Publishers for having the confidence in me to publish this book. I would also like to thank them for the great job done on layout, typesetting and editorial work.

Contents

Preface

This book answers the six vital questions everybody has about creativity: What is creativity? Why does creativity happen? When does creativity happen? How does creativity happen? Where does creativity take place? And who is creative? There are six chapters in the book devoted to addressing each of these issues. Each chapter is illustrated by practical examples of creativity and innovation in action. These range from business to science; from continuous improvement to new product development.

Creativity is creating something that wasn't there before, seeing novel relationships between things, ideas, artefacts, products, places and people. Creativity has been linked to genius, in science, business, and art, and many people have attained world fame through their wonderful discoveries and inventions. Every idea that changed the world began in the mind of someone as a thought. Modern living has been enriched and made possible through creative endeavours. Apart from making something new or original, creativity can be also about improving, refining, changing or combining things in unusual ways. Creativity is not just for the privileged few, because we all have the potential to be creative.

The debate about the contribution of nature versus nurture to creativity still goes on and evokes considerable controversy. Research shows that certain characteristics, whether from nature or nurture, or a combination of both, account for a person's creativity. These traits include having a broad range of interests, being attracted to complex issues, seeking out novel experiences, aesthetic sensitivity, and toleration of ambiguity, non-conformity, risk taking and self-confidence. Historiometry is the study of personal traits making up genius such as creativity. It covers the lifespan of people who were exceptionally creative, and the progress of their creativity throughout their lives. By studying these role models we should be able to learn about what it takes to be creative, and apply them to our own lives.

Creativity and innovation are different. Creativity is the production of novel and useful ideas in any field, whereas innovation is the implementation of these ideas. Creative companies believe in flexibility, adaptability and involvement, implemented by a policy of employee empowerment and development. Creative companies such as 3M, Apple and Google actively support a culture of creativity.

Intelligence and creativity are linked but different. Creativity is just one aspect of intelligence. Nevertheless, you need a certain amount of IQ to be creative, although people with a high IQ are not necessarily creative. Howard Gardner, who has come up with the theory of multiple intelligences, has widened the definition of intelligence to include eight aspects that have a strong creativity bias. These include spatial, interpersonal, musical, intrapersonal, linguistic, kinaesthetic, logical and naturalistic. People can develop their creative skills in any or a combination of these areas.

The barriers to creativity include conformity, fear and group think. The myths of creativity include that the right side of the brain controls creativity, and that all the best ways of doing things have already been found. Being aware of the barriers and myths to creativity will help you develop a more positive attitude to creativity and counteract any negativity.

Evidence of creativity has spanned the history of human kind, from the drawings on cave walls and the invention of the wheel to the modern wonders of telecommunications. Global competition, rapidly changing technology, and the shortening of the product life cycle, has made creativity more important in business than ever before.

Creativity is important because it creates business opportunities, visualises possibilities, fulfils design needs, meets personal ambitions, provides roles for people to play and presents career opportunities for employees. Without being creative we would be unable to solve the everyday problems of life, and the ever changing challenges of business. The people who progress in their careers are the ones who can come up with new and innovative ideas, and new and improved ways of doing things.

To survive, a business needs to work smarter and faster, continually develop new products and services, and improve existing ones. We tend to move towards those goals that we clearly visualise. If you visualise a difficult task before you do it, you are more likely to successfully complete it.

Good design is an important ingredient of creativity in business and permeates all aspects of our lives. Many successful companies are now driven by design. It is often the main competitive advantage. Good design will increase sales, create brand recognition, and should be considered an investment rather than a cost.

Travelling to foreign parts and particularly living in foreign countries seems to be an aid to creativity. Living and adapting to a new culture forces us to think and to learn novel approaches to problem solving, and behave differently to cope with a changed way of life.

In general, people will be most creative if intrinsically rather than extrinsically motivated. If you love what you do you are intrinsically motivated. The roles people adopt facilitate the process of creativity. These roles are: explorer, artist, judge and warrior. A combination of these roles is needed for creativity.

The subconscious plays a vital role in our creativity. Your subconscious is the storehouse of everything you know, even things you can't readily recall to mind. It makes patterns and connections without your conscious knowledge. It will process, recombine, adapt and consolidate ideas, images and experiences and suggest solutions. You can tap spontaneous insights by accessing the vast resources of your subconscious.

Many famous people came up with their most brilliant ideas and marvellous inventions after a daydream or a dream. When you sleep your mind doesn't turn off but instead becomes very active. Sometimes dreams are the way your mind works out solutions to difficult problems, and it taps into the creativity in your subconscious to do so. Thomas Edison claimed that most of his ideas came to him after dozing.

Similar claims have been made by other prominent scientists and authors.

Creative people are great note takers. Leonardo da Vinci kept detailed notes and drawings of his ideas that survive to this day. Charles Darwin was an avid note taker. Scientists could not keep track of their experiments and research without keeping comprehensive notes. Novelists and non-fiction writers could not produce their books without notes on their observations and research.

Many famous inventions were inspired by serendipitous or accidental events. Serendipity is the source of many ideas in consumer goods, pharmaceuticals, science, medical devices, industry and discoveries about astronomy. One of the most notable accidental discoveries was Alexander Fleming's penicillin made in 1928.

Thinking creatively can be encouraged by having the right mindset, adopting the right approach and having fun during the process. You are more likely to be creative if you are optimistic, have a strong self-belief and pursue ideas with confidence and purpose.

The five stages of creativity are preparation, effort, incubation, insight and evaluation. New ideas may be triggered off by means of the acronym CAMPERS. This stands for combine ideas, adapt, modify, put to other uses, eliminate unnecessary parts, rearrange and simplify. This simple acronym if used purposefully can be a great inspiration for creativity.

In many organisations ideas are killed before they ever get off the ground. Some of the best ideas were initially rejected but came to fruition through the persistence and determination of their owners. The 'not invented here' syndrome is a good example of a prevalent barrier to creativity.

Edward De Bono, the inventor of lateral thinking, has suggested the six thinking hats as a way for people to become more creative. Wearing these metaphorical hats gives us different perspective on a problem. The hats represent white hat thinking (logical), red hat thinking (emotional), yellow hat thinking (optimistic), black hat thinking (pessimistic), green hat thinking (creative), and blue hat thinking (control).

Brainstorming is one of the most popular methods used in companies to generate ideas. The four stages of brainstorming are: suspend judgement, freewheel, generate many ideas and cross fertilise. Other techniques of creativity include fantasy, attribute listing, metaphors, synectics, swot analysis, stretch imaging and suggestion schemes. Companies may set up suggestion schemes to encourage employees to make cost savings and improvements related to their work or the products or services of the company.

Creative Problem Solving (CPS) is another major creativity technique for generating ideas and solving problems. TRIZ is the Theory of Inventive Problem Solving developed from world-wide patterns of inventions from patent literature and it has now been adopted by many major multinationals. These two techniques have made a major contribution to creative problem solving in organisations.

Biomimicry is creativity inspired by nature. Sources include birds, the sea, plants, insects and humans/animals. Nature has evolved over 3.8 billion years to solve problems in surprisingly efficient and novel ways. A closely related field to biomimicry is bionics, which is used creatively to mend broken bodies.

Creativity starts in the brain. Both sides of the brain are needed for creativity. The entire creative process engages different regions of the brain. The neocortex is the part of the brain that distinguishes us from the other mammals. Thanks to the neocortex, humans can perform extraordinary creative and complex tasks. These include writing a book, composing a symphony, painting a landscape or building a computer. Creative people tend to lose themselves in the creative process. This is known as a state of flow.

Exercise, sleep and meditation are good for your creativity. Creativity can happen at home or at work. Creativity is needed in our personal lives to solve everyday problems. These could include household budgeting, interior design and carrying out do-it-yourself projects.

In the workplace there are numerous opportunities to exercise creativity from continuous improvements to new product developments. Simple everyday changes and improvements may reap major benefits in productivity. Responding in a creative way to a customer's request, or solving a crisis requiring a quick response, are everyday occurrences in most businesses. At a more sophisticated level new goods and services are coming on the market all the time.

Universities are designed to encourage the flow of ideas between disciplines within and outside the university. Pure research is conducted in universities rather than development. The fruits of this research benefits industry. The internet enables universities to keep up to date on the research activities of other universities at home and abroad.

Western and eastern countries differ to the extent that they are creative. Originality, initiative, fluidity and flexibility are highly regarded and respected in the west. On the other hand, eastern cultures emphasise the importance of the group over the individual, and the need for conformity, respect for tradition and social harmony. Japan has built its reputation on incremental improvements rather than invention. China is becoming a major economic force in the world.

Major cities are creative hubs. The average inhabitant of a city is three times more creative than someone living in a small town. Innovation is a prime driver of economic growth in cities and regions. Globalised cities such as New York and London now trade in creativity, ideas, knowledge and innovation.

The traits of creative people include playfulness, resilience, imagination, novelty, curiosity and energy. These traits are well worth developing. The average person underestimates how creative they are. Creativity can be expressed in our lifestyle, in the way we solve problems, in the way we dress, in the way we speak, in how we interact with others and in the way we cook.

There is a dark side to creativity. Many famous creative people show symptoms of extreme personality disorders such as schizoid, histrionic, narcissistic and manic depressive. The

DISC Personal Profile System attempts to develop a creativity quotient (CQ) similar to the intelligence quotient (IQ), but has not achieved the same level of acceptance. There are thinking style preferences in creativity such as the inventive style, the implementing style and the evaluating style. Men and women are equally creative.

Creativity lasts a lifetime despite the fact that some people consider themselves too old to be creative. Creativity is a highly desirable skill at any age even though it may vary over the lifespan of a person. Scientists, artists, politicians, entertainers and writers can remain creative throughout their lives and into old age.

Education plays a critical role in creativity. Deep knowledge of a particular domain and a fund of general knowledge is an important resource for creativity. Creative people need a store of knowledge to fall back on. An individual must have knowledge of a specific field of study to engage in problem solving related to that field, and make a creative contribution to that domain. Entrepreneurs need to know their businesses and be knowledgeable and creative if their enterprise is to survive and thrive.

1
What Is Creativity

Introduction

The word creative means to create, to make or to produce. Creativity is creating something that wasn't there before, seeing novel relationships between things, ideas, artefacts, products, places and people.

The debate about the contribution of nature versus nurture to creativity still goes on and evokes considerable controversy. Historiometry is the study of personal traits making up genius such as creativity. It covers the lifespan of people who were exceptionally creative and the progress of their creativity throughout their lives.

Creativity and innovation are different. Creativity is the production of novel and useful ideas in any field, whereas innovation is the implementation of these ideas into useful products. Creative companies actively support a culture of creativity.

Creativity is an aspect of intelligence, although people with a high IQ are not necessarily creative. Howard Gardner has widened the definition of intelligence to include eight aspects having a strong creativity bias.

The barriers to creativity can be social, corporate and psychological. The myths of creativity relate to people, ideas, business and the brain.

Exploring Creativity

The word "creative" or "creativity" comes from the Latin word "creare" which means "to create, to make" or "to produce." Beginning in the Renaissance (14th – 17th century), into the Age of Enlightenment (18th century), and continuing into the 19th and 20th century, creativity became associated with imagination, creative insights, illuminations, ingenuity, intelligence and genius. Today, neuroscience gives us new insights into the creative process. Researchers are now discovering that creativity is not just for the privileged few, but that we all have the potential to be creative. Dewitt Jones, renowned National Geographic photographer, said: "Creativity exists in each one of us. Creativity is the ability to look at what everyone else is looking at and see something different. It is the ability to look at the ordinary and see the extraordinary."

Creativity is creating something that wasn't there before; seeing novel relationships between things, ideas, artefacts, products, places and people. Creativity is often about seeing something unusual in the usual or just seeing things differently. Apart from making something new or original, creativity can also be improving, refining, changing or combining things in unusual or novel ways. It is about building on existing ideas and finding inspiration in unlikely places. In everyday life it is about coming up with an original approach to problem solving. You are creative if you:

- Create something new (creation).
- Put two previously unrelated things together (synthesis).
- Improve something or find a new application for something (modification).

Think of the word creative and other words like imagination, originality, innovation, unpredictability, divergence and lateral come to mind. These words convey the message of generating ideas, and looking at problems from different and new perspectives. It involves the flexibility of being able to switch from one perspective to another, and to make unusual links or associations between things. To be creative requires divergent thinking, or generating many unique ideas, followed by convergent thinking - meaning combining those ideas to get the best possible results.

Janusian, divergent and lateral thinking

Divergent thinking is like Janusian thinking. Janus was the Roman deity who had two faces looking in opposite directions. It is the ability to cope with conflicting ideas, paradoxes, ambiguity and doubt. Janusian thinking helps us escape the common view of a problem by exploring an opposite point of view that may present new options. Another way of expressing this idea is juxtaposition or putting opposites together. Juxtaposition of two contrasting items is often done deliberately in writing, music, or art – in order to highlight their differences and create emphasis. Use open ended questions like "what would you do if you won the lottery" to stimulate divergent thinking

Some people make a distinction between creative thinking and lateral thinking. Lateral thinking is defined as thinking up new ways of looking at a problem rather than proceeding sequentially by logical steps. Creative thinking is about introducing something new while lateral thinking is about introducing a new approach. Other people make a distinction between big C creativity which is about breakthrough scientific innovation, and small c creativity which is about everyday problem solving in business and domestic situations.

Creative thinking is not much use if we can't tell the difference between a good idea and a bad one. Our imagination should be rooted in reality. Ideas must be useful, feasible, actionable, valuable and marketable. Business people produce a prototype of their ideas and carry out market research to test their practical and commercial viability. This is where the analytical thinking process comes in.

Creativity turns problems and challenges into opportunities and solutions. Creative people go outside the conventional way of seeing and doing things. Some people call this going outside the box. Picasso was a creative genius who threw convention to the winds, but nevertheless his work was built on solid art principles. The art he produced challenged people to look at things in new, unfamiliar, unconventional and thought provoking ways.

> "Creativity, as has been said, consists largely of rearranging what we know in order to find out what we do not know. Hence, to think creatively, we must be able to look afresh at what we normally take for granted."
>
> George Kneller

Nature Verses Nurture

There is no doubt that if you inherit the right genes it is a tremendous advantage. Many talented people came from talented families. Dean Simonton at the University of California estimates that between 22% and 36% of the differences in creativity in the arts and sciences may be explained by natural endowment. The debate regarding the contribution of nature versus nurture still goes on and evokes considerable controversy. However, even if the ratio is 50/50 it still leaves plenty of scope to become creative by deliberate training, practise, passion, persistence and access to resources. Growing up in a supportive environment with mentors and role models will also help.

Research shows that several characteristics, whether endowed by nature or nurture or a combination of both, account for a person's creativity. These include having a broad range of interests, being attracted to complex issues, seeking out novel experiences, aesthetic sensitivity, toleration of ambiguity, non-conformity and risk taking, and self-confidence. All of these traits have been consistently shown to be positively related to creativity. Research further shows that the link between novelty seeking and creativity is related to an individual's dopamine levels (a neurotransmitter found naturally in the brain essential for the normal functioning of the central nervous system) that are determined by genes. These have been labelled "novelty seeking genes."

There is no doubt that a person whose nervous system is more sensitive to colour and light will have an advantage when it comes to painting. Similarly a person born with perfect pitch will do well in music and composition. A person born with a facility for words is more likely to go on and make a good writer. Similarly a person born with a facility for numbers is more likely to go on and make a good mathematician. Persons born with these dispositions will naturally gravitate and become interested in sounds or colours or words or maths. Therefore, they are more likely to innovate in music or art or words or maths.

However, nature is only part of the equation. Upbringing and family background will have a significant effect. Interest and curiosity tend to be stimulated by many factors. These include positive experiences in a family home, a supportive emotional environment, a rich cultural heritage, high expectations and exposure to many opportunities and experiences. Resources are crucial for creativity to develop. Obviously children brought up in a home with material and intellectual resources, have a head start over those who don't have such advantages. Children who are encouraged to question things are more likely to grow up with creative problem solving skills, and be in a better position to make sense of their world. On the other hand, some creative individuals with persistence and determination have emerged from the most unlikely family circumstances, where there was little emotional support and feelings of rejection.

Historiometry
Historiometry is the study of personal traits which make up genius such as creativity, charisma, leadership and openness. It covers the life span of people who were exceptionally creative, birth order, intellectual precocity, family and educational background, and the progress of their creativity throughout their lives. Most of the studies deal with the comparisons of famous or eminent people who have made a significant contribution to life or made a mark on history, such as scientists, artists and politicians. Creative genius does not

emerge from nowhere but instead builds upon the creativity displayed by previous generations. We can study their lives and use them as role models in our quest to become more creative.

It was Sir Francis Galton who popularised the subject in 1869 with his work titled Hereditary Genius. The study in 2003, Human Accomplishments, by Charles Murray classified Einstein and Newton as the most important physicists and Michelangelo as the top ranking western artist. Several studies have compared the charisma and IQ of past presidents of the United States of America. One such study classified Quincy Adams as the cleverest US president, with an estimated IQ of 165 to 175. George W Bush had an average IQ of 125, the second lowest ever, exceeding that of Warren Harding with an IQ of 124 (he was regarded as a failed president).

"Life is not a matter of holding good cards, but of playing a poor hand well."

Robert Louis Stevenson

Creativity and Innovation

Some theorists maintain that we have gone through the Industrial Age, the Information Age and that now we are in the Creativity and Innovation Age. Inspiration and innovation are frequently linked to creativity but are distinct from it. "Inspire" literally means "breathe into," and is the historical belief that the source of creativity is the whispered breath of God in the form of a sudden insight. Inspiration is often the stimulus such as the compelling need or problem that motivates us to pursue an idea. On the other hand, innovation is the outcome of creative work such as the launch or adoption of a new product or process. The word "innovate" can be traced back to 1440. It comes from the Middle French word "innovacyon" meaning "renewal" or "new ways of doing things."

Creativity and innovation are often confused but they mean different things. Creativity is the production of novel and useful ideas in any field, whereas innovation is the sifting, refining, and most critically the implementation of those ideas. Creativity is about divergent thinking. Innovation is about convergent thinking. We can see that creativity is not enough. We need innovation to turn the creative ideas into physical reality as useful and profitable products that people desire. Innovation is a far tougher proposition than creativity. It is one thing understanding the workings of the atom, but it quite another thing to apply this knowledge by building a nuclear powered electricity generation station. It is one thing to conceive a product, but it is quite another thing to bring it to fruition, identify a need for it and market it successfully and profitably.

Types of innovation

There are two philosophies of innovation: top-down innovation and bottom-up innovation. With top-down senior management select the most talented creative people, provide adequate funding, and allocate time and other resources as needed. This approach is used by Canon's Reprographic Products Development Centre. They employ teams with designers and production engineers to create beautifully designed cameras. Bottom-up innovation starts at operations and works upwards. Employees must convince managers of the value of their ideas. The best example of this is Richard Drew, a lab technician with 3M who refused to take no for an answer when developing masking and Scotch tape.

Innovation can be categorised into three types:

1. Incremental innovation enhances existing services or products, improving them or making them more useful. An example is the iPad 2 model.
2. New-to-the-market innovation delivers a new product or service that previously did not exist. This requires considerable effort, time and resources. An

example of this type of innovation is the Dyson hand dryer.

3. Breakthrough innovation is something that has never been achieved before. It cannot be compared to any existing product or service. An example of breakthrough innovation is the creation of the World Wide Web.

Innovation to succeed needs a supportive environment and company culture. There is no doubt that culture drives innovation, as evidenced in companies like Apple, Google, Samsung and 3M. These companies have a culture of strong support for risk-taking and employee participation. The organisation should be patient with failures, and have the attitude that mistakes are learning opportunities. Reflecting on mistakes often leads to useful insights showing what went wrong, and suggests a different and more effective approach. Giving employees room to make mistakes creates opportunities for serendipity, insights and valuable learning. IBM's Thomas Watson, Sr. once said that the fastest way to succeed was to double your failure rate.

Google cofounders, Larry Page and Sergey Brin, are no strangers to failure. They initially failed when they brought the entire Stanford computer network down in developing their revolutionary search engine. Failed attempts are wonderful learning opportunities when they prompt you to try a new course of action. They also didn't let rejection put them off. Their search engine was rejected by Alta Vista and Yahoo, and with hindsight it proved to be fortuitous. There is a well-known paradox in innovation – the greater the potential of an idea the more resistance there will be to it.

Attributes of innovation

Boston Consulting Group's 2013 annual list of the world's most innovative companies, placed Apple at number 1, followed by Samsung and Google at 2 and 3 respectively.

They identified five attributes which distinguish them from less innovative companies:

- Their top management is committed to innovation as a competitive advantage. Nine out of ten of the top innovators said that their leadership was more committed to innovation compared to the weak innovators.
- They leverage their intellectual property. Instead of viewing the protection of intellectual property rights as a defensive strategy, top innovators see it as a way to establish a competitive advantage.
- They manage a portfolio of innovative initiatives. Strong innovators define their project goals clearly. They have processes in place to stop projects continuing when their promise wanes i.e. when they are no longer financially viable.
- They have a strong customer focus. More than 70% of strong innovators say that the views of key customers play an important role in choosing which ideas to develop compared with 42% of weak innovators.
- They insist on strong processes, which lead to a strong performance. Top innovators are far more likely to have standard procedures in place to review projects and make decisions. Consequently more of the top innovators finish on time.

Five skills of innovators

There are five discovery skills that distinguish innovators from others:

1. Associational thinking. This happens when people synthesise and organise novel inputs. They create links between seemingly unrelated items. People with strong discovery skills are able to make connections across seemingly unrelated questions,

problems or ideas. They make associations or links where innovative breakthroughs often take place. eBay was launched when somebody couldn't find what they wanted in local classified advertisements.

2. They ask provocative questions to challenge the status quo. Questions such as Why? What if? And Why not? What are the worst things and the best things that could happen? A change in the question can revolutionise your answer. Different questions produce different answers, giving different perspectives, leading to different solutions. Michael Dell founded Dell Computers, after asking why a computer costs five times as much as the sum of the parts that makes it up.

3. They observe the world like an anthropologist (anthropology is the study of humans, past and present) to detect new ways of doings things. Creative people with great awareness observe in great detail what is happening in the world, and then imagine what could be better. Scott Cook's idea for Quicken software, making money management easy, came from observing his wife's frustration with keeping track of home finances.

4. They network with people from various walks of life with different viewpoints to gain radically different perspectives. Technology Entertainment and Design (TED) conferences on the internet bring artists, entrepreneurs, scientists, and many other extraordinary people together to present their ideas and projects.

5. They experiment relentlessly to test new ideas and try out new experiences and continually learn from the results. One type of experimentation is living and working overseas. Former Proctor and Gamble CEO, A.G. Lafley, studied history in France, and headed retail operations in a US military base in Japan.

> "Imagination will often carry us to worlds that never were. But without it we go nowhere."
>
> Carl Sagan

From the wheel to the computer

One of the greatest discoveries of all time was the invention of the wheel. The wheel on its own is not much use. It had to be combined with an axle and a box to become useful. This means that somebody had to synthesise them into the cart. Consider how difficult it would be to move things about without the wheel, even though the Inca civilisation seemed to manage without it. The wheel in turn inspired countless further inventions. All kinds of transport, machinery, instruments and equipment are based on the wheel. In fact most creative ideas are just refinements, improvements, combinations or new applications of existing things.

Other great discoveries such as fire gave us cooking and heating. The cultivation of crops gave rise to agriculture and human settlements. The invention of tools, from primitive stone based implements to the modern sophisticated versions, improved and extended our capability to do many things. The invention of language made communication easier, and facilitated the recording and passing on of information facilitating commerce. This was followed by printing which democratised books and reading. The invention of sanitation improved hygiene and health and drastically reduced the death rate. We now have electricity which has transformed our everyday lives, making way for the invention of information and communications technology.

Take the modern omnipresent computer. Thirty years ago it was so big that it needed a special purpose air conditioned room to accommodate it and an army of maintenance staff to keep it going. Today it is much smaller, cheaper, better designed, portable, and more powerful and faster than ever before. It is now as common as the radio or television was to previous generations. The technology behind it is developing so fast that it is obsolete as soon as you buy it. It comes in many incarnations such as desktop, laptop, and tablet. Computer technology in the form of silicon chips has also been incorporated into other equipment, such as cars, televisions, mobile phones, cameras, machines, robots and domestic appliances making them faster and more efficient.

The development of scientific innovation over the centuries has been steady but slow. Scientific advancement was restricted through lack of general education, superstition, lack of resources, slow communication networks and political interference. Today the pace of innovation has advanced dramatically because of higher education levels, Government support, the internet and the widespread availability of social media such as Linkedin, Facebook and Twitter. The commercial exploitation of the internet, including email and ecommerce, has seen an explosion in internet activity. Internet shopping is now a vigorous competitor to high street shopping. The success of Amazon is an example of this phenomenon.

> "Originality is nothing but judicious imitation."
>
> Voltaire

IQ and CQ

Creativity is an aspect of intelligence, although people with a high IQ are not necessarily creative. A high IQ is needed for subjects like mathematics, physics and astronomy. You don't need a high IQ for gardening, cooking or design. Many people with high IQs live unremarkable lives, never living up to their potential. There are many highly intelligent failures in the world. There is no correlation between high IQ and creativity. However, you do need an average or above average IQ to be creative. A solid 'C' student with interest, curiosity, conscientiousness and determination can make a big impact on the world. Thomas Edison, Winston Churchill and Charles Darwin were all lacklustre students when at school. Edison was expelled from school at fourteen because he was considered a daydreamer. Teachers thought he had learning difficulties due to a hearing impairment which developed into almost total deafness later in life.

Winston Churchill was not regarded to be a good student while at school although he did show signs of having a remarkable memory. Darwin's father concluded that the young Charles Darwin, when he was a student, wouldn't amount to much: "You care for nothing but shooting, dogs and rat catching and you will be a disgrace to yourself and your family." Richard Feynman, the famous physicist, who helped build the atom bomb in the 2nd World War, hadn't an exceptionally high IQ and dismissed the IQ test as unscientific. He was a brilliant communicator and teacher with a gift for making the complex simple. His curiosity which fuelled his creativity had no bounds, and his enthusiasm for science was contagious. He had great interpersonal relationship skills and consequently was a favourite with his students. He was keenly interested in his students, and had great patience and empathy when explaining complex issues to them

The Torrance tests of creative thinking invented by Ellis Paul Torrance are some of the most widely used and reliable tests to measure creativity. In 1958, 400 Minneapolis children completed a series of tasks designed by Torrance to measure their creativity quotient (CQ). Those who came up with good ideas on Torrance's tasks grew up to be entrepreneurs, college presidents, authors, doctors, diplomats and software developers. In 2010 Jonathan Plucker of Indiana University reanalysed Torrance's data. The correlation to lifetime creative accomplishment was more than three times stronger for childhood creativity than childhood IQ.

Torrance's test, a 90 minute series of discreet tasks administered by a psychologist, has been taken by millions worldwide. There is one crucial difference between IQ and CQ scores. With intelligence, there is a phenomenon called the Flynn effect – with each generation, scores go up about 10 points. It seems enriched environments are making children more intelligent. With creativity, a reverse trend has been identified with creativity scores falling. Researchers think that there are a number of reasons why this is happening. One is that children are spending too much time watching TV and playing videogames, rather than engaging in creative activities. Another is the lack of creativity development in schools where there is no systematic approach to nurture creativity in children.

Reversing the decline in creativity

Some countries are addressing this problem. In the USA numerous Fortune 500 companies, including Hewlett-Packard and Sears, have hired creativity consultants to help boost employee innovation. Also the number of business schools offering classes in creativity has increased significantly in recent years. The EU designated the year 2009 as the European Year of Creativity and Innovation, holding conferences on the neuroscience of creativity. They have also financed teacher training in creativity, and started practical problem-based learning programmes for children and adults. Research shows that you can enhance your creativity through deliberate training, through the practise of appropriate techniques and by adopting an attitude that you can learn creativity. In China there has been widespread education reform to counteract the rote memorisation style of teaching. Instead Chinese schools are adopting a problem-based learning approach.

Schools usually resist the introduction of creativity training, claiming that there is no room in the day for a creativity class because of the demands of other subjects. Children are fortunate if they get an art class once or twice a week, on the belief that arts have a special place in creativity. However, this assertion has been disproved by scientists. When scholars gave creativity tasks to both engineering and music majors, their scores turned out to be the same. Their brains behaved in a similar way when generating and evaluating ideas. Both sides of the brain are involved in creative problem solving – the right side for generating ideas and the left side for evaluating them.

Creative problem solving can be taught and improved through practise. University of New Mexico neuroscientists Rex Jung found that those who diligently practise creativity activities learn to use their brains' creative networks quicker and better. A lifetime of consistent habits gradually changes the neurological pattern. Experts maintain that it takes about 21 days of constant practise to change the habits of a lifetime and lay down a new one. Physical habits such as mannerisms and facial expressions are easiest to rectify. Mental habits like attitudes, values and beliefs are more difficult to change.

Back in 1958, Ted Schwarzrock was 8 years old and in third grade when he participated in the Minneapolis experiment. He did exceptionally well and impressed the psychologists who administered the test. They concluded that he had "unusual visual perspective" and "an ability to synthesise diverse elements into meaningful products." When he was 30 years old, Ted Schwarzrock's prospects didn't look promising. He wasn't artistic when young, and his family didn't recognise his creativity or nurture it. He was pushed into medical school by his father, a dentist, and his mother, a speech pathologist. He was unhappy, felt stifled and frequently had run-ins with his college professors. But eventually, he found a way to combine his creative and medical expertise, inventing new medical devices.

Today Schwarzrock is a wealthy man, having founded three medical product companies. His innovations in health care have been wide ranging, from portable oxygen devices to skin absorbing anti-inflammatories, to insights into how bacteria become antibiotic-resistant. Schwarzrock said: "As a child, I never had an identity as a creative person, but now that I know, it helps explain a lot of what I felt and went through."

> "We are what we think. All that we are arises with our thoughts. With our thoughts we create the world."
>
> The Buddha

Multiple Intelligences

Although IQ tests have earned a certain amount of credibility, creativity tests (CQ), emotional quotient tests (EQ), and multiple intelligence tests (MI) haven't the same acceptance. A good emotional intelligence, or being able to effectively handle interpersonal relationships and having good street smarts, is now accepted as a prerequisite for success in life. This ability includes self-knowledge, as well as being able to understand and effectively manage your own emotions and the emotions of others.

Howard Gardner has widened the definition of intelligence to include eight aspects which have a strong creativity bias. This approach is called multiple intelligences. Each of us has a combination of these intelligences with a strong preference for some. However, it is possible through practise to enhance our ability in any or all of these intelligences. People have excelled creatively in each of these intelligences.

The eight intelligences

Spatial
People with spatial intelligence are good at visualising objects, shapes, charts, diagrams, pictures and maps. They can imagine maps in their heads and thus have a well-developed sense of direction. They like to draw, paint, and design and create things. Many of the most creative minds in history, like novelists, artists, and scientists claimed that their greatest inspirations came in visual images rather than words. Well-known examples of creative people with spatial intelligence include Pablo Picasso, Van Gogh, Salvador Dali, Rembrandt, Leonardo da Vinci and Michelangelo.

People with spatial ability are excellent at visualisation, and think and remember things in the form of three dimensional pictures. Designers, graphic artists, architects, landscapers and navigators have this ability. To enhance this ability use learning maps, diagrams, graphs, flow charts and your powers of visualisation. Of course, successful professional people with this innate ability have many years of training and practise behind them.

Interpersonal

These people are good at interpersonal relationships, reading other peoples' minds and understanding their motives. They have a good sense of empathy and get along well with people. They are good at interpreting body language, facial cues and picking up hidden agendas. Many famous creative people were handicapped in their personal lives by a lack of interpersonal relationship skills. Isaac Newton (1642-1727) had one of the best analytical brains of all time but was arrogant and insensitive, and fell out with many of the great scientists of his day. On the other hand, Raphael (1483-1520), unlike his two famous contemporaries, Leonardo da Vinci and Michelangelo, was not a solitary genius but a sociable and approachable figure.

Albert Einstein's personal life was not very happy. He treated his wives and children insensitively. He was a womaniser who had little regard for the feelings of his wives (he was married twice). However he was the exception rather than the rule as research on eminent creative people, all over the age of 60, found that they mostly enjoyed stable, committed marital relationships. This in no small way contributed to the peace of mind needed for their creative work.

Beethoven (1770-1827) had low interpersonal intelligence. He had a brusque and often uncouth manner. His personal eccentricities and unpredictability were to grow, augmented by the realisation in 1798 that he was going deaf. Just like in any other aspect of intelligence you can be creative in the way you adopt, adapt and practise interpersonal relationship strategies. Modern examples of people with superb interpersonal relationship skills include former President Clinton and TV personalities Oprah Winfrey and Terry Wogan. People with this ability tend to be extroverted, and be tuned into the needs of others.

Interpersonal intelligence is highly prized by employers, but is not something that is addressed in conventional education. Personnel managers, public relations managers, training managers, salespeople, counsellors and negotiators need this ability to survive and thrive in their jobs. To enhance this ability, get involved in teams, debating societies, teach, mentor and coach others, lead seminars and workshops, resolve conflicts by negotiating successful outcomes, engage in small talk with shop assistants and socialise as much as possible.

Musical

Mozart obviously enjoyed this ability to an exceptional degree. Most of the rest of us exercise this talent to a lesser extent by listening to music, singing and humming along to a tune. People with musical intelligence are good at picking up sounds, remembering melodies, noticing pitches/rhythms, harmonising and keeping time. Composers, song-writers, musicians, singers, and pop artists have this ability. Beethoven, Elton John, the Beetles, Frank Sinatra, Elvis Presley and Luciano Pavarotti would be prime examples. Research has shown that for many people listening to music can enhance both the creative and learning process, because a combination of melody and harmony can help you solve complex problems.

To increase this ability, try relaxing to music and studying or reading with classical music playing softly in the background. In particular, Baroque music has a beat of 60 cycles per second, which is conducive to relaxation and creativity. On the other hand, if you want to get into a positive mood listen, to upbeat music. You are more likely to solve problems when in a positive state of mind. We all have musical intelligence to some degree, it just needs development. Set what you want to learn to music. Rhythm and music will make it easier to remember. Advertisers are one of the creative professions who use rhymes and music for greater impact and recall. Music reduces stress and pent up emotions, while poems and songs will help you to memorise and learn information. When Einstein got stuck on a problem he relaxed by playing the piano or violin. Similarly, when Edison got stuck on a problem he played the organ. These activities are therapeutic and act as a diversion, enabling his subconscious to work on the problem.

Intrapersonal

People with this intelligence have self-knowledge, and understand their own feelings, strengths and weaknesses. Without self-knowledge people often make very poor life choices with serious consequences. Jung classified people as introverts or extroverts. People with intrapersonal intelligence tend to be introverts. In the learning styles model, they are called reflectors. They tend to be introspective, focusing on inner feelings and intuitions. Monks, nuns and others in the religious field, through a contemplative lifestyle, tend to have developed this ability to a high degree. Freud's science of psychoanalysis emerged from his great capacity for introspection. Writers, philosophers, psychologists and counsellors need this ability to be successful in their careers. Writers in particular need the creative capacity to visualise, daydream and fantasise, particularly those who write novels and science fiction. In their work they need to create characters, context, actions and a plot.

Well-known examples would include Plato, Aristotle and Socrates. "Know thyself" was the motto Socrates is reputed to have learned from the Oracle at Delphi. In knowing oneself, he saw the possibility of learning what is really good, in contrast to accepting superficial outward appearance. To enhance this ability, reflect on your life's expectations on a daily basis and record them in a diary. Day dreaming, mediation and visualisation would also strengthen this ability. Research shows that if a person allows their mind to wander, they outperform their peers in a range of tasks where insight is important - from imaginative word games to exercises in original thinking and invention. In 2003, Shelley Carson and colleagues at Harvard University studied people who had published a novel, patented an invention or had art displayed in a gallery. She found that these people's minds wandered more frequently from the task at hand opening them up to creativity.

Linguistic

These are people who are good at reading, writing, talking, debating and languages. They tend to have a good vocabulary, be fluent speakers and good all-round communicators. Your ability in this area is likely to increase right through life and into your 50s, 60s and 70s. Creative people like poets, writers, actors, broadcasters, teachers, trainers, preachers and politicians tend to have highly developed linguistic skills. Oscar Wilde (1854-1900), the Irish poet and dramatist, was a great conversationalist and a man of wit and wide learning. James Joyce (1882-1941), the Irish-born author, was one of the most creative literary innovators of the 20th century. His books contain extraordinary experiments in language and in writing style. Other examples of people with linguistic intelligence are William Shakespeare, Winston Churchill, John F Kennedy, Bill Clinton, Robin Williams and Isaac Asimov. It is not widely known that Winston Churchill, the great English statesman, won the Nobel Prize for Literature. In the writing field, writers who are particularly creative include fiction, fantasy and science fiction writers. Linguistic intelligence is highly valued in most occupations and in life generally. Many politicians have this ability to a high degree. To enhance this ability, learn from books, DVDs, lectures and seminars. Keep a daily journal and solve problems collaboratively with a friend. Write, do crosswords and debate issues with friends. Take up part-time lecturing, debate or join toastmasters.

Kinaesthetic or tactile

Athletes, racing drivers, dancers, mime artists, boxers and gymnasts all have tactile intelligence, and some people in these fields have proved to be particularly creative. Surgeons and skilled craftspeople also have this ability. Surgeons need fine-tuned tactile skills to carry out precise operations, and skilled craftspeople need developed manual skills especially in areas of creativity such as pottery, sculpture, woodwork and textiles. US golfer Tiger Woods stunned the golfing world by winning three consecutive amateur golf tournaments and two professional tournaments by the age of 20. In more recent times Rory McIlroy from Northern Ireland has come to the fore. Other well-known creative people with this intelligence include Thomas Edison, Michael Flatley, Fred Astaire, Charlie Chaplin and Muhammad Ali. To enhance this ability role play, take part in amateur dramatics, dance and practise. The importance of practising in order to achieve success was emphasised by Gary Player, the famous golf player, who is reputed to have said: "The more I practise the luckier I get."

Analytical or Logical

This intelligence is associated with deductive reasoning. It involves the ability to recognise patterns, and to work with abstract symbols and geometric shapes. There is no doubt that some people are good at logic, problem solving and doing maths. They naturally take to using symbols and manipulating formulas, while others who lack this facility struggle. Some people are good at bringing facts together and arriving at conclusions quickly, while others miss the point. Creative thinking has two parts – a divergent and a deductive aspect. At the problem definition stage and the evaluation stages of creativity, the deductive reasoning aspect is essential. Accountants, actuaries, mathematicians, scientists and lawyers are some of the professions that value powers of logic and deduction.

Charles Babbage (1792-1871), British mathematician and inventor, who designed and built mechanical computing machines on principles that anticipated the modern electronic computer, had a superb analytical intelligence. In everyday life, people good at household budgeting, problem solving, organising and time management also have this ability. Analytical intelligence is usually noticed early in life and peaks at between 30 and 40 years of age. Like linguistic ability, it is highly valued in the academic, business and scientific worlds. To enhance this ability, do mental arithmetic, prepare a cash budget for your personal expenditure, balance your chequebook and practise a systematic approach to problem solving. To apply your analytical skills to reading operate the PEACE approach which stands for key Points, Evidence, Assumptions, Conclusions and Examples. This means that you differentiate between facts and assumptions, and that you make sure your conclusions are supported by evidence and concrete examples.

Naturalistic
Naturalistic intelligence is the eight of the intelligences described by Howard Gardner. People with this intelligence are tuned into the natural and ecological world, love the outdoors and have great powers of observation. Gardner describes the naturalist as the individual "who is able to recognise flora or fauna, to make other consequential distinctions in the natural world, and to use this ability productively in hunting, farming and biological science." Farmers, botanists, fishermen, conservationists, biologists, environmentalists and Green Party members would all have strong naturalistic intelligence. A world famous example would be Charles Darwin. Charles Darwin's theory of evolution by natural selection is probably the major intellectual contribution of the 19th century. Cultural groups possessing and valuing this form of intelligence include Native American nations, Australian Aboriginal peoples and Friends of the Earth members.

"Somewhere, something incredible is waiting to be known."

Carl Sagan

Barriers to Creativity

So far we have considered how to become more creative. The flipside to this is how to stifle creativity. There are many barriers to creativity but the following are the most important. If you are aware of these it will help you understand and counteract their negative effects. Barriers can be considered as social, corporate and psychological.

Social barriers

Social barriers include conformity, the one right answer, evaluating too quickly, being afraid to challenge the obvious, the self-imposed barrier, fear of looking a fool and fear of failure. Let's now explore each of these in more detail.

Conformity

People do not like to be different and like to fit in socially. There are all sorts of pressures and cultural norms on us to be the same. People don't like to think for themselves, they like to fit in with the crowd, and they prefer to do the accepted or conventional thing, rather than the novel or unusual. Many people feel if they don't conform they will stand out and be ostracised by the group. They thus feel it is unsafe and counterproductive to take risks.

In everyday life, fashion and mores tend to standardise the way we think. Bureaucratic cultures often reward routine and conformity, while discouraging difference and initiative. They encourage unhealthy political activity, infighting and lack of cooperation between employees. When an organisation has poor communication and structural silos, it prevents the flow of useful information while hindering initiative and creativity. Rules may be controlling and stifle creativity. Standard operating procedures are the norm. There is great emphasis on creating sameness, and on increasing standardisation, and reducing variability in all aspects of social and business life.

Management was born from the desire to optimise productivity and control. Consider the work of Frederick Taylor, who promulgated the scientific approach to management through work study. He also emphasised the benefits of specialisation, standardisation and simplification. He believed that workers should have no say in the design of their work. This was the sole responsibility of management. This approach is the antithesis of creativity and initiative. Conformity is comforting, while change is often threatening and traumatic. Whistle blowers who challenge the status quo are often shunned, avoided and ostracised, rather than welcomed and celebrated for their courage to stand up for what they believe is right.

There are people in the world who may be more intelligent, better educated and better disciplined than you, but who have not mastered the art of the fresh, unconventional look at old knowledge. We must be happy, playful and adventurous like children to be creative. Thomas Edison said that the greatest invention in the world is the non-conformist mind of a child. Einstein maintained that he thought like a child because children see new relationships in seemingly unrelated things. So we should think like children if we desire to be creative.

Children are innocent and free, don't know what can't be done and see the world as it is. They have fresh, original ideas unfettered by rules and boundaries. They ask questions all the time. On the other hand, adults think too much, see the world as they believe it to be, and are burdened with too much knowledge as well as being constrained by culture and convention. The idea for the first Polaroid camera came not from a scientist in Edwin Land's laboratory, but from the unconventional source of his three year old daughter. When he was on holidays at the Grand Canyon in 1943, his daughter asked him why she couldn't see immediately the picture he had just taken. This was his eureka moment which prompted him to invent the instant camera.

The one right answer

All our early schooling and subsequent training and education are logical rather than creative. Our education is largely concerned with language and numbers. We are taught to be rational, convergent, conventional and predictable, rather than imaginative, creative, controversial and lateral. At school and college we are taught that there is one right answer to all problems, which conveniently resides in the teacher's head, or at the back of the textbook. In examinations we are rewarded for neat writing, relevancy, good presentation and regurgitation of facts, not for creative and lateral thinking. We are not taught to think for ourselves or develop our creativity. The great American psychologist, Abraham Maslow summarised the limits imposed on us by the one right answer mentality when he said that: "If the only tool is a hammer then you tend to see every problem in terms of nails."

However, in real life there are many different solutions to most problems, and many grey areas rather than black and white answers, and very few people have all the answers. The human mind is surprisingly adroit at supporting its deep-seated prejudicial ways of viewing the world, while shifting out contrary evidence. Even when presented with overwhelming facts supporting an opposite point of view, many people, including the well-educated ones, simply won't abandon their deeply held views and habitual ways of doing things. If the reason for a given process is because you've always done it that way, you have a habit. It is healthy to recognise and challenge your habits. There are always different perspectives, alternatives and better ways of doing things.

Evaluating too quickly

Be the angel's advocate rather than the devil's advocate. When you generate ideas write down as many as you can think of while suspending judgement. Let the ideas flow rather than cut them short by being critical and dismissive too early and too quickly. One person's question or comment can easily stimulate another's imagination. Ideas can piggyback on other ideas. Let the creative juices flow – time enough to play the devil's advocate and be critical and rational later. In the meantime, be playful, adventurous and have fun.

It is estimated that children at the age of 5, ask about 120 questions a day. At age 6 they ask only 60 questions a day, and at the age of 40 adults only ask about 4 questions a day. Adults need to behave like children and ask many questions, instead of trying to find immediate answers. Ask questions such as 'what if,' and 'why not.' Unless you ask lots of 'why' questions you won't generate creative insights. The objective should be to crystallise as many ideas as possible in writing, as unless you record them they are unlikely to be examined and will be forgotten. The human memory is exceedingly fallible. Quantity rather than quality, and encouragement rather than judgement, should be the key at this stage.

Being afraid to challenge the obvious

A questioning approach is essential to unearth issues, and see novel relationships that have not been thought of before. Sometimes we fail to see the obvious even though it is staring us in the face. The movements of the moon, and the rise and fall of the tides at sea were known since antiquity. However, it was only in the 17th century that the astronomer Kepler connected these two unrelated facts, and discovered that the moon controlled the tides.

Try to see things from different perspectives. Reframe by changing your point of view. You can do this by seeing it from another's perspective or put it into a different context. This helps you see the world around you in a brand new light. One way of doing this is to reframe problems by using different words. For example, we don't have a health care crisis; we have a sick care crisis. By refocusing our resources from treating illness to prevention, diagnosis and early treatment, we can keep our older workers healthy and out of hospital, free up hospital beds and improve productivity.

Similarly, we do not have an obesity problem; rather we have a willpower, lifestyle, exercise, nutrition, and overeating problem. Greater willpower, more exercise, sensible eating and dieting are the solution. One plus one is not always two. With a bit of creativity and playfulness it may be eleven, a cross, a T and so on. This type of provocative thinking will help your imagination generate different possibilities and perspectives.

The self-imposed barrier

Sometimes barriers are traditional and psychological rather than real. Take the QWERTY which was originally designed for typewriters so that keys wouldn't stick. This design has now been adopted in computer keyboards even though it is inefficient and not ergonomic. It still holds sway because existing users of computers have been trained in the QWERTY method and so there is a reluctance to change. Designers maintain that the QWERTY system could be improved by a more ergonomic layout but manufacturers are reluctant to change their keyboards because of vested interests and customer resistance. A new design called the Dvorak keyboard claiming to be more efficient hasn't really caught on and the QWERTY system still reigns supreme.

There are times when you have to go outside the box to get a new perspective, and to break away from conventional constraints. For many years it was accepted to be physiologically impossible to run a mile in less than 4 minutes. Then Roger Bannister came along in 1954 and broke the physiological and psychological barrier. In the years that followed numerous runners broke this self-imposed barrier. Similarly, it was thought that it was impossible to fly until the Wright brothers came along and proved otherwise. Since then air travel has made the earth seem much smaller. Air travel has improved communications and opened peoples' minds to other cultures.

Our peers and bosses can also impose barriers on us. Two research scientists had an irritating boss who was always saying 'you can't make a silk purse out of a sow's ear.' They were determined to prove him wrong, and bought 100 pairs of sow's ears from the local abattoir. Treating them chemically, they extracted a silk filament, which they then made into a silk purse much to their delight, and the surprise, annoyance and dismay of their boss.

In fear of looking a fool

Fear of failure, fear of ridicule, fear of judgement, fear of not being original, fear of losing control, fear of the first step, fear of hard work, fear of the unknown, and lack of self-esteem and confidence are major barriers to creativity. Some people are often inhibited to suggest ideas, because they fear a negative reaction, or that they will be laughed at. The inner critic may say to you; 'they'll think I'm foolish,' 'it will never work,' or 'it has been tried before.' This may be the position in a group of staff, peers and managers at work who are extremely cautious and conscious of their status, and have a vested interest in the status quo. Some people have a fear of sharing their ideas in case others might steal them without giving them the credit.

Employees are afraid to offer ideas in front of their managers, in case their ideas are thought to be ridiculous, and thus their chances of promotion in the future will be adversely affected. On the other hand, managers are reluctant to make suggestions, in case they look foolish in front of their peers and staff. People must trust and respect each other, have faith in their own judgement, and feel safe, confident and secure enough to express new ideas freely without fear of censure. Turn your inner critic into an inner guide through constructive suggestions, encouragement and positive thoughts.

Cynicism, criticism, jealousy, envy and apathy towards your ideas stifle creativity and encourage conformity. People who are cynical know the price of everything but the value of nothing. People who criticise have a false sense of superiority. They often lack confidence and project their own faults, shortcomings and feelings of inferiority onto others. You don't really need the approval of others. So don't take criticism to heart. Opinions are subjective and may have no basis in fact. Think of all the people who were criticised and went on to become successful. However, constructive criticism may be useful. Personally I would only offer criticism if asked, and I would only give an opinion if it's positive and encouraging. Envious people are jealous of another's talent, success, energy and ambition. Envy is often a way of shielding their own inadequacy. Apathy may be a disguised form of envy. People who are apathetic towards you may have incompatible personalities, interests or background.

Fear of failure

Failure should be viewed as a stepping stone to success. It ought to be seen as something that didn't work the first time around. Your efforts may need a few changes and more perseverance. Henry Ford said that failure is only the opportunity to begin again more intelligently. Innovators and entrepreneurs are less fearful of failure and more open to opportunities. They feel the fear and do it anyway. Many are propelled forward by the frustration of putting up with the status quo and trying to change it. Frustration causes us to look at problems with a new urgency and perspective. In addition, you will need to take calculated risks from time to time but always learn from your mistakes.

Sometimes you must have the humility to admit your ideas aren't working and accept the ideas of others. Think collaboration rather than competition. Abandon the "not-invented-here" syndrome, where people are reluctant to consider any ideas other than their own. Look for opportunities and cede control to other people to gain new perspectives. Be prepared to brainstorm solutions from the bottom up rather than the top down. There is a fund of ideas out there that you can tap into.

Many people are frozen by the thought of taking the first step. Writers fear being confronted with the blank page; speakers fear their first presentation, teachers fear the start of the new term, new employees are fearful about their first day at work, and even seasoned managers fear the first day of a new project. There comes a stage when you need to stop planning and just get started. Too much planning is often an excuse for procrastination. A journey of a thousand miles begins with a single step. So just start doing it. Find a small piece of the work that you think is feasible and can tackle straight away. Break challenges into small chunks or steps so that you gradually build up your confidence as you successfully complete each step. This will help you overcome your fear of taking on bigger and bigger challenges.

Some people are afraid of hard work. We hear stories about flashes of inspiration but we forget about the years of experimentation and hard work it takes to bring ideas into fruition in the form of commercial products or viable services. Edison had this in mind when he said that creativity was 1% inspiration and 99% perspiration. He had a hands-on approach, learning from trial and error experiments. He certainly wasn't afraid of hard work or making mistakes. He said: "I make more mistakes than anyone else I know, and sooner or later, I patent most of them."

Sometimes we have to go outside our comfort zone to confront our fear of the unknown. We have to leave our comfortable surroundings and venture outside. The real world is unpredictable, messy and chaotic. But it is here that you will get new creative insights and breakthroughs rather than in the cosy comforts of your office. Talk to your existing and potential customers to find out what their concerns, desires and needs are. Talk to your employees and see what their views are. This feedback from the bottom up will give you new insights.

Corporate barriers
Corporate barriers include functional fixedness, group think, taboos and copyright and patent production. Let's now consider each of these in more detail.

Functional fixedness
This is the term invented by psychologists to describe the condition whereby individuals from departments are constrained and stymied from thinking of novel ideas by their unique departmental culture, perspective, philosophy, specialised knowledge, expertise and experience. Experts may

also suffer from functional fixedness because of their specialist training. We only see the obvious way of looking at a problem – the same comfortable way we have always looked at it. Individuals who want to be creative should maintain a fluid and flexible approach, and avoid relying too heavily on habitual ways of doing things, or on a particular perspective.

Bureaucracies with their hierarchical grading structures have a habit of killing off ideas before they get a chance to grow. Command and control cultures will not help creativity, although setting goals, targets and boundaries, like operating within budgets, and defining the problem will often encourage creativity. What you need to do is to control expenditure while at the same time avoiding putting out the creative fires. Living within your means can be a spur to creativity. Thus formal management controls can have a positive impact on creativity by providing the necessary structures. These will help to convert creativity into value that otherwise would be dispersed into uncoordinated and unfocused efforts. This can be done by creating new products, improving an existing product or process, or by identifying and meeting customer needs. It can also be achieved by exploiting new opportunities and new technologies to serve emergent customers or markets.

Group think
This is the tendency for like-minded people, within a cohesive group, to agree on issues without considering alternatives, or challenging each other's ideas rationally. There is an erroneous perception of unanimity while simultaneously filtering out divergent views. People have a natural tendency to support the majority viewpoint and set aside their own personal views. If a group is completely absorbed with its own maintenance, members and priorities, it can become dangerously blinkered to what is going on around it. Such groups may confidently forge ahead in the completely wrong direction. It is the opposite of creativity. The suppression of individual opinions and creativity can result in stupid decision-making and inept problem-solving.

The phenomenon of group think may arise in groups such as a political party, or a board of directors influenced by a strong charismatic leader. The German people seemed to be spellbound by the charisma of its Nazi leader Adolf Hitler, and liked what he said because his message of superiority appealed to their egos, making them feel more important and confident. Hence institutions, contrary to declared ethical and moral values, often show more concern to protect their corrupt and misguided leaders than to serve the interests of their customers. Groups can start pursuing their own ends rather than the interests of the organisation. The group think process can be checked and counteracted by appointing a devil's advocate to challenge ideas, consider alternatives, question facts and logic, and provide constructive criticism. In addition, a good gender and ethnic mix will help groups form more balanced decisions. The old boys club is not a good recipe for rational thinking.

Symptoms of group think
The symptoms of group think include self-censorship, stereotyping, rationalisation and a sense of invulnerability. Self-censorship means that members of the group want to maintain consensus at all costs, and so put pressure on dissidents not to "rock the boat". The club mentality prevails. Stereotyping is seeing others as outsiders and opponents. This is vilifying them as the "enemy," – a "them versus us" perception. Rationalisation means that inconsistent facts are ignored so as to quash doubt or remorse. Invulnerability means that the group is very optimistic and is willing to take undue risks in the belief that it is not answerable to anybody. They are thus blind to the risks and dangers involved when pursuing their "pet" strategies.

Examples of group think
Irving Janis, the psychologist who identified the phenomenon of group think, gives several historical examples of group think including the following:

- President Kennedy's decision to launch the Bay of Pigs invasion of Cuba. He accepted stereotypes of Cubans and didn't question information from the CIA.
- The decision not to fly reconnaissance missions north of Hawaii just before the Japanese attack on Pearl Harbour. The US Government were aware of the possibility of an invasion, but believed that the Japanese wouldn't dare to attack the US because of its military superiority.
- The collapse of Swissair. This company felt it was invulnerable because of its financial strength – it was known as the "Flying Bank." Because it failed to question poor decisions and gross mismanagement, the airline eventually went bankrupt.
- The Challenger Disaster (1986). NASA decided to throw caution to the wind because of time pressure about concerns regarding possible failure of the O-rings.

Taboos

These are hot potatoes that companies avoid discussing, because they are politically dangerous, too sensitive, culturally unacceptable, too difficult to solve, or just too dreadful to contemplate. People often turn a blind eye to some feature of a process that is too cumbersome to a manager whose autocratic style is driving staff demented, and even causing some to leave, or to go to a competitor who is gradually eroding market share.

These are the things that remain unchallenged and unsolved, and create serious barriers to creativity and business success. These problems are left to fester, when they could have been nipped in the bud. In the long-term they develop into major issues, when it is either too late or too difficult to address them. The worst thing about elephants in the room is that if you ignore them long enough, they become invisible because they blend into the background, and thus the problem remains unnoticed and festers away.

Copyright & patent protection
Too much legal protection makes it harder to be truly creative. Creativity is a cumulative process involving tweaking, adapting, and combining existing creations. Older works are often the building blocks of newer ones. Patent and copyright laws are aimed at promoting creativity. In practice, they often have the opposite effect by stymieing new work because they require the creators to obtain permission for existing creations they wish to use, refine and adapt. This is why copyright and patent protection doesn't last forever, and only last for a certain number of years before they expire. Nevertheless, some people are more concerned with the good that their invention can do rather than protecting it or enriching themselves. For example, Jonas Salk endeared himself to the public by refusing to patent his polio vaccine. He had no desire to enrich himself from the discovery, but merely wished to save as many lives as possible.

Psychological barriers
Psychological barriers include anxiety, phobias, beliefs, Pygmalion effect, mindset and inhibitions. Let's now discuss these barriers in more detail.

Anxiety
Too much and too little anxiety can inhibit creativity. An optimum amount of anxiety is needed for best results. An extreme example of anxiety is the experience of self-doubt felt by many people known as the imposter syndrome. Creatively successful people may feel they are a fraud and that they are really incompetent and unworthy of their success. They feel that they will eventually be exposed as the fraud that they really are. This is ironic as true frauds and incompetents rarely experience the imposter syndrome. Bertrand Russell said: 'The trouble with the world is that the stupid are cocksure and the intelligent are full of doubt.' Be aware and accept that the

imposter syndrome is a natural part of gaining experience, and becoming successful – most people feel the same.

If you're upset, your brain focuses only on what you're worried about, and can immobilise you against doing anything creative. Anxiety is related to the fear of the unknown. Anxiety and creativity go hand in hand. To do something creative we run the risk of failure, rejection and being laughed at. This doesn't stop people who are truly creative, but makes them more determined to pursue their ideas. Give yourself permission to fail by labelling your next attempt as something like an experiment. This gives you a creative license to try without feeling bad if you fail. Look on failure as a stepping stone on the path to success.

Overcoming phobias
Albert Bandura, a world-renowned psychologist and Stanford professor, carried out experiments where he helped people overcome lifelong snake phobias, by guiding them through a series of increasingly demanding interactions. It is a technique of taking small incremental steps when doing tasks that you fear. Bandura calls this process "guided mastery." He found that small successes boost confidence and increase self-belief and feelings of self-efficacy. People were not only cured of their snake phobia, but also had more success in other parts of their lives, which normally would have caused them great anxiety. They took up horseback riding and public speaking. They tried harder, persevered longer, and were more resilient in the face of failure.

Actors like Al Pacino, Robert DeNiro and Jack Nicholson, instead of denying their anxiety, acknowledged it, and channelled it into superior and dynamic acting performances. They use their anxiety to fire up their creativity. It is often a question of feel the fear and do it anyway! In a training session setting 'ice-breakers,' humour, and energisers, can be used to break down barriers, relax people and stimulate them to be more creative.

> "Anxiety is part of creativity, the need to get something out, the need to get rid of something or to get in touch with something within."
>
> David Duchovny

Belief

Without self-belief, optimism and confidence in your unique talents and ability to generate worthwhile ideas for change, you are unlikely to get very far. If you think you can be creative you will be, while if you think you can't you won't. Thinking negatively about creativity may become a self-fulfilling prophecy and hinder your ability to be creative. To offset this tendency just think back about times when you were creatively confident – as a toddler when you learned to walk and talk, as a young child when you learned to cycle and as a young adult when you learned to drive. In between you learned how to make relationships work successfully, and learned how to think and solve problems. You took all of these challenges in your stride, building up your creative confidence as you accomplished one task after another. You didn't let other people define your creative confidence as a youngster and don't let them do it now!

Society has a negative view of older people. It is part of conventional wisdom that people should consider retiring from age 60 on. Old age is stereotyped as a time of mental decline. Old people are seen as a burden on society rather than a source of wisdom, learning and experience. Society expects old people to become passive and inactive. If you are getting on in years and you buy in to the societal expectation that mental decline is inevitable then it is more likely to happen. However, if you believe it is possible to remain alert and creative irrespective of age then this is more likely to be the case.

Pygmalion effect

People live up to their own expectations and the expectations of others. This is known in psychology as the Pygmalion effect and is a self-limiting belief. Beliefs are old programs imbedded in our subconscious through the influence of our parents, teachers and peers, who taught us to conform rather than question and be creative when we were young children. While very young our critical faculties are insufficiently developed to question such beliefs. However, you can program your mind using Neuro-Linguistic Programming (NLP) or self-hypnosis with positive self-talk to change such beliefs counteracting the damage done. Tell yourself you have great ideas. Program your mind with positive affirmation such as 'I'm becoming more creative with each passing day' or 'I'm unique, original and creative'. Program your mind to see challenges and opportunities, where others only see problems and obstacles.

Always bear in mind that creativity is a learnable skill. Anticipate obstacles and put strategies in place to deal with them. Imagine you have successfully overcome these anticipated problems and obstacles, as the mind doesn't distinguish between a real and an imagined thought. Strong positive beliefs pursued energetically have changed the course of history. Innovation is all about the confidence and determination to pursue your ideas.

Growth versus Fixed Mindset

There are two types of belief systems – one called a growth or achievement mindset and the other called a fixed mindset. The growth mindset believes that creativity can be improved by acquiring knowledge, experience and undertaking challenging assignments. This encourages you to keep going as creativity is malleable and can be enhanced through training and practise. Creativity is something you practise rather than a talent you are born with. The growth mindset thinks about possibilities and opportunities rather than limitations.

On the other hand, the fixed mindset believes that creativity depends on innate ability and is thus outside your control and sphere of influence, and so cannot be improved irrespective of how hard you try. This means that people with a fixed mindset do not embrace change as an opportunity for creativity with the challenges and new possibilities that change presents. They are thus more likely to leave things as they are rather than challenge things and seek out novel solutions to problems. They just give up and fail to recognise and exploit their special creative abilities that could help them make a mark on the world.

Some people have an attitude that they are too busy to sit back, reflect, innovate and dream. They feel they are too busy to draw up plans to turn their dreams into reality. They are too busy caught up in the day to day events of their lives to devote the necessary time to their dreams and aspirations. They don't realise that anything worthwhile takes considerable effort to do, and nothing gets done until you devote sufficient time and effort to do it.

Michelangelo took 4 years to finish the ceiling of the Sistine Chapel in the Vatican, and invented the painting technique of fresco in the process. This is the art of painting on fresh moist plaster with pigments dissolved in water. Some of the great cathedrals of Europe have taken centuries to finish. You need to do something each day to move you closer to your goal. Many famous writers stuck rigidly to a daily routine to get their work done. For example, the poet W.H. Auden was obsessively punctual, living to an exacting timetable during his lifetime.

Martin Luther King Jr. had a growth mindset with a dream that the United States could become a society free from racial prejudice, segregation and injustice. Despite fierce opposition and even imprisonment he went on to substantially achieve his objective. He was inspired by Gandhi's philosophy of non-violent protest. Following the Civil Rights Act of 1964, which helped stifle discrimination against black people, King was awarded the Nobel Peace Prize for his work towards social justice. Before this, in 1963 he was named Man of the Year by *Time* magazine. Similarly, Mahatma Gandhi had a growth mindset, winning independence for India from British rule by peaceful means. His belief in the effectiveness of non-violent protest changed the course of history and brought down the might of the British Empire.

Inhibitions

People don't like being observed or under scrutiny when attempting to be creative. It makes them nervous or on edge. Research shows that people in such circumstances are less creative. To be creative you need to be relaxed. Similarly when people feel they are being tested, they are less creative. In a work context, people reporting to an authority figure, who exercises tight control, are less likely to be creative. In addition, you are more likely to be creative if you have a say in your choice of work. People need the freedom to use their initiative and exercise their discretion if you want them to be creative.

> "All human development, no matter what form it takes, must be outside rules; otherwise we would never have anything new."
>
> Charles Kettering

Myths of Creativity

There are many half-truths and myths about creativity in circulation. Being aware of these myths will help you develop a more positive attitude to creativity and counteract any negativity. Myths can be categorised as people, ideas, business, and brain.

People myths

People myths include, only experts create anything meaningful, creative people are a gifted minority, you have to be mad to be creative, and most people seek creativity in drugs and alcohol. Let's explore these issues in further detail.

- *Only experts create anything meaningful.* In fact many of the great inventions of history were done by amateurs and people with a particular interest in the topic. They were driven by passion, desire and compulsion. The vast majority of inventions were created by unknown inventors. Some of these inventions were critical to the success of the human race like the plough, simple hand tools, the wheel and fire. We have evolved from crude primitive fire torches, to candles, to gas and electric lighting. However, sometimes it takes the unique perspective and fresh eyes of an outsider to solve a problem, particularly one that is thought to be unsolvable. Business history is filled with examples of outsiders who were dissatisfied with the status quo, and consequently helped to create new industries, products and services. Motivation and drive are more important than expertise and education – too much expertise and education can stifle creativity. Some US companies post their most difficult research and development problems on an internet site called InnoCentive, a crowdsourcing website for solving their most difficult problems. According to a survey 30% of the most difficult problems posted on the site were solved within 6 months. The secret is outsider thinking. Similarly, don't rely solely on experts within your company to solve problems. Bring in people who don't understand your problems from a corporate viewpoint, such as outsiders with an interesting different perspective, like customers, suppliers, or others in the value chain.

- *Creative people are a gifted minority.* Everybody is creative to some degree or another. You don't have to have a high IQ to be creative. A solid "C" student with curiosity and determination can make a bigger impact on the world than an "A" student. Creativity depends on a number of things: experience, including knowledge and technical skills, talent, an ability to think in new and unusual ways and an intrinsic interest in what you are doing. Common sense and the ability to relate successfully with other people will take you a long way. You don't need to write a symphony, carve a sculpture or paint a work of art to be creative. Simple everyday acts can be creative, such as how you express yourself, how you solve everyday problems, and how you engage with other people. However, there is no doubt that some people are more creative than others. Having the right genetic makeup can help. The rest of us have to learn to be creative. In any event, the important thing is to develop the creativity you have by further training and practise. Bear in mind that originality is just a combination of previous ideas brought together in new and unusual ways.

- *You have to be mad to be creative.* Creative people are not emotionally disturbed. They are not the slaves to, but rather the masters of, their imagination. There is plenty of evidence to suggest that creative individuals are just as healthy, both psychologically and physically, as non-creative individuals, and tend to have more energy and stamina. Most highly creative people are socially adjusted, have empathy, sensitivity, rationality and are open-minded. They tend to be hard-working and very diligent about what they do. Creative people tend to be good problem solvers. Certainly there were some creative people who were a bit idiosyncratic to say the least, but these were the exception rather than the rule. For example, the artist Vincent Van Gogh (1853-1890), cut off part of his ear with a razor and spent some time in psychiatric hospitals. In addition, there is no doubt that many famous creative people like Churchill, Beethoven and Hemingway had bipolar like symptoms. People suffering from bipolar disorder tend to have high self-esteem, be energetic and motivated and engage in fast and divergent thinking. However, research shows that most creative people are healthy and this leads to happiness and personal satisfaction rather than depression.

- *Most people, particularly writers and musicians seek creativity in drugs and alcohol.* However, research shows that there is no evidence that mood-altering substances can promote creativity. In an interview with Larry King on CNN, the famous rock star Mick Jagger admitted that performing under the influence of drugs limited his sense of control over his craft. Even though some artists claim they got good ideas while inebriated, creativity itself requires a lucid mind. It is true that Robert Louis Stevenson was known to take cocaine. W.H. Auden (1907-1973) relied on amphetamines to maintain his energy and concentration. Auden regarded amphetamines as one of the "labour-saving devices" in the "mental kitchen," alongside alcohol, coffee and tobacco. However, he was aware in his own words that "these mechanisms are very crude, liable to injure the cook, and constantly breaking down." Other writers were also known to be fond of alcohol, but it proved their downfall rather than a help. For example Brendan Behan (1923-1964) the Irish playwright and author was addicted to alcohol and died at 41 years of age cutting short a very promising career. He also had diabetes which didn't help, but refused to look after his health during his short life.

Idea myths

Idea myths include, when you come up with a brilliant idea people will beat a path to your door, ideas are magic and divinely inspired, the best ideas come from individuals, great ideas are instantly recognised, creativity is good and creativity means complexity. Let's explore these issues further.

- *When you come up with a brilliant idea people will beat a path to your door.* Ideas require hard work and dedication if they are to be implemented in the form of a worthwhile product or service. It takes a lot of research and development, product testing, advertising and marketing to bring ideas to fruition. Unless people are aware of your idea they are unlikely to be influenced by it. This suggests that advertising and marketing are ways of making your ideas known to the public. Many brilliant ideas never see the light of day because of lack of publicity. Many brilliant innovators never get the recognition they deserve because of lack of publicity. Take the case of Nikola Tesla, probably one of the greatest inventive geniuses of all time. Among other things he discovered alternating electricity and invented the electric motor. Even Marconi who won a Nobel Prize in Physics for inventing radio based his idea on Tesla's work. Tesla died broke and alone in a New York City hotel.

- *Ideas are magic, divinely inspired and you don't have to work for them.* The creative act is often seen as divinely inspired. This view dates back to the ancient Greeks, who believed that creativity required the intervention of the muses. In mythology the muses were the nine goddesses who symbolised the arts and sciences. People do have 'Eureka' moments, but they usually come after considerable hours of discussion, debate, reflection, research, experimentation and hard work. Insights need time to incubate in the subconscious before they emerge as suitable projects to pursue. The Wright brothers tinkered with the design of their flying machine for years, revising and improving each element again and again. For the wings alone, they tested more than 200 designs in a wind tunnel they built. Each attempt led to new ideas that eventually resulted in a machine that actually flew. Even Mozart said that people who think composition came easily to him were wrong. He claimed that he devoted more time to his composition than anybody else, and studied the music of other famous masters over and over. Gertrude Elion (1918-1999) earned a Nobel Prize in Physiology or Medicine in 1988 for her work in the discovery of drugs to treat leukaemia and herpes, and to prevent the rejection of kidney transplants. She said: "Don't be afraid of hard work. Nothing worthwhile comes easily. Don't let others discourage you or tell you that you can't do it. In my day I was told women didn't go into chemistry. I saw no reason why we couldn't."

- *The best ideas come from individuals.* In modern times great innovations are often the work of dedicated research and development teams. Most of the great discoveries and inventions of the 20th century including computers, telecommunications, commercial aviation, space flight and the breaking of the genetic code have come from inspired teams. All inventions build on the ideas of others. Take electricity. Frenchmen discovered alternating current. Germans invented the Leyden jar and the vacuum pump. The Danes were the source of many electric theories. An Austrian invented the first electric-powered machines. Alan Turing was the architect of the modern computer and came up with the concept of artificial intelligence. The creators of many inventions are teams of people who often remain anonymous. Corporate entities often take the credit for the inventions of their employees who are paid a salary. Even Edison had a team supporting him. The Beetles as a group were heavily influenced by the Beach Boys' *Pet Sounds* while recording Sgt Pepper. Their harmony was influenced by the Everly Brothers.
- *Great ideas are instantly recognised.* In fact great ideas are often mocked, laughed at, ridiculed,

rejected, and undermined. It often takes great persistence and determination on the part of the inventor to gain recognition and acceptance and see them through in the end. Alexander Graham Bell was laughed at during the first demonstration of the phone. Van Gogh never sold a painting even though they are now selling for millions each. Pasteur was mocked by the medical community when he claimed that vaccination could protect people from diseases.

- *Creativity is good.* Some creativity is bad. Thieves, murderers, unethical bankers, accountants, lawyers and other professionals often do bad things which are highly creative. The American scientists who invented the atomic bomb were horrified at the devastation and loss of human life caused when it was dropped over the Japanese cities of Hiroshima and Nagasaki in August 1945. The financial instruments designed by bankers were certainly very creative in their design but destructive in their outcome. However, they contributed in a significant way to the economic recession that the western world was plunged into in 2008. Enron was brought down by creative accounting. Terrorists used creative skills in a destructive and evil way to attack the World Trade Centre in New York. The lifestyles of famous inventors and scientists are often obsessive with long working hours leading to the neglect of their families. In addition, sometimes their interpersonal relationships skills are inadequate. The media often surround experts with the Halo Effect. In other words they treat them as if they are experts on all topics and issues in the world. In fact they don't have a magical insight on issues outside their domain. Outside their area of expertise their knowledge is limited and their views are no better than a layman's.

- *Creativity means complexity*. This is not necessarily so. The best ideas are simple and are often overlooked because they seem to be so obvious. Take the lowly tin can. This is a simple idea which revolutionised the world. It facilitated production, storage and distribution of food. It made armies and individuals more mobile and virtually eliminated botulism – a potentially deadly bacterium. Another simple but very effective idea was the flush toilet, which improved sanitation and hygiene resulting in a huge improvement in peoples' health, and a significant fall in mortality rates. There is a scientific principle which backs up the idea that the least complicated idea is often the best. This principle is known as Occam's Razor. Scientists believe that all things being equal, the simplest explanation is usually the correct one.

Business myths
Business myths include that competition facilitates creativity more than collaboration, it pays to be first into the market, all the best ways of doing things have already been found and constraints hamper creativity. Let's explore these issues further.

- *Competition facilitates creativity more than collaboration*. Competition is often a spur to creativity but generally the opposite is true, particularly in relation to teams. People in teams need the trust and confidence to collaborate with others to generate, share and build on each other's ideas. People who compete for recognition stop sharing ideas because of self-interest, envy and jealousy, and thus hinder the generation of further ideas. No single person in an organisation has all the information necessary to solve difficult problems.
- *It pays to be first into the market*. This may be true if you are patenting a blockbuster drug and therefore

monopolise the market. Pharmaceutical companies invest heavily in applied research, have long new-product development cycles and rely on legal protection through patents to safeguard their investment and competitive position. However, this is not always the situation in other industries, so followers can adopt a policy of wait and see and learn from the mistakes of the first entrants. In a 2010 study, University of Chicago researchers found that companies that enter new industries at an early stage actually operate at a disadvantage, and fail at a much higher rate that those who wait and see. It seems that the first-to-market pioneers suffer from higher costs which undermine their profitability. Consequently, over the long-term they are less profitable than second or third generation followers. There are many ways of outcompeting pioneers such as improving or simplifying a product, giving better service, tempting financial arrangements, more attractive packaging or by outmanoeuvring them in the marketplace. Consumers can get exhausted by complexity, giving other companies the opportunity to simplify products and thus gain the upper hand in the marketplace. For example the average user only uses 5 per cent of the functionality of Microsoft Word. A similar percentage would apply to Excel and PowerPoint. Apple's equivalent products are simple to use.

- *All the best ways of doing things have already been found.* This is not true as there are always better ways of doing anything. Many products are improvements of existing products. Most inventions build on ideas that came before. Many machines are refinements of existing ones. Continuous improvement is part of progress. Alexander Graham Bell described his invention of the telephone as an improvement in telegraphy. The improvement allowed electrical signals sent over a wire to be converted into sound. The modern aeroplane is a vast improvement on the Wright Brother's invention, but it took over 100 years of incremental improvements to come to this stage. Similarly, the modern car has come a long way from the Model T Ford produced at the start of the 20th century.

- *Constraints hamper creativity.* The opposite is sometimes the case. In fact constraints such as time deadlines and lack of money and resources often spur people on to greater creativity. Necessity may be the mother of invention. Great innovations are often made during times of great adversity such as wars, natural disasters, illness and competition. Working under time pressure a NASA team came up with a solution to fix the air filtration system aboard Apollo 13. The pressures of World War 2 and the fear that the Nazis would make the breakthrough first prompted the allies to produce the Atomic bomb quickly. Similarly World War 2 gave us the bouncing bombs invented by Barnes Wallace used to demolish strategic dams and defeat the Nazis. On the other hand, more often than not creativity needs an incubation period, which means people need to reflect on a problem for a considerable period of time in order for the idea to grow and develop. It took Newton 17 years to confirm his theory of gravity through complex calculations. Darwin's period of incubation was probably even longer. He had spent many years travelling and studying plant and animal specimens before a book by Malthus that he happened to pick up, and similar research by Alfred Russel Wallace, prompted him to publish.

Brain myths

Brain myths include, the right side of the brain controls creativity and that brain power is fixed at birth. Let's explore these issues further.

- *The right side of the brain controls creativity.* In fact, creativity is a whole-brain process, requiring the engagement of the left side of the brain as much as the right side. Writing a novel or creating any great work of art requires the integration of inputs from both sides of the brain. Professional musicians and designers have more efficient integration of the creative and rational parts of the brain than others. This means that high levels of creativity require divergent thinking mixed with convergent thinking. Divergent thinking is needed to generate alternatives, while convergent thinking is needed to evaluate and implement them.
- *Brain power is fixed at birth.* Neurological studies show that the brain is malleable and can lay down new brain cells as we gain more knowledge and experience. This means that we can increase our brain power through continuous learning and experience as we go through life. Since creativity is part of our brain power it follows that we can improve our creativity through continuous learning, experience, training and the application of creativity techniques.
- *Old people can't be creative.* Society expects them to be stuck in a rut. They are stereotyped as having fixed attitudes and being unable to learn new things. Instead they should be revered for their lifelong experiences and wisdom. In fact, older people can remain creative right into old age provided they remain healthy, and engage in lifelong learning and challenge themselves with new experiences.

> "Imagination is the beginning of creation. You imagine what you desire, you will what you imagine, and at last, you create what you will."
>
> George Bernard Shaw

Summary of Chapter 1

Creativity is not just for the privileged few, because we are all creative. Creativity is often about seeing something unusual in the usual or just seeing things differently. Apart from making something new or original, creativity can also be improving, refining, changing or combining things in unusual or novel ways.

Research shows that certain characteristics, whether from nature or nurture, or a combination of both, account for a person's creativity. These include having a broad range of interests, being attracted to complex issues, seeking out novel experiences, aesthetic sensitivity, toleration of ambiguity, non-conformity and risk-taking and self-confidence.

Creativity is the creation of an idea whereas innovation is the practical application of that idea. The creative company believes in flexibility, adaptability and involvement, implemented by a policy of empowering and developing their employees.

Intelligence and creativity are linked but different. You need a certain IQ to be creative, although people with a high IQ are not necessarily creative. The theory of multiple intelligences has widened out the scope of intelligence and creativity to include spatial, interpersonal, musical, intrapersonal, linguistic, kinaesthetic, logical and naturalistic.

The barriers to creativity are social, corporate and psychological. There are many half-truths about creativity. These relate to people, ideas, business and the brain. Being aware of these myths will help you develop a more positive attitude to creativity and counteract any negativity.

2
Why Does Creativity Happen?

Introduction

Evidence of creativity has spanned the history of human kind, from the drawings on cave walls and the invention of the wheel to the modern wonders of telecommunications. Creativity has been linked to genius, in science, business, and art, and many people have attained world fame through their wonderful discoveries and inventions. Modern living has been enriched and made possible through their creative endeavours.

Creativity is important because it creates business opportunities, visualises possibilities, fulfils design needs, meets personal ambitions, provide roles for people to play, and presents career opportunities for employees.

To survive, a business needs to work smarter and faster, continually develop new products and services, and improve existing ones. If you visualise a difficult task before you do it, you are more likely to successfully complete it. We tend to move towards those goals that are clearly visualised.

Good design is now more important than ever and permeates all aspects of our lives. Many companies are now driven by design. It is often the main competitive advantage.

The people who progress in their careers are the ones who can come up with new and innovative ideas, and new and improved ways of doing things.

Travelling to foreign parts and particularly living in foreign countries seems to be an aid to creativity. Many writers have produced their greatest works while being exiled abroad.

In general, people will be most creative if intrinsically rather than extrinsically motivated. The roles people adopt facilitate the process of creativity. These roles are explorer, artist, judge and warrior.

Business Needs

The basic reason companies facilitate creativity is because it is good for business, good for innovation, good for the morale of employees, and good for the reputation and image of the organisation.

Professional business people do not see themselves as creative – yet coping with change, innovation and competition is part of their business life, and demonstrates that they are creative. In order for businesses to survive they must work smarter and faster and come up with innovative strategies to match and beat the competition. They must improve the efficiency and productivity of their business by continually improving systems and procedures and operating to the highest standards. This means keeping up to date as regards information and communications technology. In the marketplace their products and services must meet the changing needs of customers.

Creativity isn't just about inventing new products and services. Creativity is also about identifying and developing new uses for existing products and services thereby creating new markets. During times of rapid change, management must design creative communication strategies to convince employees of the benefits of change, and win them over to accept the change programme. Creativity also helps people solve the problems and challenges of everyday life, and make more informed decisions.

The importance of creativity in the modern world cannot be disputed. In 2010, IBM conducted a poll of 1,500 CEOs who identified creativity as the number one leadership competency of the future. Since then other surveys have supported this finding. It is not only in business that creativity is needed but also in every walk of life. Broader societal needs include the threat of terrorism, global warming, political instability, poverty, pollution, renewable energy sources, finding alternatives to our diminishing primary resources and global warming. Solutions will emerge from people with original ideas who are also open to the ideas of others.

All of these issues need to be addressed and demand creative solutions. These issues impinge on a business as well, demanding creative solutions such as green technology and policies to protect the environment. Specifically in business, global competition, rapidly changing technology, and the shortening of the product life cycle, has made creativity more important than ever. A business needs creative people who are prepared to take calculated risks, and challenge conventional wisdom. Such people can identify and exploit opportunities to create new products, new markets, and new customers, to enhance profitability.

Creativity is needed throughout a business, from the top to the bottom, at strategic management, middle management, lower management and operational levels. The chief executive and the senior management team, should actively support creativity, and promulgate its importance throughout all levels of the organisation. Without creativity, a firm is unlikely to be innovative, and without innovation it is unlikely to be commercially viable. Creative solutions to problems can increase efficiency, productivity and profitability, and save companies substantial sums of money. A study by the Innovation Network in 2012 found that 88% of public companies identified innovation as a strategic priority. However, only about 5% had any specific programs or initiatives in place to make innovation a reality. Those who have made innovation a priority are reaping the benefits in terms of economic growth.

Specifically, creativity is needed in areas of business such as research and development, training and development, management services, systems analysis, product and market development, strategic planning, manufacturing processes, marketing, advertising, design and development. In a changing world, new products, services and technologies are appearing all the time. Apart from new inventions, there is continuous improvement on existing products, processes, systems and services. In addition, if a company is losing money creativity is needed to reverse its fortunes and make it profitable again.

Inventiveness and creativity is becoming more important in computer programming as well. As the routine work of testing, maintaining and upgrading software is moved to low-cost countries like India, engineers with the ability to invent new software applications are in high demand. Even when the new products have been invented they need to be launched, marketed and explained, and this requires ingenuity, customer service skills and empathy to build rapport with customers, investors and stakeholders. People also need to be trained in how to use them.

Visualisation

If you visualise a difficult task before you do it, you are more likely to successfully complete it. Athletes in various sports use this technique. They can rehearse critical movements in their heads which is almost as good as actual practise. In creative problem solving you can visualise a successful outcome. In engineering a similar approach may find a creative solution to a difficult problem. You visualise solutions no matter how absurd they may appear to be. Visualisation works because it programmes the mind to work as programmed.

The mind cannot perceive the difference between an actual event and one that has been imagined. Self-image determines what we are. You can improve your creativity by imagining that you are creative. You can imagine that you are good at generating ideas. You will then act like the person you imagine yourself to be. You can change your life by changing the way you think about yourself. Of course, this creative image should be backed up and reinforced by creative deeds. Nothing gets done until you act.

In addition, we tend to move towards those goals that are clearly visualised. Visualise your goals and your mind will figure out how to achieve them. The most successful companies are those that are driven by a compelling vision, such as Apple or Google. The idea of visualisation is well supported by research. For example, there is a well-known research study undertaken with three groups of basketball players. The first group physically practised and their skill improved by 24 per cent. The second group didn't practise and showed no improvement. The third group visualised practising in their heads and their skill improved by 23 per cent. Experiments with dart throwers produced similar results. Mentally throwing the darts was just as effective in improving skill as physically throwing them. Visualisation is now an integral part of sport and athletic training. Divers visualise the dive. Tennis players visualise the slam. Golfers visualise the putt. Boxers visualise the knockout punch. Footballers visualise the goal. They all do this with the expectation that their skill will improve and that their expectations will become real outcomes.

Every idea that changed the world began in the mind of someone as a vision. Many famous scientists visualised the solution to problems they were working on. Einstein maintained that he never thought in words. Ideas came to him in images which he later expressed in words and formulas. Companies visualise and produce a prototype before they commit resources to large scale production. They can test out a prototype of the product on a limited scale with customers and redesign if necessary before they commit to a final launch. This is the way to cheap, fast and successful innovation and the avoidance of unnecessary costs.

Steve Gass, who manufactured saws, visualised the most absurd concept. He wanted to develop a saw that would cut wood without cutting off the user's finger, if the blade came in accidental contact with it. Gass visualised in his mind a way to develop a revolutionary safety system that stops and retracts the blade of a 10 inch cabinet saw within 5 milliseconds of contact with the skin. A common technique used by creative people like Steve Gass when confronted with a problem, is to block out all verbal thoughts and concentrate instead on visual images.

> "If students are to trust their creative ability, we must teach them to slow down, gather sensory data, notice relationships, and use their imaginations to visualise."
>
> Betty K. Garner

Design Needs

Good design is often the driver behind creative ideas. Good design is now more important than ever and permeates all aspects of our lives – from the houses we live in and how we furnish and decorate them, to the products and appliances we use and consume. It's no longer sufficient to just create reasonably priced, useful and user friendly products. They must also be aesthetically beautiful, unique and appeal to the senses and emotions, and fit easily into peoples' lifestyles. Even the most humble kitchen utensils must satisfy the new middle-class obsession with good design. People now want lighting, décor, furniture, fabrics and products of good design that will enhance the home environment.

Many organisations now understand the importance of good design, and have entered into ongoing partnerships with poets, designers, architects, dancers, musicians, theatre professionals and visual artists to improve their artistic and design capabilities. Some firms spend considerable sums of money on designing eye catching corporate logos. These give the company instant recognition in the market place. After all, branding and good design are different sides of the same coin. One provides recognition and the other creates attraction while strengthening customer loyalty. Companies create loyalty by getting customers to fall in love with their corporate logos, brands and designs.

Good design is what differentiates your products from the competition. Good design is not merely the package for a product, but a way to drive sales. Good design will increase sales, create brand recognition and should be considered an investment rather than a cost. Good design gets things noticed.

Coca Cola's famous iconic bottle shape created instant brand recognition and huge sales volume for the brand worldwide. Car manufacturers have long understood the importance of design, and the contribution it makes to the success and profitability of a company. In the early days Italian car manufacturers built their market niche on the design of their cars. Other car manufacturers quickly followed.

The mini is considered a British icon of the 1960s and is still going strong as the revamped mini cooper. Similarly, the Volkswagen Beetle is considered a German icon, and is the longest-running and most-manufactured car of a single design platform worldwide. BMW's goal for their cars is to produce the ultimate driving machine. Their designers have a great sense of passion and pride in their designs. They consider their goal of perfection as an almost spiritual quest. Well-designed products can be sold at premium prices.

Good engineering design means designing things with the needs of the customer or end user in mind. People like to own products that are enjoyable to use and easy to learn. This means empathising with the user and trying to see things from their point of view. Products should be easy to use and be built to withstand everyday misuse and the damage such misuse can cause. The emphasis should be on simplicity rather than complexity. Designs should be emotionally appealing to the user as well as functional.

Making your product too complicated to use with unnecessary features will hinder the adoption of your creation, no matter how brilliant or useful it might be. Microsoft Word is a case in point; it is badly designed not because it is complicated but because it is too complicated. The average user doesn't know half the things it can do. On the other hand, Apple's business success lies in the simplicity of its design. Business analysts attribute a significant share of the company's growth to the creative artistry of Steve Jobs, and his abilities to make products that consumers deeply desire, love and find easy to use. An example of superb design is the Mac personal computer which has gone through many incarnations and is still popular today.

People who design computers should take the advice of Cordell Ratzlaff, the designer of the Mac OS X, to heart:

"People don't use a computer to enjoy the operating system; they don't care about choosing what kinds of scrollbars they want. They use a computer because they want to create something; they want to express their own personality, everything from writing a novel to balancing their cheque book – some more than others, but it's all about accomplishing something that really doesn't have anything to do with a computer. The computer is just a tool. As interactive designers, we need to remember that it is not just about the interface, it's about what people want to do! To come up with great designs, you need to know what they are really trying to accomplish."

Companies driven by design

The fashion industry would not survive without constant creativity and innovation. Successful fashion companies reinvent their product line and thus their brands every season. It repeatedly brings out products that consumers didn't know they needed, often creating such high demand that the previous year's fashions are made obsolete. A fashion company that fails to innovate and please customers will not survive in business.

Nike is a company driven by design. It has an in-house think tank, called the Innovation Kitchen, to generate ideas for its innovative footwear. The Kitchen is completely separate from the day-to-day business, and in the past has come up with footwear innovations such as Flywire and Lunarlite super resilient foam. The Innovation Kitchen has evolved into a multidiscipline innovation and sports performance organisation that drives Nike's agenda for all footwear and some sports apparel. It is very concerned with developing environmentally friendly practices, and has a team comprised of 13 experts in environmental science, engineering, chemistry, toxicology, and product development to drive efforts to reach the company's sustainability goals. Nike knows their customers well and they develop products around their customers' needs. Consequently, they have a reputation for producing innovative, customer focused and market-led products.

IDEO, the largest design-consulting firm in the USA, have used creative idea generation techniques to develop new and innovative products. In the past, they have included Crest toothpaste tubes, the original Apple computer mouse, Nike sunglasses, a motor scooter and a carbon-fibre bicycle wheel. IDEO believes bureaucracy stifles creativity. It has no permanent organisation charts, no titles, not even permanent offices. Employees' file cabinets and bookcases are on wheels, so they can be easily moved to another office more convenient for the project team. IDEO lives by the five brainstorming rules when conducting brainstorming sessions. These are: "Have one conversation at a time. Build upon the ideas of others. Defer judgement. Encourage wild ideas. Stay focused on the subject." It attributes its considerable success at design to sticking to these principles. Brainstorming is explored in more detail in Chapter 4.

Good design is the output of good design thinking. Good designers study how people use things in practice, and then use their skills to improve those things, making them easier to use. IDEO believes that the methods and approaches that good designers use to solve problems include understanding and anticipating user needs, prototyping to evolve ideas and using storytelling to bring ideas to life. They believe in making prototypes quickly and testing out their products on a small scale, getting feedback and refining the product, before they commit to large scale production and marketing. When you have a prototype you have something physical to discuss and debate about. Innovation is all about experimentation and improvement. A viable product will get you feedback as regards customer acceptability, and save you considerable time and cost in the long-term. At the end of the day innovation is all about quickly turning ideas into action, rather than getting side-lined by complicated planning. The best failures are quick, cheap and early so that you can learn from your mistakes and take them into account in subsequent redesigns.

One project IDEO undertook was making an MRI scanner more acceptable to paediatric patients or children. They found that many children were scared of the machine and therefore very reluctant to use it. The solution was to redesign the experience as a pirate ship or spaceship. In other words, they reframed the experience and designed it with a child's perspective in mind. They redesigned it as a fun and playful experience that children would enjoy. Children then had no bother using the machine, and even asked their parents when they would have an opportunity to return and use it again.

The IDEOs Embrace Infant Warmer is a low cost incubator. It has saved the lives of babies in remote areas in poor countries with little modern infrastructure. Embrace is an alternative to expensive incubators for babies born prematurely, who are unable to maintain their own body temperature. This low cost product maintains premature and low birth weight babies' body temperature, and helps them survive and thrive. Embrace has been acclaimed as a major success in health and human-centred design. It has gone through a number of changes in fabrics, materials, shapes and warming elements, learning and adapting from testing and feedback. It has gone through and is still going through a process of continuous improvement. It can keep infants warm for up to 6 hours at a time.

Ikea is an international home products retailer that sells furniture, accessories, and bathroom and kitchen items. The group's emphasis on providing home furnishing products of good design at low prices has been the main reason its products are so popular. It is considered to be at the forefront of an urban design revolution. The customer plays a vital role in keeping costs down. Ikea relies on customers to choose, collect, transport and assemble Ikea products themselves. Ikea's mission is to "create a better everyday life for ordinary people." Head designer Marcus Engman says that "Ikea isn't just about making things; it's about making things better." Ikea is also concerned about protecting the environment through its sustainability policy. For example, the group has installed more than 550,000 solar panels in its stores and buildings throughout the world, and invested in 137 wind turbines.

> "Good design is good business."
>
> Thomas Watson JR.,
> Chairman and chief executive IBM

Career Opportunities

The people who progress in their careers are the ones who can come up with new innovative ideas, and new and improved ways of doing things. The people who get noticed and promoted are the ones who continually challenge existing processes and methods. They are prepared to suggest better and more efficient ways of doing them, even in the face of ridicule and strong opposition. These people are confident about the feasibility and quality of their ideas, and have the determination and persistence to pursue them and push them through in the face of opposition.

These are the people who stand out from the crowd because of their creative problem solving skills, and ability to learn on their own. They stand out because they are unique and make a unique contribution to the firm. Even in routine jobs, creative people will be continually questioning things to find better ways of doing them. They are never satisfied with the status quo. The idea of continuous improvement comes naturally to such people.

When creative people don't find the creative opportunities they desire in their existing employments they look elsewhere to meet these needs. This could be through taking up hobbies that interest them or seeking employment where their creative talents would be used. In exceptional cases they even set up their own businesses to meet and exploit their creative needs.

> "Problems don't get solved by the smartest or the fastest or the strongest; they get solved by the one who sees the possibilities."
>
> Dan Roam

Creativity and Travel

Travelling to foreign parts and living in foreign countries seems to be an aid to creativity. The aphorism which says that travel broadens the mind is not true. According to recent research it is not travel but living abroad that helps people to be more creative. Research published in the Personality and Social Psychology Bulletin in June 2010 found significant links between living abroad and creativity. It seems that living abroad can be a most creative experience for ordinary people provided they immerse themselves in the local culture.

Living in and adapting to a new culture requires people to learn novel approaches to problem solving, and behave in a flexible and different way to cope with a changed way of life. On the other hand, travelling from place to place and staying in hotels doesn't have the same effect as it may not move people very far out of their comfort zone. Although anecdotally travel would appear to broaden your knowledge base and give you new perspectives. In addition, when you're far away you begin to see issues at home in a new light and not as compelling as when you are close up to them.

Artists and writers always said that living abroad helped them to be more imaginative and creative. We just have to think about artists like Picasso, and writers like Ernest Hemingway, James Joyce and Samuel Beckett. Picasso spent most of his life in France. Ernest Hemingway spent time in Italy, France, Spain, Cuba as well as the USA. He also spent time shooting wild game in Africa.

James Joyce spent considerable time in Paris and Zurich. His books were banned for a time in the USA and the UK as well as being banned in Ireland. Samuel Beckett eventually settled down in Paris just like James Joyce. He wrote his original works in French even though his native language was English – the accepted international language of the 20th century. However, he said that he wanted the discipline, flexibility and economy of expression that a new language would force upon him.

Many organisations recognise the benefits to employees of job assignments abroad. They hope employees will use the opportunity to become more creative and innovative, and introduce new ideas into their companies when they come home. Universities also maintain that students involved in study programmes abroad increase their knowledge, which in turn helps them become more creative.

Creativity and Motivation

The motivation for creativity can come from many sources including, internal, external, management theory, emotions, necessity, commitment and persistence and goals. Let's now consider each of these in more detail.

Intrinsic motivation
Intrinsically motivated people have the confidence and self-belief to be creative, and so there is a self-fulfilling prophecy in operation. They take a pride in their work. They are totally committed and love the work that they do, and have a strong desire for self-actualisation – becoming what they are capable of becoming. They are totally interested and emotionally absorbed in their work, find it satisfying and enjoy the challenge that it offers. They are drawn to their work like a magnet because of the prospect of discovering something new and exciting. Scientists are often intrinsically motivated by the prospect of expanding the frontiers of understanding and knowledge and improving the lives of ordinary people.

Those lucky enough to have a career rather than a job are likely to be more creative. People with a job view it just as a means of making money, to provide for themselves and their family. On the other hand, those with a professional career or vocation have found their purpose and mission in life. For example, a nurse may have a mission in life to help those under their care to overcome their sickness and return to health. They really enjoy their work and the financial rewards are only secondary. Their career provides them with the opportunity to acquire and practise the essential skills and knowledge of medicine, to help those who are too ill to recover without their help and intervention. Their mission in life provides them with an inherent source of motivation and great job satisfaction.

People are most creative when they're passionate about their work, and they're stretching their skills. If the challenge is far beyond their skill level, they tend to get frustrated, while if it's below their skill level, they tend to get bored, and so the right balance needs to be struck for best results. In fact, a challenging job offering satisfaction is more important than monetary compensation. The Wright brothers were motivated not by the desire to get rich, but rather by the technical challenges and sense of adventure in the quest for human flight.

John Irving, the famous novelist whose screenplay adaptation of his novels has won Oscars, maintains he loves writing despite the long hours involved. He says: "The unspoken factor is love. The reason I can work so hard at my writing is that it's not work for me." Research has found that Nobel Prize winners were proud of their work not for the awards they received, but for the intrinsic satisfaction of the work. Albert Einstein talked about intrinsic motivation as "the enjoyment of seeing and searching." Arthur Schawlow (1921-1999) who won the Nobel Prize in Physics in 1981 said: "The labour-of-love aspect is important. The most successful scientists often are not the most talented, but the ones who are most impelled by curiosity. They've got to know what the answer is."

The pros and cons of money as an extrinsic motivator

Though few creative people are motivated by money, the importance of money cannot be denied. Money brings you financial independence and freedom to pursue the work that you really want to do and enjoy. With money you can buy the necessary materials and equipment that you need to do your work, employ mentors and travel to places and people that you can learn from.

Many of the famous creative people in history such as Darwin were financially independent, and so had the time and resources to commit to their lifetime passions. Most of the rest of us have to work for a living and pursue our interests on a part-time basis, unless we count ourselves among the fortunate few who happen to have jobs that they are passionate about. If survival needs consume all our attention we have little energy left to be creative and innovative.

If you don't find work particularly satisfying you should look for those aspects of the work that you find appealing rather than boring in order to be motivated. On the other hand, intrinsic motivation can be undermined by extrinsic motivators that make people feel externally manipulated, bribed and controlled in their work. Extrinsic motivation or being rewarded by a third party is not as effective and can be counterproductive. In fact, the prospect of monetary rewards for creativity could make you less rather than more motivated.

Management theories on motivation
Financial rewards do not in themselves make employees passionate about their work, and thus may hinder creativity in the long-term. This is no surprise as the pioneering work of Frederick Herzberg showed that learning and being challenged motivate workers more than money. In addition, if you reward some people and don't reward others, the people who aren't rewarded feel that they have been punished and feel like losers. At the same time, people may feel underappreciated if their creative efforts are ignored. This would suggest that genuine praise, if given in the appropriate circumstances, is effective. Richard Branson said: "When you lavish praise on people, they flourish; criticise and they shrivel up." He walks the talk by giving compliments to his staff. In addition, other kinds of non-financial rewards such as

promotional titles, certificates of appreciation and badges and emblems can be effective.

Another management theorist Abraham Maslow saw creativity as a journey in his "hierarchy of needs" theory of motivation. According to Maslow an individual's creative journey is an upward progression. It begins with the need to meet the survival needs of food and shelter. It then progressively goes through a process of meeting safety, belonging, self-esteem and ultimately self-actualisation or creativity needs. The theory presupposes that it is difficult to move forward until each stage has been completed. Inspiration and creative innovation naturally evolve as physiological needs such as food and shelter are met. In the work context this means that the basic and emotional needs of employees including security and self-esteem must be met before their creativity blossoms. If these needs, including a supportive environment for creativity, are not satisfactorily met employees are unlikely to have the motivation to be creative. Because their work is an important part of their identity, creative people are often motived by recognition, praise and a sense of achievement.

If you promote and reward people who are creative it will demonstrate that creativity is valued and recognised. This, in turn, will encourage other ambitious people in the organisation to be creative. In addition, if you provide challenging work for employees and give them the freedom to pursue their own ideas you are more likely to foster creativity. This shows that the organisation values creativity and recognises its role. Thus creativity depends more on internal validation rather than external validation by teachers, bosses or family. Awareness of possible evaluation or the possibility of being watched reduces creativity. On the other hand, in certain circumstances extrinsic rewards can have a positive effect if the measures are linked to things other than creativity such as reaching targets, overtime hours or accuracy of output.

Emotions

According to research, emotions are contagious, so people in the workplace have the tendency to mimic or copy the emotions of work colleagues. In a series of studies published in the journal *Motivation and Emotion*, researchers found that simply placing participants in the same room as a highly motivated individual improved their drive and enhanced their performance. But when they paired participants with a less motivated individual, their inspiration fell and their performance deteriorated. This means that the behaviour of work colleagues can have a positive or negative effect on our creativity and work performance.

The impact of motivational synchronicity is greatest in organisations that rely on creativity and problem solving to succeed. Creativity doesn't just happen but requires a particular state of mind such as openness, curiosity and exploration. Fostering creativity in the workplace is a major source of innovation and profitability for companies. Our work colleagues shape our thoughts, influence our creative thinking, and ultimately determine the quality of our work. So it pays to create an environment in work that encourages, fosters and celebrates creativity.

In certain circumstances anger can be a strong motivator to creativity as it may energise us to action to take steps to rectify perceived wrongs. Sometimes people are so angry by injustice in the world that they decide on extraordinary measures to counteract it by fighting for social justice. There is a strong correlation between anger, rage and creativity, provided the anger is channelled in a focused, controlled, appropriate, non-destructive and productive way. Just think of people who suffered physical and sexual abuse in lay and religious institutions, and set up organisations as adults to expose and seek justice for the wrongs done to them during the most innocent and vulnerable periods of their lives.

Other people witness extreme poverty in the world around them and decide to do something about it by setting up organisations to combat poverty. Some works in literature and art were inspired by a sense of anger against the world such as works by the writer Virginia Woolf and the artist Frances Bacon. Even some inventors are motivated by anger. British inventor James Dyson claims anger motivated him to produce the ball-barrow and bag-less vacuum cleaner. Frustration with existing poor designed products is often the motivator for better and improved ones.

Even moods can affect your creativity. When individuals are in a good mood they are more motivated, and their creative thinking and problem solving skills are enhanced. They make more connections and associations between different things, and see things with a broader perspective. Moods are contagious, so a supervisor's positive mood will be transmitted to employees.

Competition can be a prime motivator for invention. Edison was aware of the work of others on the light bulb at the same time and this prompted him to move more quickly. The Wright Brothers realised they were in competition with other teams to be the first to achieve powered flight. Watson and Crick, the discoverers of DNA, knew they were racing Linus Pauling to discover the helical structure of DNA. Winning the race was a powerful motivator for them. Similarly, Darwin released his theory of evolution when he realised that Alfred Russel Wallace had arrived at similar conclusions and was about to do the same, and so it is often competition that spurs innovators into action. The race to get patent recognition is also a factor.

Necessity
There is an old saying that necessity is the mother of invention. Indeed it was necessity that motivated Mary Anderson to invent windshield wipers. It was during a trip to New York City when she noticed that car drivers had to open their windows when it rained to see. This inspired her to invent a swinging arm device with a rubber blade that was operated from inside the car using a lever. She received a patent for her invention in 1903. Initially many people were wary of Anderson's invention, claiming that it would distract drivers. However, by 1918 windshield wipers were standard

on most vehicles. It was also a woman named Charlotte Bridgwood who invented the automatic windshield wiper in 1917.

Josephine Cochrane (1839-1913) invented the dishwashing machine. Her motivation was also necessity. She did a lot of home entertaining, and found that her servants chipped her fine china much to her annoyance when washing up by hand. She took on the chore herself, but found it very time-consuming. She thought to herself that there must be a better way. She worked out a design employing water jets with trays to hold the plates, cups and saucers. Soon after she began working on the design her husband died and left her with debt. This gave her the drive to create a successful model of her machine.

In 1886 she succeeded and patented her invention. In 1893 her machine won an award for its design and durability at the Chicago World Fair. Initially she sold the machine to friends, calling the machine the "Cochrane Dishwasher." The public generally were slow to take up her invention, as they claimed that they preferred to wash the dishes by hand. It was not until the 1950s that the machines popularity skyrocketed. Women's' attitudes to housework had changed, detergent had arrived and the machines were more user friendly. Today the dishwasher is a part of the typical modern home. Her company eventually became part of the Whirlpool Corporation.

Commitment and persistence

People who want to see their creative ideas implemented must be highly motivated, committed and enthusiastic to win the support of potential backers. Commitment is the prolonged effort needed to solve complex problems. It is a specific, more developed, form of motivation. There is an analogy about the bacon-and-egg breakfast. The chicken is interested but the pig is committed. Your ability to network and build strong relationships, and win the support of the right people is essential if you want to get your idea implemented. The social nature of creativity is important and the ability to network with others can't be underestimated. Having an idea is the easy part. Convincing others about the merit of your idea is the hard part. To win support of potential investors your idea must be capable of being transformed into a viable and profitable product or service.

Motivation and persistence go hand in hand. It takes many years to build up the knowledge and experience necessary to make a major creative contribution in any field. This time is spent in constant experimentation, revising, discarding and learning new and more efficient ways of doing things. Research sounds exciting and inherently motivational. But this is not always the case. Just like most jobs, research can involve a lot of routine monotonous work that is not very motivational. Patient endurance is needed to stick to the task. Edison learned 1,800 ways of how not to build a light bulb before he got it right. Clarence Birdseye had his flash of insight forty years before he established the frozen food industry. It took Bill Bowerman and Philip Knight more than twenty years to turn their technical knowledge into a viable shoe. Twenty or forty years is a long time to wait for a reward. It shows that creative people are not merely motivated by rewards, but more motivated by the challenge of the task they are pursuing.

Goals
People are motivated by goals. Goals should be challenging but attainable, specific and measurable. Written goals are unlikely to be forgotten. Goals focus attention and effort by providing clear targets for individuals to direct their energies. Goals regulate action by directing people's attention; determine how hard they work, and how long they persist on a task. People should have goals beyond their present goals. This will give them a sense of purpose, interest and enjoyment throughout their lives. Goals will ensure that you have always something to accomplish in life, and therefore you will always have something to do.

Goal setting leads to goal achievement, which results in satisfaction and pride and increased happiness and confidence.

On the other hand, immobilisation leads to non-achievement, boredom and depression and feelings of worthlessness. Having goals makes life interesting and challenging, leading to personal growth and self-esteem. Doing nothing leads to despondency and hopelessness. Which would you prefer?

Research shows that individuals who were set goals for creative performance increased their creative output. On the other hand, if goals for creativity are not set, then people are less likely to be creative. Edison was probably one of the most creative people who ever lived. He continually set himself and his team creative goals to be achieved, and surrounded himself with support staff and experts in a workshop to do so. Just like Edison, leaders should make it known to employees that creativity is demanded and needed to perform the job effectively.

> "There is no doubt that creativity is the most important human resource of all. Without creativity, there would be no progress, and we would be forever repeating the same patterns."
>
> Edward de Bono

Adopting Certain Roles

The roles people adopt during their lifetimes facilitate the process of creativity. Four roles have been identified as explorer, artist, judge and warrior. All these roles are necessary in combination to convert creative ideas into worthwhile products.

- *The explorer.* An explorer is hungry for adventure and discovery. Explorers see problems as challenges and are curious and open. They search, look and probe for information. They read around the problem and talk to lots of different people to get different perspectives. The explorer searches continually for new challenges and opportunities, and is not overly concerned with the risk involved.

They continually wander off track just like real explorers to surreptitiously discover unusual things. The explorer constantly asks questions and discusses issues. Well known explorers include Christopher Columbus who discovered America, Marco Polo; synonymous with travel and adventure and known for his travels throughout China, and Charles Darwin for his historic voyage aboard the Beagle. It was during this time that Darwin conducted explorations that led to the development of his controversial theory of evolution by natural selection.

- *The artist.* Combines and transforms information in new and interesting ways to create new ideas. Artists are flexible, open, persistent, playful and imaginative. They are keen to experiment and are continually modifying things. They are unconventional and uninhibited and can tolerate ambiguity. Artists look at information from different perspectives and pursue different approaches to find unexpected connections. Artists challenge the status quo and don't really care what other people think about them. They trust and rely greatly on their powers of intuition. They are not afraid to let their imagination run riot to visualise new possibilities. Picasso experimented with his style frequently and it is difficult to realise that his works of different periods are by the same artist.

- *The judge.* The judge evaluates and offers constructive criticism. The judge assesses the idea in a logical, objective and realistic way. The judge considers the pros and cons of each idea. Is the idea feasible? Will the idea give you the return on investment you want? Do you have the resources to make it happen? The judge acts as a devil's advocate and continually questions assumptions. He will check evidence and look for counterarguments before arriving at sound conclusions. It is important not to exercise judgement at the earlier stages of idea generation. Criticism at this early stage can stifle ideas, and so can be counterproductive. The judge provides constructive criticism and makes sure that the product is practical and commercially viable. At the end of the assessment the judge will do one of three things – implement the idea, change it or reject it.

- *The warrior.* The warrior puts ideas into action by taking the idea started by the explorer, developed by the artist and evaluated by the judge as worthwhile and realistic. Warriors are persistent, tenacious, self-confident and courageous. Warriors have a can-do attitude. They see each obstacle as a challenge to be overcome. They take the product to market by overcoming resistance, dealing effectively with competition and convincing others of its merits. To do so you will need a strategy and plan of action. You must be able to sell your ideas and overcome obstacles and objections. The warrior must follow through to make sure that the plan of action has been successfully implemented, and learn from feedback about mistakes made on the journey.

The journey from explorer to artist to judge and warrior is not sequential, but may go back and forth depending on the need for further clarification, information and consideration. The main thing is to be aware of is which role you are performing at any one time. You should have the necessary skills for each role, and play each one competently at the appropriate time. In practice you may have a preference for any one role. All the roles are equally important and each plays a significant part in the overall success of the project. When you adopt the explorer and artist role you are involved in divergent thinking, or generating and exploring new ideas. When you adopt the judge and warrior roles you are involved in convergent thinking, or seeking a conclusion.

> "Sceptical scrutiny is the means, in both science and religion, by which deep thoughts can be winnowed from deep nonsense."
>
> Carl Sagan

Summary of Chapter 2

Global competition, rapidly changing technology, and the shortening of the product life cycle, has made creativity more important in business than ever.

Every idea that changed the world began in the mind of someone as a thought. We tend to move towards purposeful goals that we clearly visualise.

Good design is what differentiates your products from the competition. Good design will increase sales, create brand recognition, and should be considered an investment rather than a cost.

The people who get noticed and promoted are the ones who continually challenge existing processes and methods. They are adept at continuous improvement and the development of new products and services.

Living in foreign countries increases creativity. Living and adapting to a new culture requires people to learn novel approaches to problem solving and behave differently to cope with a changed way of life.

People are motivated more by the interest and love of the work that they do rather than monetary rewards. Adopting the roles of explorer, artist, judge, and warrior will make you more creative and channel your creativity in an appropriate way.

3
When Does Creativity Happen?

Introduction

The subconscious plays a vital role in our creativity. Your subconscious is the storehouse of everything you know, even things you can't readily call to mind. It makes patterns and connections without your conscious knowledge.

Some famous people came up with their brilliant ideas and marvellous inventions after a daydream or a dream. Thomas Edison claimed that most of his ideas came to him after dozing. Creative people are great note takers. Leonardo da Vinci kept detailed notes and drawings of his ideas that survive to this day.

Many famous inventions were inspired by serendipitous events. One of the most notable accidental discoveries was Alexander Fleming's penicillin made in 1928. This is just one of the serendipitous events which inspired major breakthroughs in business and science and consumer goods.

Thinking creatively can be encouraged by having the right mindset, adopting the right approach and having fun during the process.

Role of the Subconscious

Sometimes problems get solved when people are working on other problems, thinking about other issues, or engaged in recreational pursuits. People have even solved problems after sleeping on them! Bertrand Russell reported how, when he was writing *Principia Mathematica,* he would frequently go to bed having failed to solve a problem despite much effort. On waking the next morning the solution to the problem unexpectedly popped into his head. His subconscious biological computer had solved the problem during his sleep. Your subconscious is the storehouse of everything you know, even things you can't readily call into awareness. It makes patterns and connections without your awareness. Some people are more creative late at night, while others are more creative early in the morning. Research has established that early birds find more original solutions late at night, while night owls do better early in the morning.

Ideas often come to us at the most unexpected times and in the most unexpected places. It is said that the Greek scientist Archimedes discovered the principle of buoyancy when stepping into his bath, when he noticed the level of the water rose as he got into it. King Hieron had posed the problem for Archimedes to solve that the King's new crown was definitely made of solid gold. He suspected the artisan who made the crown of being deceitful by alloying or corrupting the gold in his crown, but had no way of proving it. Archimedes couldn't simply break open the crown as that would have destroyed it. Instead he realised that the problem could be solved, by measuring the volumes of water displaced by the crown and an equal weight of gold. By comparing densities he could determine the gold content of the crown and thus solve the King's problem.

Your subconscious will process, recombine, adapt and consolidate ideas, images and experiences and suggest solutions. It is a way of accessing the vast resources of the subconscious, and tap spontaneous useful insights. This is why daydreaming is so effective for producing creative ideas. It is also natural to daydream. Psychologists and neuroscientists estimate that we spend between 15 and 50% of our waking hours daydreaming – that is we stray away from reality and focus instead on our inner thoughts, feelings and fantasies.

Inspired By Dreams

Many scientists have been inspired by their dreams to make wonderful discoveries and inventions. When you sleep your mind doesn't turn off. Instead it becomes very active during dreaming. Sometimes dreams are the way your mind works out solutions to problems you may have, and taps into the creativity in your subconscious to do so. For many writers and inventors their dreams can be powerful inspirational tools. There is an old adage "to sleep on it" which means that if you go to sleep thinking about a problem, you may wake up in the morning with the solution. So if you plant a seed before you sleep the mind works on it as you sleep.

Daydreams also help us to build and practise our social skills. We can rehearse social encounters in a virtual imaginative world such as difficult encounters with the boss, making fun of the teacher, and potential conflicts with our enemies without risk or consequence.

Instead of being a waste of time, daydreams are now seen as a potential door to the Nobel Prize. Many famous scientists used visionary daydreams to help them win the coveted prize. For example, Einstein conceived the theory of relativity while working in a routine job at the Swiss patent office.

Rene Descartes is known as the "father of modern science." What isn't widely known is that the essence of what we now know as the "scientific method" was revealed to him in a dream. The scientific method is where a new model or hypothesis is developed to explain a natural phenomenon. This is then supported through experiments to test the model. Descartes was an exceptionally bright young man and dropped out of school at the age of 17 when he realised that he wasn't learning anything. He then decided to retire at the tender age of 20, and for the next two years did little else but stay in bed, read, reflect, dream and write. It was during the second year of his retreat that the scientific method came to him while dreaming.

Take the case of Elias Howe, who invented the lock stitch sewing machine, and claimed to have hit on the idea after a nightmare. He dreamed that while cannibals were boiling him alive he noticed that their spears had holes in the tips. This proved to be the novel solution to his problem of where he would put the eye of the needle of his sewing machine.

August Kekule, a famous German chemist, discovered that many organic compounds are formed of rings, rather than open molecules. He was inspired by a dream of a snake swallowing its tail, with the realisation that the Benzene chemical compound had a circular rather than a linear structure. He thus solved a problem that had been confounding chemists for a long time. In addition, don't ignore your intuition or sixth sense, as gut feelings sometimes are inspirational, and the idea generated may have practical validity. Our intuition may serve us well in some circumstances by harnessing the subconscious processing part of the brain.

Otto Loewi (1873-1961), a German born physiologist, won the Nobel Prize for medicine in 1936 for his work on the chemical transmission of nerve impulses. His discovery was inspired by a dream. In 1903, Loewi had the idea that nerve impulses had a chemical rather than an electrical cause, which was the conventional wisdom at the time. However, he didn't know how to prove his idea. He left the idea incubate for 17 years, until he had an inspirational dream about how he could draw up an experiment to prove his thesis. It took Loewi another 10 years before he could carry out the tests to prove his theory to the satisfaction of his peers and critics.

You must pay attention to your daydreams if you are to reap the benefits of potential creative insights. Jerry Swartz, is the inventor of the first hand-held barcode laser scanner, and the first commercial wearable computer. He always carried index cards with him, so that he could record any ideas occurring to him while daydreaming lest he forget them. We should model this behaviour, as otherwise what good are ideas emanating from daydreams, if we don't take the trouble to record them?

Writers inspired by dreams

Joseph Heller (1923-1999) the famous American author, who wrote the best seller *Catch-22*, maintained that his best ideas came to him when engaging in controlled daydreaming and directed reverie. He had worked in advertising, and claimed that the discipline of writing advertising copy to strict deadlines may have developed this capacity.

Creative writers never lose their childhood ability to daydream, dream and fantasise. For example, the three Bronte sisters created make-believe characters and worlds in their novels, while living in their parsonage on the Yorkshire moors. Their books such as *Jane Eyre, Wuthering Heights* and *The Tenant of Wildfell Hall* and other works are considered masterpieces of literature. Mary Shelley in her introduction to *Frankenstein* claims that her book was inspired by a dream about a man assembled from bits of dead people.

In his autobiography Robert Louis Stevenson describes how he used dreaming to produce his literary works including such famous novels as *Kidnapped, Treasure Island* and *The Strange Case of Dr Jekyll and Mr Hyde*. The novelist Stephen King said the storyline for his book *Misery* came to him after he fell asleep on a plane journey. Generally he uses dreams as a valuable resource for his writing.

Stephenie Meyer maintains that she got the idea for *Twilight* from a dream she had on 2 June 2003. She awoke from the inspirational vivid dream and began to write, having never written a book before. After three months of writing each day, she produced a 498 page manuscript about teenage vampires. She didn't tell anybody about the manuscript except her sister who urged her to get it published. She sent it to 15 agents. Nine didn't reply. Five rejected her work. One expressed interest and signed her on. The book titled *Twilight* is one of the bestselling books of all time and led to three sequels and five movie adaptations. It has sold over 100 million copies with translations into 37 different languages.

The great American caricaturist Al Hirschfeld (1903-2003) was inspired by his dreams. According to his wife he used to dream about various ways of designing his drawings. Even his subconscious didn't give him any time off. In the morning, holding onto a dream he would rise at first light, and race to his drawing board to jot down his dreams before he forgot them.

Relaxation and creativity

Relaxation helps us generate creative insights. Albert Facey had no pressures on him when he wrote the bestseller *A Fortunate Life*. He never meant it to be published. Relaxation also helps recharge your batteries when you feel you are tired. This is why Google puts Ping-Pong tables and other recreational facilities in their headquarters to encourage breaks and reinvigorate employees. They also include a large cafeteria with food service for employees and their guests. If you want to encourage insights then you've got to encourage people to relax. Nolan Bushnell, the founder of the Atari Company, got the inspiration for one of his best-selling video games while playfully kicking sand on a beach.

Mozart maintained that his best musical ideas came to him when least expected, while travelling alone, or walking after an enjoyable meal, or during periods of wakefulness at night when he could not sleep. Tchaikovsky believed that walks were essential to his creativity. He would walk twice a day and occasionally stop to jot down ideas that he would later flesh out at the piano.

Einstein got his theory of relativity while taking a relaxing walk in the mountains.

> "There is only one way in which a person acquires a new idea: by the combination or association of two or more ideas he already has into a new juxtaposition among them of which he was not previously aware."
>
> Francis H. Cartier

President Kennedy was famous for taking power naps in the middle of the day. This was Kennedy's method of getting into a creative state. This was his way of intentionally switching off and a source of renewed energy and fresh perspectives. A report in the June 2009 Proceedings of the National Academy of Science confirmed the hypnagogic state. It found that naps can help people separate the gist of new information from extraneous details, and that catching some REM sleep makes people better at finding connections between weakly related words. This is a sure sign that napping helps creativity. The same report showed that a nap with REM (rapid eye movement) sleep improves people's ability to integrate unassociated information for creative problem solving.

The poet Samuel Taylor Coleridge and the inventor Thomas Edison said that most of their ideas came to them when they were dozing. Edison was considered a daydreamer at school, and was expelled but used this facility to good effect when he grew up. He would think about his problem before he dropped off, and would keep a diary nearby to record the outcome. He would doze off in his chair with his arms over the armrests. In each arm he held two ball bearings. He would place two plates on the floor underneath his arms. As he drifted off his hand would relax, and the ball bearings would fall and hit the plates with a loud bang. Awakened by the noise, Edison would immediately write down any ideas that had come to him in his dreamlike state. Psychologists call the drowsy state just before we fall asleep as the *hypnagogic state*. They call the drowsy state just before we wake up the *hypnopompic* state.

Edison induced the hypnagogic state on purpose by taking frequent naps. During the hypnagogic state people can experience novel ideas and thoughts that might never occur otherwise. The mind is at its most flexible during this time combining things in the most unusual ways. This drowsy creative state happens just before we go to sleep at night, and before we wake up in the morning. This is also a good time to programme our minds with positive affirmations, so that we develop a positive attitude in our lives.

Besides Edison, many other famous people used the hypnagogic state to inspire their creations. These included artists, writers, composers, philosophers and scientists such as Salvador Dali, the Spanish surrealist painter, Edgar Alan Poe, the American writer, Beethoven, the German composer, Aristotle, the Greek philosopher and August Kekule, a famous German chemist. These people claimed they were inspired by flashes of genius which came to them during a hypnagogic state.

Salvador Dali used a similar technique to Edison to induce the hypnagogic state to inspire ideas for his painting. He would lie on a sofa and hold a spoon in one hand, balancing it over a glass placed on the floor. As he drifted off to sleep, he'd inevitably let the spoon fall and the noise of the spoon hitting the glass would awaken him. He would then sketch the bizarre hypnagogic images he saw.

"The future belongs to those who believe in the beauty of their dreams."

Eleanor Roosevelt

Notes to Inspire

Keeping notes is a feature of people who achieve creative greatness. Just like the creative geniuses of history meticulously keep a complete record of your dreams, ideas and insights. You never know when they might come in very useful. Things change quickly and ideas currently impracticable may come of age at some future date. Also keep a treasure file of unusual stories, insights and snippets of information that you might be able to use later. These ideas may come through purposeful research of books, magazines, newspapers, encyclopaedias and surfing the internet. Libraries, bookshops, Wikipedia and Google are good starting points for your research.

B.F. Skinner, the most influential behavioural scientist of the 20th century, believed that we all have good ideas, but must remember to capture them when they come, as otherwise we will forget them. He realised that human memory was fickle, and so always carried a small notebook with him so that he could write down ideas as they came to him. Many people produce a to-do list to remind them about the things they need to do each day to achieve their purpose. The list acts as a constant reminder of what needs to be done. Most people fail to turn their creative dreams into deeds because of lack of discipline, commitment and follow through.

Novelists and non-fiction writers could not produce their books without the ability to produce notes on their observations and research. Many like to use mind maps to record their notes. Famous people, and the not so famous, conscientiously keep diaries to record the events in their lives. This is a valuable source of factual everyday information about their lives, and helps as a reference and aide-memoire when writing their autobiographical books. Some famous creative geniuses maintain that they get their best ideas during the drowsy states just before they fall asleep, and just before they wake up in the morning. They keep notebooks near their bedsides to capture these ideas as otherwise they will lose them.

Charles Darwin was an avid note taker. When researching scientific literature over many decades he kept detailed notes of his findings. When he went to the Galapagos and other exotic destinations on the HMS Beagle he kept detailed notes of his observations about plant and animal life. These notes form the basis for his revolutionary theory of evolution and natural selection. Even when back at home in England he kept detailed notes about his observations on plant, insect and animal life.

Leonardo da Vinci kept detailed notes and drawings of his ideas. Many of his notes have survived to this day. They show the broad interests of this famous renaissance figure. There are hundreds of pages of his notes including sketches, doodles and musings. At the time of his death in 1519 Leonardo had earned a great reputation as an artist, but the legacy of notes that he left behind showed that he also had capabilities as an engineer, scientist, astronomer and inventor.

His notes contain information on mathematics, geometry, astronomy, botany, zoology, and the military arts. Included in his notes are illustrations of gliders, flying machines, a parachute and an underwater diving bell. On the military side he designed a giant crossbow and a spring catapult to hurl boulders. He also designed siege machines to breech city walls and span moats. During his lifetime Leonardo made no attempt to publish his notes, despite the fact that printing had been invented, and so he could have published them if he wanted to.

Galileo's confirmation of the Copernican view that the sun was the centre of the universe rather than the earth would not have come to light if he didn't keep copious notes. More importantly was his discovery of the four moons in orbit around the planet Jupiter. This gave credence to the Copernican model that displaced the Earth from the centre of the universe. Galileo kept careful notes of his observations about Jupiter's moons over many nights and published the data with his interpretation. He was the first to do so. In addition he kept meticulous notes about his discoveries, wrote letters to his benefactors and published twelve written works between 1564 and 1642.

"Creativity is just connecting things. When you ask creative people how they did something, they feel a little guilty because they didn't really do it, they just saw something. It seemed obvious to them after a while. That's because they were able to connect experiences they've had and synthesise new things."

Steve Jobs

Serendipity

Serendipity has been defined as the ability to make fortunate discoveries accidentally. Irving Langmuir, 1932 Nobel Prize winner in chemistry, defined serendipity as "the art to profit from unexpected occurrences." Serendipity needs three elements to happen: action, recognition and insight. Action sets the stage, recognition allows one to see and not overlook what is happening, and insight is the 'eureka' moment or understanding when a possible application is seen. Many of the Nobel Prizes for discoveries in physics, chemistry, and medicine, ranging from x-rays to penicillin were the result of serendipity.

Serendipitous people are not afraid to try something new. Instead they think: 'Isn't that interesting?' 'Isn't that a possibility?' 'I'd like to give that a try.' If you are psychologically prepared for the possibility of serendipity you are likely to find more of it and exploit it. You must recognise what is happening, and realise the significance of it. As Pasteur said chance only favours the prepared mind.

A prepared mind is one that is curious and always asking 'why?' or 'what? The prepared mind ponders and investigates the unusual occurrence, and sees an opportunity where others only see an obstacle or a mistake. The prepared mind is usually one with extensive training and experience. The word 'serendipity' was first coined by Horace Walpole, an 18th century British diarist, who wrote about the Persian story of the three Princes of Serendip (now Sri Lanka). These fairy tale characters were always having the good luck of making fortunate discoveries through chance. Mystery writer, Lawrence Block said: "One aspect of serendipity to bear in mind is that you have to be looking for something in order to find something else."

In science, carefully planned experiments are designed to systematically test a hypothesis or prove a scientific claim. However, they often yield unexpected but potentially useful results not specifically expected or looked for. We should not view chance events as random and meaningless. On the contrary, serendipity provides a framework for understanding, working and accepting such phenomena when they occur. The sign of a good scientist is having the presence of mind to recognise and pursue the unexpected results to make a worthwhile discovery; to see an opportunity rather than just dismiss it as an irrelevant anomaly.

Scientists must have knowledge, curiosity and flexibility of mind, motivation and perseverance to exploit these opportunities when they arise. They must have an in-depth knowledge of their subject, and continually keep up to date about new advances in their field. Knowledge provides the fuel for their imagination, while imagination is the catalyst that transforms knowledge into ideas. For example, the pharmaceutical industry is a knowledge based industry. Its scientists are drawn from different disciplines, and its success depends on its ability to use the latest scientific knowledge and techniques. In addition, scientists should have a broad knowledge of other subjects which may help them develop new perspectives and ideas. Reading widely and using search engines like Google will help them in this process. This bank of knowledge helps them to explain their observations and interpret their results.

Practical discoveries made through serendipity
There are many examples of products discovered through serendipity in pharmaceuticals, vaccination, medical devices, astronomy, industry and commerce. Although fortune favours the brave, it also favours those who know what they want and work hard and persevere.

Serendipity and pharmaceuticals
It takes a curious and flexible mind to follow up unexpected results to understand what is happening. Serendipity doesn't come from being the first to notice a particular result. It comes from being curious enough to doggedly pursue it. Many people notice things but do nothing about it. Being in the right place at the right time is insufficient. More importantly, it takes knowledge, curiosity and persistence to turn

serendipitous opportunities into meaningful and valuable discoveries. Serendipitous discoveries make a significant contribution to the advancement of science, and often provide the foundation for intellectual leaps of understanding.

One of the most famous accidental discoveries was Alexander Fleming's penicillin made in 1928. This is an antibiotic widely used today for the treatment of infections. Fleming had left open a petri dish of Staphylococcus bacteria by mistake. When he returned, the mould penicillin was killing the bacteria on the petri dish. Fleming recognised and realised the significance of what was happening. He could have treated the incident as a mistake but his curiosity motivated him to investigate the matter further. However, it took many years and contributions from other scientists before penicillin became commercially available. It took Fleming to see the opportunity, and Howard Florey and Ernest Chain to convert the observation into a therapeutic product. The three shared the Nobel Prize for Physiology or Medicine in 1945.

Viagra, the first treatment for erectile dysfunction, was developed accidentally at Pfizer Laboratories. It's a good idea to keep your eyes open for surprises. Its intended use was as a cardiovascular drug to lower blood pressure. An unexpected side effect was that men who took the drug were getting erections which were harder, firmer and lasted longer. It was approved by the FDA for use in 1998. Since then it has helped millions of men throughout the world with erectile dysfunction. In the process it has catapulted Pfizer from a small, little known company into one of the top pharmaceutical companies in the world. Former presidential candidate Bob Dole, who suffered from the condition after surgery for prostate cancer, has appeared in a commercial supporting its use.

Viagra is not the only drug where an unexpected side effect has been found. Ritalin was initially designed to treat depression. However, it was found that it helped people with Attention Deficit Hyperactivity Disorder (ADHD). It has since been found that Ritalin makes people without ADHD cleverer as it boosts concentration and cognition. Because of this reason it has become a favourite drug with students preparing for examinations.

Dramamine is a medicine for treating motion sickness. Doctors at Johns Hopkins were working to alleviate allergic disease symptoms. A patient reported that after taking Dramamine her allergy was not relieved but the car sickness she suffered from was cured. The doctors followed up with this chance observation, and a medicine for treating motion sickness was identified.

Cisplatin is a synthetic chemical used in the treatment of some types of cancer. In the 1960s researchers at Michigan State University made an exciting serendipitous discovery. A team led by Dr Barnett Rosenberg were trying to find out if an electric current affected the growth of cells. During the experiments they found that some bacterial cells, when exposed to an electric current, died, while others grew to 300 times longer than normal. Their curiosity motivated them to investigate further. They discovered that it wasn't the current that was increasing the cell length, but rather a chemical produced from the reaction of the platinum electrodes with the solution containing the bacteria. The chemical was cisplatin. Further research suggested that the cells that survived were getting longer because they were unable to divide. Rosenberg then concluded that cisplatin might be useful in treating cancer, which results when cell division is rapid and out of control in the cancerous cells. He tested cisplatin on mice and found that it was an effective treatment for some types of cancer. In 1978 cisplatin was approved as a chemotherapy drug for treating cancer in humans.

The long road to the discovery of insulin started with a serendipitous observation. In 1889, Joseph Mering and Oscar Minkowdki noticed flies swarming around a dog's urine. The urine, when tested, proved to have a high concentration of sugar - a sign of diabetes. The scientists subsequently found a connection between the pancreas and the metabolism of the sugar, as well as a relationship between the lack of a pancreatic secretion and diabetes. Over the following years many unsuccessful attempts were made by other scientists to isolate the secretion. Eventually Frederick Banting and Charles Best took up the challenge and after many years of hard work and dogged determination succeeded in discovering insulin. They won the Nobel Prize in Physiology and Medicine in 1923 for their work.

The story about ether anaesthesia is interesting. In the 1830s students were aware of the fun effects of ether and used it playfully to get high at parties. It was commonly known as laughing gas and was demonstrated by marketers for entertainment around the United States. Customers were charged 25 cents to watch fellow members of the audience take the gas and make fools of themselves.

In 1844, a dentist named Horace Wells attended one of these demonstrations. A man under the influence of the gas fell and badly injured his leg but felt no pain. Wells was convinced that the gas could be used as an anaesthetic for dental surgery. He was so committed to his idea that he used himself as a guinea pig by getting his assistant to extract one of his teeth. He felt very little pain. He realised the potential of the gas as a general anaesthetic for surgery in hospitals. On 16 October 1846, the first public demonstration of ether anaesthesia, took place at Massachusetts General Hospital. Horace Wells failed to secure a patent for his discovery because of ether's ancient origins. Before the discovery of the benefits of anaesthesia, surgery was extremely painful. Anaesthesia has revolutionised modern surgery.

Serendipity and vaccination

A chance meeting with a young milkmaid gave Edward Jenner (1749-1823) the inspiration to develop his first vaccine in 1796. She told him how people who contracted cowpox, a harmless disease picked up from contact with cows, never got smallpox – a deadly disease which killed one in three who caught it. This claim was widely supported by an old wives tale that milkmaids could not get smallpox. Instead of dismissing this information as make believe he decided to pursue it further. As an experiment he injected an eight year old boy with cowpox. The boy developed a slight fever but nothing more. A few months later Jenner injected the boy with smallpox. The boy failed to develop the disease and the idea of modern vaccination was born. The word vaccination comes from the Latin 'vacca' which means cow. In his day Jenner was publicly humiliated when he brought his findings to London. The medical community could not accept that a humble country doctor could make such an important discovery. Vaccination is now a common and effective practice worldwide. In 1980 the World Health Organisation declared that smallpox was extinct throughout the world.

Louis Pasteur (1822-1895) is best known for the process of pasteurisation which is named after him but less well known for his work on vaccination. Pasteurisation helped to limit the spread of tuberculosis and typhoid. Even though he was a chemist, his most significant breakthrough was in medicine, when he developed a vaccine against rabies. In 1880 Pasteur was to recognise and manipulate a chance occurrence that he noticed in his laboratory. Some chicken cholera bacteria had accidentally been left alone for a long period. He noticed that when he injected this into chickens they did not develop the disease. When he later injected the same chickens with fresh bacteria, they survived. Others who had not received the vaccine quickly died. He went on to successfully produce a vaccination against anthrax, a disease which mostly affects sheep and cattle. By 1885 he had developed a vaccine, extracted from the spines of infected rabbits, to successfully treat animals for rabies. He then successfully treated humans who had been infected by rabies.

> "The seeds of great discoveries are constantly floating around us, but they only take root in minds well prepared to receive them."
>
> Joseph Henry

Serendipity and medical devices

Wilhelm Roentgen accidentally stumbled on x-rays in 1895 while working in his laboratory. He called the strange rays he had found 'x' because he didn't know what they were, and 'x' was the mathematical symbol for unknown. Ironically he delayed publication of his finding because he was afraid that his colleagues would laugh at them. On the contrary, they were published to wide acclaim throughout the world. The x-ray images of his wife's hand, complete with wedding ring, became an iconic image throughout the scientific world. In 1901 he was awarded the first Nobel Prize for Physics. The benefits of x-rays in medicine were quickly recognised and brought into common use.

Rene Laennec (1781-1826), when searching for a way to hear the sounds of the heart, found the answer when he noticed two boys playing in an unusual way with a see-saw. One boy was hitting one end of the wooden see-saw with a stone. The other listened with his ear pressed close to the opposite end of the see-saw. This inspired the idea of the stethoscope to his mind. He called the instrument a stethoscope from the Greek word "stethos" meaning chest. He rolled sheets of paper into a cylinder and applied the roll to the chest of the patient, listening with his ear pressed to the other end. This worked quite well and from there he went on to improve his stethoscope using different materials. Before the invention of the stethoscope, doctors used to place their ears directly on the patient's chest. This was ineffective if the patient was obese, and was impermissible if the patient was a female. So Laennec invented the device that no modern doctor can live without.

Wilson Greatbatch (1919-2011) was the inventor of the implantable pacemaker. While building a heart rhythm recording device, he reached into a box of parts for a resistor to complete the circuitry. He pulled out the wrong one and when he tested it, the circuit produced intermittent electrical impulses. He immediately linked the timing and rhythm of the pulses with a human heartbeat. His pacemaker breakthrough is an example of Pasteur's observation that chance favours the prepared mind. He patented more than 325 inventions. The most notable was the long-life lithium battery used in a wide range of medical implants. Mr Greatbatch often told his students that 9 out of 10 of his ideas failed. He once said: "To ask for a successful experiment, for professional stature, for financial reward or for peer approval, is asking to be paid for what should be an act of love."

Serendipity and astronomy

Arno Penzias and Robert Wilson made one of sciences greatest discoveries by accident. While tuning a small horn antenna they heard a constant low level noise disrupting their reception. They checked the equipment to make sure it wasn't a malfunction. Furthermore, the noise continued irrespective of the direction that the antenna was pointing. On further investigation they came to realise that they had stumbled upon the most conclusive evidence to date to support the Big Bang Theory. They had discovered leftover radiation from early in the Universe's history. This supported the notion of an expanding universe and evidence against the steady state model. The discovery was of huge interest to cosmologists and earned Penzias and Wilson the Nobel Prize for Physics.

The Northern Ireland astronomer Joselyn Bell discovered pulsars, while completing her PhD at Cambridge University, in the late 1960s. The pulsars were discovered serendipitously in 1967 in the course of an experiment to detect interplanetary scintillation (the transmission of electromagnetic waves through the atmosphere) – an entirely different phenomenon first discovered three years earlier. She made the discovery after analysing miles of print-outs from the telescope after noticing a few unusual signals. Bell and her supervisor Anthony Hewish concluded that these signals must have come from rapidly spinning, super-dense, collapsed stars. Anthony Hewish went on to be awarded a Nobel Prize for his work along with Martin Ryle while Bell was ignored despite having discovered pulsars. Some scientists maintain that it was the most significant astronomical discovery of the 20th century.

USA military satellites accidentally discovered gamma ray bursts in the 1960s while monitoring the Earth for nuclear weapon explosions. In more recent times, networks of astronomers have used both ground-based and satellite-based instruments to study gamma ray bursts as they occur.

William Herschel (1738-1822), a German born English astronomer was looking for faint stars when he happened to come across the planet Uranus and its two moons. It was named Uranus after the ancient Greek deity of the heavens. In 1781 Herschel, using a telescope that he had built, carried out two preliminary surveys of the heavens. During his third survey he discovered Uranus and its two moons. He was the first astronomer to suggest that nebulae are composed of stars. He also discovered the two moons of Saturn, and coined the term "asteroid." The first asteroid called Ceres was accidentally discovered by the Italian astronomer Giuseppe Piazzi (1746-1826) in 1801 when he was creating a star catalogue. Herschel maintained that the solar system is moving through space and determined the direction of that movement. In January 1986, the unmanned US spacecraft Voyager 2 visited Uranus. It discovered 10 new moons in addition to the five already known, and a system of faint rings around the planet.

Serendipity in industry
Alfred Nobel, who founded the Nobel Prize, is the inventor of dynamite. According to lore Alfred was working with nitro-glycerine, a highly explosive and unstable substance, when the vial slipped out of his hand and crashed to the floor. Alfred expected the worst but fortunately the nitro-glycerine landed on sawdust and rather than explode, the liquid was soaked up. Alfred realised that mixing nitro-glycerine with an inert substance held the answer to its stability. He tried mixing it with many substances but the results were unsatisfactory. He then had the bright idea of trying the mud outside his door. This worked, which meant that at last he had a stable explosive. He was granted a patent for dynamite in 1867. He is now remembered as the founder of the Nobel Prize. This is given annually to individuals who have contributed the most to literature, physics, chemistry, medicine and peace.

James Watt (1736-1819) is often wrongly attributed with the invention of the steam engine. In fact it was invented by Thomas Newcomen who invented it nearly a quarter of a century before Watt was born. However, Watt did improve it considerably. His discovery was a happy accident. In 1764, Watt was asked to repair a scale model of Newcomen's engine used by the University of Glasgow for teaching purposes. On closer examination of the model while repairing it, Watt realised that it was grossly inefficient. The biggest weakness was in the heating and cooling of the engine's cylinder during every stroke. This wasted enormous amounts of fuel, as well as time, in bringing the cylinder back up to steam producing temperature that limited the frequency of the strokes. He realised the key to improved efficiency lay in condensing the steam in a separate container, thereby allowing the cylinder and the piston to always remain hot.

George Westinghouse (1846-1914) discovered the idea of the air-brake. When casually flipping through a journal he came across an item saying that compressed air power was being used by Swiss engineers in tunnel building. Westinghouse revolutionised the railroad industry, making braking safer and thus permitting trains to travel at higher speeds. He subsequently made many alterations that improved his initial invention.

Quite independently, Super Glue led to another fortuitous discovery in the late 1970s. Laurie Wood, an English policeman, found that fumes from the glue condensed around his fingerprints. He had stumbled on a forensic technique called fingerprinting which is now used worldwide by the police to identify criminals and solve major crimes.

In the early 1920s Richard Drew, a young lab assistant in 3M, was given the task of improving 3M's sandpaper. While testing the sandpaper, he noticed a different problem – paint sprayers had difficulty covering areas which did not require painting. He brought this to the attention of his boss who wasn't interested and told Drew to stick to his terms of reference. Drew persevered and worked in his own time to develop a new tape. He persuaded auto body workshops to test his new product, and he eventually got several orders for it. Drew's boss realised his mistake and gave him permission to continue work on his new tape. The new product, now known as masking tape, went on to become a real money spinner for 3M. Drew went on to develop other products such as cellophane. He was rewarded for his creativity with eventual promotion to 3M's chief science officer.

Serendipity and consumer products

The discovery of safety glass, which doesn't shatter when exposed to impact, was the result of a clumsy accident by a French scientist named Edouard Benedictus in 1903. He inadvertently knocked a glass flask to the floor, and much to his surprise the glass flask remained intact. The flask which had recently held a solution of cellulose nitrate, a liquid plastic, hadn't been washed properly. There was still a thin coating of plastic on the flasks interior. Coincidentally, the same week a Paris newspaper had run a series of articles about car accidents, where the drivers were seriously injured by shattered glass windshields. Edouard knew that his unique glass could prevent this happening and save lives. However, at the time, safety was not a major issue with car manufacturers. In World War 1 the safety glass proved its worth in gas masks. However, it was not until 1927 that it was adopted into car windshields. In addition to windshields, safety glass is now used in goggles, protective screens in banks and in windows and doors.

Cellophane is used widely to cover food and keep it fresh since it is airtight and waterproof. This was not what the inventor Jacques Brandenberger, a Swiss chemist, had in mind when he discovered it in 1908. He was looking for a way to make a stain proof tablecloth, after witnessing the aftermath of a spillage in a restaurant. He tried coating the tablecloth with a thin coat of viscose film. Nobody was interested in his tablecloth, but he saw other possibilities for his discovery. It took him a further 10 years of experimentation and development before he was able to bring the product to the market commercially. In 1927 a waterproof lacquer coating was developed which made his product more useful.

In 1954, French engineer, Marc Gregoire created the first pan coated with Teflon non-stick resin under the brand name of Tefal. He had been using the material to coat his fishing tackle when his wife suggested that he try it on her cooking pans. He accepted her intuitive advice and went on to develop non-stick cookware. A simple idea revolutionised and made life easier in the kitchen. Today non-stick cookware can be found in every modern kitchen in the world.

Harry Coover invented the incredibly stable adhesive known as Super Glue. During World War 2 he was part of a team conducting research with chemicals known as cyanoacrylates. These chemicals were extremely sticky, making them very difficult to work with. The team didn't recognise their value, and rejected them and moved on with their research. In 1951 Coover and his team rediscovered the cyanoacrylates and came to recognise their potential. They had unique properties in that they required no heat or pressure to bond. He knew they were on to something big, and began developing the product for commercialisation. Super Glue has numerous applications, ranging from simple woodworking and appliance repair to industrial binding. Since then cyanoacrylates have been discovered to have medical uses. Some of these include re-joining veins and arteries during surgery, sealing bleeding ulcers, and use during dental surgery.

Charles Goodyear invented the process of vulcanisation after years of research, experimentation, hard work and a single fortuitous stroke of luck. Although in this instance luck was opportunity meeting preparation. In 1839 Goodyear visited a general store to sell his product. When the locals laughed at his samples he began gesturing wildly, when a lump of rubber in his hand accidentally flew onto the hot surface of a stove. He scraped the rubber off, and found to his surprise that it had become remarkably tough. It took another five years of experimentation before Goodyear finally perfected the process later known as vulcanisation. This process made rubber durable and resilient enough for industrial use. Goodyear tyres are now famous throughout the world.

Louis Daguerre (1787-1851) was a French artist and physicist and is credited with the invention of photography. He invented film when, having failed to produce an image on an iodized silver plate, he put the plate away in a cabinet filled with chemicals when the fumes from a spilled jar of mercury produced an image on a plate.

James J. Ritty (1837-1918) had a problem. He ran a successful bar and restaurant but his cashiers were light-fingered and stole much of the cash. He was subsequently travelling on a transatlantic steamer to Europe when he became fascinated by a device used for counting and recording the turns of the propeller. This was his "Eureka" moment as he went on to use the same principle, after much trial and error, to build the first successful cash register. He patented the design in 1879 and sold on his cash register business. It went through many incarnations to become the National Cash Register Company. Today NCR makes business machines including cash registers using the latest computer and electronic technology. The lesson from this story is to look to other disciplines or fields when you have a problem. The best ideas cross disciplinary boundaries.

Percy Spencer noticed that the microwaves from the radar he was working with had melted the chocolate bar in his pocket. He wasn't the first to notice that microwaves generate heat. However, he was the first to visualise the possibility of using microwaves to cook food. His curiosity motivated him to pursue the idea further, resulting in the eventual invention of the microwave oven that so many of us take for granted today. It was probably the greatest invention in cooking since the fire and has made all of our domestic lives easier.

Constantin Fahlberg was a Russian chemist who discovered saccharin, an artificial sweetener, by accident in the late 19th century. He had been working with coal tar and its derivatives before he sat down to have his supper. He forgot to wash his hands, and was amazed to find that the bread he had touched and was eating tasted very sweet. He immediately recognised that he was on to something big. After many months of further development he went on to set up a factory to produce it and become very wealthy in the process. Initially when he published his research, some people laughed at it and thought it was a scientific joke, while others thought it had no practical value.

In 1827, an English pharmacist named John Walker was the first to discover the strikeable match. He had just finished stirring a pot of chemicals when he noticed that the stick he had been using to stir the pot had a dried lump on one end. When he dragged the stick across the floor it burst into flames. At first his matches were temperamental and failed to light consistently. He failed to patent his invention, so various improvements by others followed. The first safety match using red phosphorous was developed by a Swedish match factory owner named Johan Edvard Lundstrom in 1855. Lundstrom separated the elements of matches parting the tip from the striking surface. The result was a match that couldn't spontaneously combust.

Corn Flakes were invented through a fortuitous accident by Dr John Harvey Kellogg. He and his brother Will were Seventh Day Adventists, and they were trying to find wholesome foods to feed patients to comply with a strict Adventist vegetarian diet. Will boiled some wheat and then left it to sit while attending to other things. When he returned it was stale. Rather than throw it away, the brothers decided to put it through rollers, hoping to make sheets of dough but instead they got flakes which they toasted. They tasted the flakes and liked them. They then tried them out on patients who also liked them. In 1906 Will created the Kellogg's company to market the cereal. On principle John refused to join the company, objecting to the fact that the health benefits of the product were lowered because sugar was added to the product.

"The seeds of great discoveries are constantly floating around us, but they only take root in minds well prepared to receive them."

Joseph Henry, physicist

Thinking Creatively

Thinking creatively can be categorised under mindset, approach, and having fun. Let's now consider each of these in more detail.

Mindset

Believe that you are creative. Expect to be creative and you are more likely to be creative. Chekhov said man is what he believes. Similarly, Jean-Paul Sartre concluded that man is what he conceives himself to be. Practise being creative. Your mind is like a muscle. The more you use it the stronger it becomes. Be positive but realistic about your ability to be creative. Believe you have a growth mindset rather than a fixed mindset.

Be open to new ideas. Look to nature, history, geography, other cultures and famous creative people as sources of inspiration. Reframe or redefine problems in order to see things in unusual ways. Continually look for a better way of doing things. No matter how efficient a process is, there is always a better way of doing it. Turn things on their heads. Think about the opposite. Take the familiar and look at it in a different way. Don't look at things as they are or always have been but as they might be. See things from other points of view. Also, sometimes we see things we expect or want to see rather than reality. Learn to separate perception from reality.

Get into a creative state when you need to. To do so, remember a time when you were in a creative state. Visualise intensely what it felt like. Anchor the feeling by pressing your thumb and forefinger together. Practise this a few times. Re-experience this state at any time by pressing your thumb and forefinger together.

In business one sacrosanct assumption is that the customer is always right. Marketing people often conduct surveys to find out what people actually need. The problem with this approach is that some people don't know what they want and reject ideas that they don't understand or can't relate to. For example, in the early 1990s, the initial reaction by consumers to mobile phone text messaging was, "Why would you want to send messages by phone?" They couldn't imagine a phone being used for anything but conversation. Texting caught on gradually when people discovered how useful and economical text messaging was. Today most people use text messaging in addition to talking on their phones. This is now a significant source of telecom revenue. Sony launched the Walkman even though consumer surveys suggested it would not succeed.

Challenge your preconceptions or stretch your mind by going outside your comfort zone. In other words, avoid getting into a rut or ineffectual habitual ways. If you keep on doing the same old thing you are surely going to get the same old results. So do something different! To start the process you could visit places you've never gone to before such as a gallery, a store or a museum. You could visit a foreign country and have a wide variety of experiences. On an everyday note you could drive a different way to work, or eat out in a different restaurant, and try a dish you haven't experienced before.

Competition may be an antidote to creativity. Two groups of employees were asked to solve the same problem. One group was told prizes and recognition would be awarded to those who produced the best result. Competition was not mentioned to the second group. They were only told to have fun and enjoy themselves. The outcome was counterintuitive. When both groups' solutions were studied, the second group's solutions were more creative than those of the first group who were operating under a competitive mindset.

Approach

Build on existing ideas and inventions. We can all be inspired creatively by the people and things around us and by what has come before us. Writers are influenced by books they have read, or by other writers that they know. Painters draw on the tools, techniques, approaches and ideas of other artists.

Musicians build on the style of other musicians, so that their own style can be a blend of others. Inventors build upon the creation of others. Henry Ford is often credited with inventing the automobile. This is not true. Cars developed out of a combination of bicycles and tricycles. These involved wheels and a geared mechanism. These were combined with engines for propulsion to create cars. In 1795, Joseph Cugnot, invented a steam driven cannon carriage, a type of tractor, for the French army which is credited by some as being the forerunner of the automobile. In fact, the history of the automobile is an evolution that took place over centuries worldwide. It is estimated that over 100,000 patents contributed to the modern automobile. Steam driven cars were not the only type of cars invented in the early days, there was also the electric car which today is making a comeback. Steve Jobs of Apple was inspired from knowledge taken from diverse fields to design and create his iPad. He famously remarked that creativity was just connecting things. He was very good at adapting the ideas of others. Apple didn't invent MP3 players or tablet computers. They just made existing products better by combining things, and adding unique design features.

Have considerable knowledge in your particular domain and generally through a wide range of interests. The greater knowledge you have the greater your ability to generate ideas, to combine ideas from different areas, and make creative breakthroughs. It is difficult to appreciate the applications and ideas in other fields to your own area, if you are unaware of them. This isn't easy as it takes about 10 years of disciplined study to build up sufficient knowledge in your particular domain. Reading is an easy and enjoyable way of acquiring a diverse source of knowledge. Read history to learn about the past. Many ideas of the past were abandoned because the technology didn't exist to support them. The time may be just right to revisit these ideas because current technology may support them. There is nothing new under the sun. New ideas are just combinations of old ones. Read science fiction. With science fiction you can allow your imagination to wander freely without restraint. Many of the impossible innovations predicted in previous science fiction works are now reality. The writer Jules Verne in his books anticipated the submarine, and landing a man on the moon.

Work smarter, not harder. You need to be efficient and effective at doing the right things. There are always better ways of doing anything. Consider if all steps are necessary in your processes. Are some unnecessary and deliver no value? Is there a better way? The great Peter Drucker reminds us that sometimes the best course of action is to do nothing. The "bias for action" is popular, but in some circumstances inaction and reflection may be the best choice.

Take time to think and reflect. Incubation is a vital aspect of the creative process. You need time to test your hypotheses, question things, bounce your ideas off your colleagues, get different perspectives and compare your ideas with what is known in the literature.

Develop a tolerance for ambiguity. Accept that there is risk and uncertainty in life, and that there are times when you must embrace it if you want to succeed. Jonas Salk the developer of the polio vaccine said: "Risks, I like to say, always pay off. You learn what to do or what not to do."

Work alone or in a group. Many creative people prefer to work alone. If you want to work with others, seek out positive people rather than negative people. Have a clear vision about what you want to achieve. With vision and passion you can overcome any amount of negativity. If you have a tendency to engage in negative self-talk, turn it into positive self-talk. Your mind cannot think of more than one thing at a time. In other words, you can't hold a positive and a negative thought in your mind at the same time. This means that you can control what you think about. So think positive thoughts! Through persistent programming, positive self-talk becomes automatic and rooted in your subconscious mind so that your outlook will improve.

Use all your brain. This includes the right side or creative side and the left side or logical side. You need the right side for coming up with ideas and you need the left side for problem definition and evaluation. Learn to access the subconscious mind through fantasy and daydreaming, as it is a huge storehouse of information. Research by Jonathan Schooler at the University of California, Santa Barbara, has found that people who daydream more score higher on various tests of creativity. Creativity is only limited by the paucity of your dreams and drive. Some great discoveries were made after dreaming. As discussed previously, Elias Howe invented the sewing machine and August Kekule discovered the benzene ring. Keith Richard of the Rolling Stones composed the song 'I Can't Get No Satisfaction' after a dream. The tune for 'Yesterday', one of the most recorded songs in history came to Paul McCartney of the Beatles fame in a dream. Keep a pad at your bedside to capture your dreams. Each night just before you fall asleep tell yourself that you will remember your dreams. When you wake up, jot down your dreams. The more ideas you generate the better, as 95% of ideas fail to become positive outcomes.

Give and receive feedback. Most people want to do excellent work, exceed the expectations of others and especially their own. Most companies treat feedback as a formal process to be given only after yearly or half-yearly performance appraisal sessions. This is much too infrequent and too late to modify behaviour and be beneficial. Feedback should be given as near to the event as possible, so that corrective action can be taken to improve things or put things right. Creative cultures thrive on timely, frequent and spontaneous feedback. Feedback should be realistic to provide direction, and help people raise their own expectations. B.F. Skinner found that random rewards lead to desirable behaviour. This is why the gaming machines in Las Vegas are programmed to reward punters randomly. This provides them with the incentive to keep on spending their hard earned cash.

Enjoyment

Have fun. Develop a sense of humour. We experience some of our best ideas when we are happy, relaxed and having fun. Creativity is positively associated with joy and love, and negatively associated with anger, fear and anxiety. Happiness and humour builds rapport and promotes openness to new ideas, by relaxing people, and making them less likely to criticise ideas. This leads to risk taking, which is the basis of creative thinking. You are more likely to come up with a creative idea if you were happy the day before. This is a kind of virtuous cycle. One day's happiness often predicts the next day's creativity. In addition, you are more likely to generate ideas during play, games, role play or laughter. Laughter is good for your health. Laughter is cathartic, releasing negative and destructive feelings. It boosts the immune system and stimulates the lymphatic system. It makes you feel good and positive, and helps you put problems in perspective. It loosens up the subconscious mind, and helps you develop novel perceptions. Probably the single most important thing a manager can do to encourage creativity is to make it fun to work on a project.

Do the things you enjoy and enjoy the things you do. Immerse yourself in what you are good at. Passion is one of the main reasons for creative success. It helps us overcome our limitations by turning negatives into positives. Think about possibilities rather than problems. Obstacles become problems to solve or opportunities to exploit. Passion is contagious like laughter. Find your passion and ignite the passion in others by inspiring and engaging them in your vision. Organisations like Google, Apple and Virgin let their employees know what they are passionate about. This helps their employees buy into the vision. Google has a passion for information; Apple has a passion for design, while Virgin has a passion for customer service.

Have a curious mind. In one of his journals Leonardo da Vinci wrote about having "an insatiably curious attitude to life, and unrelenting quest for continuous learning." To build information about your subject, ask challenging questions. Questions may help you answer some overlooked relationship, or discover some nugget of information that you need to solve a problem. Continually ask the question 'why'? 'how might you?' and 'what if'? Consider 'why'? as a prompt to learning more. Consider 'how might you?' and 'what if'? as a prompt to open up possibilities. Creative people have a childlike wonder. They look at things in new ways, see things that others do not see, see things that are not there, and question what they don't understand. They continually challenge assumptions. Challenging long held assumptions is not as easy as it sounds. Even prominent scientists resist looking beyond long-held scientific assumptions, particularly if they feel that new thinkers are threatening their position.

Be willing to be different by challenging the status quo and questioning the norm. From an early age we are taught to conform. This begins in school, is reinforced by the norms of society, and the culture of workplace organisations. Defy the conventional and be non-conformist. You are happy to go it alone without popular support. People who follow the status quo or a consensus group view, are less likely to be creative.

"The number one premise in business is that it need not be boring or dull. It ought to be fun. If it's not fun, you're wasting your life."

Thomas J Peters

Summary of Chapter 3

Your subconscious will process, recombine, adapt and consolidate ideas, images and experiences and suggest solutions. You can tap spontaneous insights by accessing the vast resources of the subconscious.

People can be inspired by their daydreams and dreams. When you sleep your mind doesn't turn off but instead becomes very active during dreaming. Sometimes dreams are the way your mind works out solutions to problems you may have, and taps into the creative resources in your subconscious to do so. For many writers and inventors their dreams can be powerful spurs to inspiration and creativity.

Psychologists call the drowsy state just before we fall asleep the hypnogogic state. They call the drowsy state just before we wake up the hypnopompic state. It is during these states that we have our most creative moments. Elias Howe, who invented the lock stitch sewing machine, claimed to have hit on the idea after a nightmare.

The ability to keep clear notes is the foundation of creativity. Charles Darwin was an avid note taker. Novelists and non-fiction writers could not produce their books without notes on their observations and research.

Many great inventions were inspired by accidental discoveries. This is known as serendipity. Serendipity is the source of many ideas in pharmaceuticals, vaccinations, medical devices, industry and discoveries about astronomy.

To think creatively you must have the right mindset, adopt the correct approach and enjoy the process.

4
How Does Creativity Happen?

Introduction

The five stages of creativity are preparation, effort, incubation, insight and evaluation. New ideas may be triggered by means of the acronym CAMPERS. This stands for combine ideas, adapt, modify, put to other uses, eliminate unnecessary parts, rearrange and simplify. The 4 Ps of creativity are people, processes, product and place.

In many organisations ideas are killed before they ever get off the ground. Creativity killers include begrudgery and pessimism. Persistence, determination, and resilience, will see ideas through in the end.

Edward De Bono, the inventor of lateral thinking, has suggested the six thinking hats as a way for people to become more creative. The hats trigger off a particular mood. A person wearing a white hat focuses on factual information. A person with a red hat focuses on emotional intuition. A person with a yellow hat adopts a positive perspective. A person with a black hat is cautious. A person with a green hat is creative, and finally a person with a blue hat exercises control.

The range of creativity paradigms are paradigm preserving, paradigm stretching and paradigm breaking. In paradigm preserving techniques the boundaries around the problem remain the same. People do not go outside their own perspectives in exploring the situation. Consequently, they develop existing ideas but do not change them significantly. Paradigm stretching techniques encourage the participants to broaden their existing ways of thinking and looking at something. Paradigm breaking techniques encourage people to look at situations from a number of different perspectives, and so come up with unique and novel ideas.

The four stages of brainstorming are suspend judgement, freewheel, generate many ideas and cross fertilise. Reverse brainstorming and brainwriting are variations on the brainstorming theme. Other techniques of creativity include fantasy, attribute listing, metaphors, synectics, swot analysis, stretch imaging and suggestion schemes.

Creative Problem Solving (CPS) is another major creativity technique used in organisations but can also be used for solving difficult personal problems. TRIZ is the Theory of Inventive Problem Solving, used by many major companies throughout the world, developed from world-wide patterns of inventions from patent literature.

Biomimicry is creativity inspired by nature. Sources include birds, the sea, plants, insects and humans/animals. Bionics is a type of biomimicry used to mend broken bodies.

Five Stages of Creativity

The five stages of creativity are preparation, effort, incubation, insight and evaluation. These are the stages you go through when being creative. Let's now consider each of these stages in detail.

Preparation
Preparation includes all of the experience, formal education and research a person has done to date on the problem. This includes a deep understanding of a particular discipline which takes 10 years to develop. As stated earlier, Louis Pasteur observed that fortune favours the prepared mind. A prepared mind is one that is curious and persistent and always asking "Why?" and "What?" Although serendipity, or the making of fortunate discoveries by chance, does happen you must be tuned into the problem to recognise the solution when you come across it accidentally. Preparation includes being in the right receptive mood, or studious frame of mind, to think deeply about the problem in hand. Research shows that being

in a positive mood enhances creativity, while being in a negative mood adversely affects it.

You take ownership of the problem by thinking about it continuously, and making it part of your thinking. You become goal-oriented, obsessed, challenged, motivated and stretched, by the desire to solve the problem. You must allow your mind to roam free while playing with the problem and sleeping on it. Try and imagine looking at the problem from as many different perspectives as possible. View the problem from above, below and from the sides. View the problem from the inside and from the outside. Let the problem brew and gestate in your mind.

Redefining the problem can be helpful; using the words 'how to,' and 'in how many ways can we.' At this stage you must read widely around the problem. Read how some of the great ideas were discovered. Chester Carlson who invented the electrostatic photocopier said if "things don't come to mind readily all of a sudden, like pulling things out of the air. You have to get your inspiration from somewhere and usually you get it from reading something else." Appreciate how great inventions were made through a combination of knowledge, original thinking, hard work and persistence. Ask yourself has anybody solved a similar problem before? If so, you may already have a ready-made, proven answer. This will save you wasting the time involved in reinventing the wheel. To promote creativity, diversify your interests and read outside your comfort zone to generate divergent views and analogies. Read to generate ideas rather than just for information.

Stand on the shoulders of giants by consulting experts and reading the best specialist authors on the subject pertinent to the problem. Collect all information and relevant facts about the problem, including first hand and desk research. Consult friends and colleagues to get fresh and different viewpoints. All of these preparations and approaches will help you find an optimum solution.

Effort

Don't engage in "either/or" thinking. That kind of mindset will severely limit your options. For example, instead of petrol powered car or an electric car, there is now a hybrid in which the two sources of power are combined together. These result in significant savings in fuel costs and a reduction in exhaust fumes.

Leonardo da Vinci believed that in order to solve a problem you had to restructure it in many different ways. When you initially look at a problem you are prone to see it in the usual manner. What you need to do is look at the problem from different perspectives and move from one perspective to another. With each move your understanding of the problem will deepen, and you will begin to see the essence of the problem. Leonardo called this thinking strategy "knowing how to see."

Just like Leonardo you will need mental effort to generate as many ideas and alternatives as possible. Record these ideas as you go along. You may use the technique of brainstorming to generate numerous ideas. Brainstorming is a type of discussion process, in which members of a group are encouraged to generate as many ideas as possible. They do so within a defined period of time with the guidance of a facilitator.

The facilitator records these ideas for subsequent scrutiny, evaluation and criticism. The initial emphasis is on quantity rather than quality, so suspend judgement and let the creative juices flow. Seemingly unusual and crazy ideas may form the germ of perfectly practical solutions. The technique of brainstorming is covered in greater detail later on in this chapter.

Incubation

Incubation brings to mind a hen sitting on an egg waiting for it to hatch. Nothing seems to be happening for a long time, until suddenly a new life breaks through the shell. Similarly, you should reflect on the problem in your mind and let it gestate. In the meantime, do something interesting, distracting and relaxing, so that the subconscious mind takes over the hard work of problem solving for you. This may include general reading as your mind needs information to work with, as new ideas are often a combination of old ideas from diverse sources. Lloyd Morgan said: "Saturate your mind with your subject, and then wait." Many new products on the market are just variations on what already exists. Once you let go of the problem, fresh perspectives will develop, and the solution will often spontaneously come to mind.

The subconscious mind is far better at coming up with creative insights than the conscious mind. People asked to consciously solve problems can make worse decisions than those simply asked to sleep on it. In the subconscious mind ideas are free to recombine with other ideas, in novel patterns and unpredictable associations. It is also the storehouse of everything you know, including things you've forgotten and can't readily bring into conscious awareness. Further, the subconscious engages us beyond words including emotions and the deep imagery of the senses.

We are more open to insights from the subconscious mind when we are relaxed and not thinking of anything in particular. One of the paradoxes of creativity is that even though it often involves hard work and persistence, ingenuity stems from a relaxed mind and letting go. That is why daydreams are so useful for creativity. We need to give the subconscious mind a chance to come to the surface. An idea that is eventually recognised by the conscious mind as a solution may have originated in a dream. The subconscious mind is discussed in detail in Chapter 3.

"For me, the creative moment almost always occurs during a dream state. I wake up certain that I have created something but I am unaware of what it is at the time. The creation becomes realised during a later conscious state in its entirety. But I recognise it as the memory of an earlier idea."

Ally Sheedy, actor.

Insight

The 'eureka' feeling of euphoria is felt when a novel solution has been arrived at, or a unique discovery has been made. Eureka means I have found it. This is a sudden flash of illumination, and a release of tension, when a difficult and seemingly insurmountable problem has eventually been solved. The brain releases dopamine during these 'aha' moments of inspiration. Insights come during periods of great contemplation, introspection, inspiration and critical thought – a vital part of being creative. They usually occur during the most unexpected times, such as when exercising, during holidays, taking a shower or bath, driving; commuting by bus, playing golf, or while you are doing something repetitive, such as shaving, housekeeping, knitting, mowing the lawn, painting, or cooking. You may even get your ideas at the most unusual times. Grant Wood (1891-1942) the famous American artist, whose most famous work is called *American Gothic,* said his best ideas came to him when milking a cow.

It is now thought that the brain's right hemisphere specialises in pattern recognition and divergent thinking. This seems to offer a physiological explanation for the eureka phenomenon. After the left hemisphere has analysed a problem logically into its components, the right hemisphere may suddenly perceive a hidden pattern, just like you are able to suddenly pick out and recognise a familiar face in a crowd. Scientists using functional magnetic resonance have found that insight is a process mostly involving the right side of the brain.

Gutenberg came up with the idea of the printing press using movable type while attending a nearby wine festival to sample the latest wines. He wrote: "I watched the wine flowing, and going back from the effect to the cause, I studied the power of the wine press, which nothing can resist." This provided him with his eureka moment. It occurred to him that the same process could be applied to his printing press. And so with a few modifications the printing press was born. Gutenberg combined the mechanisms for producing playing cards, pressing wine and punching coins to create movable type. It is often the bringing together of ideas from completely different subject areas that creates powerful new concepts.

Chemist, Kary Mullis, came up with the basic principle of the polymerase chain reaction (PCR), on a spring evening, while driving up the northern California coast. PCR is the fundamental technology that makes genetic tests possible. It is considered one of the most significant scientific discoveries of the 20th century. In 1993 he was awarded the Nobel Prize in Chemistry. Henri Poincare, a French mathematician, got an important insight into a mathematical problem he was trying to solve while stepping on a bus. He believed you should immerse yourself in the problem, and then relax and do other things when you hit an impasse. It is during the most unexpected times that solutions will come to mind.

James Watson, the co-discoverer of the structure of the DNA-helix with Francis Crick, had his eureka moment in 1953 when he saw Rosalind Franklin's new X-ray diffraction picture of DNA, realising that the patterns could only arise from a double-helical structure. Nine years later he shared the Nobel Prize in Medicine with Maurice Wilkins, for solving one of the most important biological riddles; now a vital element in modern medicine and forensic science.

Evaluation
This is the verification stage and a return to logic for evaluating and criticising the solution. During the previous stages you suspended the inner critic to encourage and release the playful child within. However, at this stage you must become the devil's advocate by criticising the idea. You become a judge by evaluating the merits and demerits of an idea. Test the idea in order to see that it works. Can you implement the idea in a practical way? Unless you can it will never see the light of day.

Discard ideas that are too costly, unacceptable, unprofitable, inappropriate, or unethical. Tease out the solution against the stark realities of life – organisational politics, cost, opposition, compromise and expediency. At the end of the day unless the idea is commercially viable it is of little use to the business. Synectics groups recommend using NAF criteria. Is the idea **N**ovel, **A**ttractive, and **F**easible? Is it likely to be a good idea? Give each criterion a score out of 10. So a change might get 8 for Novelty, 7 for Appeal and 3 for Feasibility. For real innovation you obviously want a high rating for Novelty and Appeal. If the score is low on Feasibility then you should go back and ask why? Synectics is a method of identifying and solving problems that depends on creative thinking, the use of analogy, and informal conversation among a small group of people with diverse experience and expertise. Synectics is explored in more detail later on in this chapter.

> "You see things; and you say, 'Why?' But I dream things that never were; and I say, 'Why not?'
>
> George Bernard Shaw

Practical Creativity

New ideas may be triggered off by means of the acronym **CAMPERS**. This stands for **c**ombine ideas, **a**dapt a product, **m**odify a product, **p**ut to other uses, **e**liminate unnecessary parts, **r**earrange, and **s**implify. Consider if you made something smaller, bigger, a different shape, a different colour, a different package, lighter, heavier, less reliable, more reliable and so on. Consider if you made the product more expensive, less expensive, broke the product into parts and bundled it with other products. You could improve the product's functionality, durability, ease of use, or the way it fits with other products. **CAMPERS** is a systematic way of considering all these changes. This simple technique can be used to generate ideas, or to prevent ideas from being forgotten.

- Combine two different ideas to create a new whole – for example, drug development requires the best ideas of biologists, chemists, geneticists and clinicians. Their insights combine and create novel solutions none of the scientists could come up with on their own. Somebody a long time ago combined fire and food together and got cooking. In electronics, radios have been combined with CD players to create music centres, while televisions have been combined with DVD players. Mobile phones have been combined with the conventional phone, cameras and the internet. A clock has been combined with a radio to produce the clock radio. A camper combines a car and a home. The Sony Walkman combined walking and stereo. The shovel was combined with a cake to produce a cake server. Various foods and drinks have been combined with vitamins to create health products with added value. John, Paul, George and Ringo combined to form the greatest pop group in history called the Beatles. The Austrian monk Gregor Mendel, combined mathematics and biology, to create the modern science of genetics. Innovation is mostly about combining existing products and using technologies in new ways. Combining ideas and making connections are key practices of creativity employed by architects, artists, designers, cooks, musicians and scientists. Some companies have created links to universities to support, share and exploit research findings and ideas. If you want to create a breakthrough start looking for new connections, or uncommon linkages between existing things. In a sense the old saying that there is nothing new under the sun is true.

- **A**dapt an existing product to meet the identified customised needs of people – for example, cars can be adapted with special features to meet the personal requirements of disabled drivers. Personal computers can be built to order and this was the market that Dell initially exploited profitably. Customised cars to meet the discretionary needs of wealthy clients, where expense means nothing, can be built to order. These customised cars have unique features which can't be bought elsewhere. Mobile phones have enlarged key pads to meet the needs of older customers who are visually challenged. Generally, products are adapted to meet the needs of customers with diverse needs in diverse markets. You could adapt a service by adding something unusual such as bed and breakfast with tax advice for customers. Books can be adapted for release into film, DVD or e-readers. Seeing is usually much more entertaining than just reading.

- **M**odify and improve an existing process or product to meet a new purpose. People can now print off their colour photographs themselves, in self-service machines designed for digital output. These machines are available in many retail outlets. Cameras have undergone many changes in line with technological developments and customer needs during the past few years. Today we have compact, disposable, and digital cameras. Smart phones with cameras are commonplace. Even Coca-Cola has built on previous success by bringing out Coca-Cola with Lemon and other varieties, with varying degrees of commercial success. Many new products and services are built on existing products or the work of others. Continuous improvement is now part of modern living. Under this heading we could also include magnify and minify. Magnify means making something bigger, stronger and thicker or making it last longer. Minify means making it smaller, shorter, condensed or more streamlined. A good example of this is nanotechnology, such as the silicon chip, which has made mobile phones and computers smaller and smaller. At the same time it has increased their capacity and capability.

- **P**ut to other uses than the original intention – for example, memory cards are now used instead of film for storing pictures in a digital camera. Computer chips are now used in domestic appliances, televisions and cars. As already discussed elsewhere, Viagra was originally a drug to treat high blood pressure, but is now used to help men with erectile dysfunction. G.D. Searle and Company, a pharmaceutical company, was doing research on a new anti-ulcer drug. Through chance they discovered a new substance that didn't cure ulcers, but instead tasted very sweet. Even though the company was not in the food business, they recognised the commercial potential of the product, and eventually developed and marketed the substance as an artificial sweetener with the brand name, NutraSweet.

- Eliminate the need for particular inputs and outputs, or for unnecessary parts or processes and procedures. For example, you might redesign a form by eliminating information that is no longer required, or that duplicates information elsewhere on the same form. In a procedure you might eliminate unnecessary operations, transports and delays and consequently improve efficiency, cost and productivity. Value analysis is a technique used by engineers to reduce the number of parts in machinery and equipment. Unnecessary parts or features are eliminated after careful examination for greater efficiency and cost reduction. Value analysis asks a number of basic questions like: "What is it?" "What does it do?" "What does it cost?" "What else could do the job?" "What would that cost?" Reverse engineering, where a company takes a competitor's product and disassembles it to see if it could be improved in any way, is another application of this idea. World class manufacturing (WCM), and total quality management (TQM), are used in manufacturing companies to eliminate waste and improve productivity.

- **R**earrange to create a new synthesis by interchanging components, re-sequencing steps, or enabling steps to be completed by different people, in new ways, in new locations or at different times. This may also include new patterns and new layouts. For example, supermarkets many years ago introduced the self-service model, thereby delegating the task of picking groceries to customers, and reducing the number of employees they needed to operate the business. Today supermarkets are offering a wide variety of services in addition to groceries. Tesco, the supermarket chain, has combined products and services in new and unusual ways. It has introduced credit cards and insurance into its range of products, and also stocks hardware, clothing, electronic equipment, books, CDs, DVDs and computers. It has extended opening times with some outlets even staying open 24 hours a day. It has internet shopping and delivery services to customers. Building societies are now offering current accounts, while banks are offering mortgages. Amazon.com has built up a very successful retailing business by combining books and other products with the internet. It has reframed its business to include electronic books, and has even marketed its own electronic reader. Modern information and communications technology means call centres can operate anywhere in the world, offering a wide variety of customer services and technical support. You can also reverse things such as putting them upside down, inside out and sideways. Bottles of ketchup are now stored upside down to facilitate the flow of sauce. Some coats have a dual role – they can be worn conventionally or the inside can be turned out to give a different colour. The engine in the famous Mini car was put sideways to save space.

- Simplify an existing procedure by reducing unnecessary complexity, introduce improved methods and make it more efficient – for example, James Dyson, the English inventor, introduced his revolutionary bag-less vacuum cleaner on to the UK market in 1993. He noticed that the conventional vacuum lost suction when the bag started to fill and get clogged, reducing its effectiveness. Rather than finding a way to improve the bag, Dyson thought more broadly about what the vacuum was trying to do. He realised that the vacuum pulls in a combination of dirt and air while needing to separate the two. He was reminded of sawmills, which use industrial cyclones to separate sawdust from air. Inspired by this and after much trial and error, Dyson developed a small version of the industrial cyclone in his portable vacuum cleaner, and in the process developed the bag-less vacuum cleaner and a very successful, profitable company. Personal computers and software packages, such as Microsoft Office, are continually being updated and simplified, and are now much easier to use than previous incarnations. Steve Jobs removed the physical keyboard from the smartphone because he intuitively knew that's what people wanted. He stripped the iPad of features to make it easier and more pleasurable to use. His gift wasn't in invention but in improving, refining and simplifying existing technology.

"Think left and think right and think low and think high. Oh, the things you can think up if only you try."

Dr. Seuss

The 4 Ps of Creativity

Creativity includes novelty and usefulness and can be productively approached through the 4 Ps as follows:

- *People.* We should learn to identify the different characteristics, abilities and styles of people. People differ in the amount of creativity that they possess, and how they choose to exercise their creativity. Nevertheless, organisations should believe that creativity skills can be enhanced through training and encouragement. They facilitate creativity through the appointment of champions and make sure that employees are trained in creative problem solving. A champion is a person who is personally committed and enthusiastically supports creativity and innovation. The champions play important roles as enablers for creativity and innovation. The champion is particularly effective and supportive when good creative ideas face major opposition. Applying a creative problem solving approach encourages people to use a common problem solving framework when they are confronted with novel, complex and ambiguous challenges and opportunities. With this approach people are encouraged to generate alternatives, evaluate them and finally implement them in a systematic fashion. This approach helps people to come up with useful ideas and develop ways to implement them.

- *Processes.* This includes the systems, procedures, processes and operations performed. Can the tools, techniques and methods that people apply be improved? Organisations that excel in innovation and growth have good procedures for managing the generation and implementation of ideas. They know the importance of searching for ideas, understanding unmet needs, and meeting those needs with new and improved systems and procedures. Innovation and incremental improvement is the key to productivity and economic growth. New technology is often the spur to new discoveries and inventions. Take the case of the telescope, which opened up the wonders of the universe to astronomy, and the mathematical and classifying powers of modern computers which help solve complicated problems too difficult for the human mind.

- *Product.* How can we apply our creativity to come up with new products and services or to improve existing ones? Unless a company is continually renewing itself in the form of new and improved products and services it will not survive in the long-term. Competition will undermine its position in the market place and it will go out of business.

- *Place.* Does the culture, context, norms or climate of the company inhibit or foster creativity? How can we establish conditions that encourage and incentivise creativity and innovation? One way is to purposefully design the work environment. The natural flow of traffic through the building should facilitate employees from different functions to accidentally bump into each other, and thus encourage informal conversations, serendipity and creativity. Leaders should act as role models for creativity by providing a supportive environment and giving positive feedback. They do this by the way they organise, motivate and inspire their followers. Ideas and suggestions from employees should always be welcome. Employees who are made to feel a high sense of self-efficacy and self-esteem tend to be more creative. Self-efficacy is the extent to which employees believe they have the ability to produce creative outcomes. A climate that increases the level of participation in the company increases employee engagement and job satisfaction. Leaders with high emotional intelligence will empathise with their workers, sense their moods and know how to rectify sources of dissatisfaction. Happy workers are more creative workers. Unfortunately most workers feel alienated and disengaged from their work resulting in a huge source of creativity being underutilised or ignored.

How to Kill Creativity

In many organisations ideas are killed before they ever get off the ground. Persistence, determination, and resilience, will see ideas through in the end. People who are sensitive about criticism will have a tough time being creative. Killing creativity can be categorised under selling, pessimism and business.

Selling

- *'It won't sell.'* Decca Records rejected the Beatles in 1962, and instead signed Brian Poole & The Tremeloes. They said that groups with guitars were going out of fashion. Columbia and HMV, subsequently turned them down as well. They were finally offered a recording contract by Parlophone, and went on to become the most famous rock 'n' roll group in history. Jim Denny of the Grand Old Oprey, Nashville, fired Elvis Presley after his first performance, and advised him to go back to driving a truck. Even market surveys can get it wrong. They said that the ultimate demand for computers would be five units. They said that people didn't need Xeroxes because they would never need more than three copies of anything, and anyway carbon copies could adequately do the job. They said that the demand for mobile phones would be limited and that the Sony Walkman would be a flop. James Dyson set up his own manufacturing company for his bag-less vacuum cleaner after the major manufacturing companies refused to take on his invention.

- *'We tried that before and were unsuccessful.'* Dr. Seuss's first book, *And to Think I Saw It on Mulberry Street*, was rejected by 27 publishers. Seuss was so depressed that he considered burning the manuscript. However, he went on to become the author of more than forty best-selling children's books, including *The Cat in the Hat*, *Green Eggs and Ham*, and *The 500 Hats of Bartholomew Cubbins*. Abraham Lincoln is remembered as one of the greatest leaders of the USA. He started many businesses which failed and was defeated in numerous runs for public office before he eventually succeeded. Many business people went through bankruptcies several times before they eventually became successful. Many scientists made numerous attempts over many years before they finally succeeded.

- *'It won't travel.'* Western Union came to the conclusion in 1876, that the telephone had too many drawbacks to be taken seriously as a means of communication, and concluded that the device was of no value to them. In 1927 H.M. Warner, of Warner Bros, said that people would not be interested in hearing actors talk. When advising Henry Ford's lawyer not to invest in the Ford Motor Company, the president of the Michigan Savings Bank maintained that the horse was here to stay but the automobile was only a fad. F. Zanuck, head of 20th Century Fox, reached similar short-sighted conclusions about TV in 1946: "People will soon get tired of staring at a plywood box every night." Some people thought that data processing was a fad that wouldn't last, and concluded that there was no reason for any individual to need a computer in his home. In 1943 Thomas Watson, chairman of IBM, concluded there would only be a total world market for five computers. Even Bill Gates of Microsoft in 1981, thought that 64K would be enough processing power for anybody. Then along came Apple and the rest is history! When the Eiffel Tower was built in Paris people thought it should be pulled down. It is now the greatest tourist attraction in France.

Pessimism

- *'It's too obvious and simplistic.'* Post-it-Notes, by 3M, have gone on to become one of the most lucrative products of all time. The company was looking for a new type of strong glue. One type of glue produced was too weak and this less aggressive glue was adapted for a new market, and the Post-it-Note, after many years, was eventually born. Because the adhesive was barely sticky, it would adhere to a page but wouldn't tear it when removed – the ideal product for bookmarks or notes left around. Market surveys for the Post-it-notes were negative and major office suppliers told the creator of the notes that they were silly. In fact, some of the simplest ideas often turn out to be the most successful and profitable.
- *'There are too many difficulties.'* Potential difficulties didn't deter the first manned lunar mission in 1969. NASA failed 20 times during their first 28 attempts to send rockets into space, but learned from their mistakes and eventually succeeded.

Complications didn't deter Charles Lindbergh. He became the first person to fly solo, non-stop across the Atlantic Ocean, and received the Congressional Medal of Honour from President Calvin Coolidge for his achievement. The difficulty of the task didn't deter Edmund Hillary when he became the first to conquer Mount Everest in 1953 after several failed attempts. Similarly, Robert Peary made 7 unsuccessful attempts to reach the North Pole until finally he succeeded on his 8th attempt in 1909.

- *'It's impossible.'* On 17 December, 1903 the Wright brothers made the first powered aeroplane flight in history. Although attended and witnessed by five people the press ignored the momentous event. At the time conventional scientific thinking assumed that such a flight was impossible. Lord Kelvin, president of the Royal Society, declared in 1895 that heavier than air flying machines could not fly. In fact, as late as 1905, Scientific American magazine still condemned the reports of the Wright brothers' success as a hoax. The Wright brothers offered their invention to the US War Department, but were dismissed as cranks. It was not until their flight in Le Mans, France in 1908 that their achievement was universally recognised and celebrated. History is littered with things that were once thought impossible, but which eventually became possible. Pierre Pachet, Professor of Physiology at Toulouse, declared in 1872 that Louis Pasteur's theory of germs was ridiculous fiction. People at the time thought that a wireless was an impossible and ridiculous idea, but Marconi proved them wrong. The safety blade was invented by King Gillette. In 1895 he had a revelation: if he could put a sharp edge on a small square of sheet steel, he could market a disposable safety blade which would replace the dangerous blade in use at the time. Gillette visited metallurgists who assured him it was impossible. This didn't stop Gillette from continuing with his vision. It took Gillette six years to find an engineer who could produce the blade that he wanted.

- *'Yes, but'* is a famous killer phrase, and denotes a negative attitude of mind. It is just one of the typical destructive statements that stultify creativity and personal initiative in a company. It is a manifestation of the not invented here syndrome. This is a dismissive attitude about ideas or improvements suggested by others. The attitude is, if they were worthwhile, we would have already thought of them. Why not substitute, 'Yes, and' which suggests positivity, expansion, and an opening up of possibilities. Why not be generous with your praise and support to encourage creativity in others? Why not accept that other people might have better ideas than you?

For those individuals who take pride in being different from the norm, rejection can inspire more imaginative thinking according to a Johns Hopkins University study conducted in 2012. It seems that rejection helps independent-minded people to think more creatively. Take the case of Colonel Sanders of Kentucky Fried Chicken fame. Sanders had a very difficult time selling his famous chicken recipe at first. It was rejected 1,009 times before a restaurant accepted it. Sanders finished up a multi-millionaire.

Business

- *'It's against company policy.'* Donald Fisher, a real estate developer, was refused when he tried to change a pair of Levi's jeans for a different size in a department store in San Francisco. Frustrated by his experience he opened up his own store specialising in jeans and called it the Gap. This is now one of the most successful speciality stores in retailing history. Frustration is often a great spur to creativity.
- *'It will cost too much.'* Walt Disney's first cartoon production company, *Laugh-O-Gram*, went bankrupt. However, he didn't let this get him down. He subsequently went on to create *Micky Mouse* which became the most famous cartoon name in film animation. He produced *Snow White and the Seven Dwarfs*, *Pinocchio*, *Fantasia*, *Bambi*, and

Cinderella and founded Disneyland. The Ford Motor Company once controlled 60% of auto sales. However, Ford's attitude that the customer could have any car provided it was black lost him the number one spot to General Motors. They had no hesitation in offering colour options to customers and were more in tune with the needs of customers. Ford's sales fell to 20% of new car sales in the 1940s.

- *'Competitors will copy our idea quickly.'* Bill Gates founded Microsoft Corporation with Bill Allen. Gates designed the software to run the first microcomputer, signed agreements with computer companies to use his software solely on their machines, and became the world's richest man, and one of the world's most benevolent philanthropists. Patent and copyright laws will help to protect your invention from unauthorised use, but it is not a complete safeguard as similar laws may not operate in other countries.

- *'It will upset the boss.'* EMI dropped the first Sex Pistols UK single from their second label. The BBC banned their second single 'God Save the Queen (She ain't a human being)'. They believed it would upset the British Monarchy. The Sex Pistols went on to become one of the most famous punk rock bands in the world. Richard Drew, a lab technician with 3M, refused to take no for an answer when his boss initially rejected his idea about masking tape. It is now one of the best sellers in the 3M range of products.

"The creation of something new is not accomplished by the intellect but by the play instinct acting from inner necessity. The creative mind plays with the objects it loves."

Carl Jung

Creative Perspectives

Edward De Bono, the inventor of lateral thinking, has suggested the following approach – known as the 'Six Thinking Hats' – to make people more creative and aware of other people's unique perspectives. The hats are imaginary or metaphorical. It has been incorporated by many companies into their creativity workshops, and is a way of solving problems by adopting different insightful viewpoints. It is a type of role play which gives you the freedom, without fear or criticism, to take on different viewpoints as appropriate.

We each have a dominant thinking style followed by a preference for one or two others. Hats are referred to by their colour and give you the permission and persona to adopt a particular thinking style, depending on the colour of the hat that you decide to choose. The hats also trigger off a particular mood. A person wearing a white hat focuses on factual information. A person with a red hat focuses on emotional intuition. A person with a yellow hat adopts a positive perspective. A person with a black hat is cautious. A person with a green hat is creative, and finally a person with a blue hat exercises control.

In a team each participant is given the opportunity to adopt each of the six hats during the creativity session. During the process participants can be asked to vary their different thinking styles, thus helping them empathise with different perspectives. The neutrality of the colours allows participants to choose roles objectively without embarrassment. Thinking becomes a game governed by defined rules. At any stage the facilitator can instruct the group to take off a particular hat, and put on a different one to change their mode of thinking, and thus get a different viewpoint. For example, if you have a proposal that you want everyone to examine for potential problems, then you can ask them to put their black hat on.

The facilitator describes the concept of the six hats, defines the scope of the problem and assigns the white hat to each participant. Then the facilitator assigns a red hat to every participant. Then they all put on the next hat and so on. The hats can be actual or metaphorical. Some facilitators use six hats with six detachable coloured tassels to facilitate people to change quickly from one role to another. Everybody puts on one hat so that everybody thinks in the same way at the same time. This means that ideas are channelled in a more effective and productive way.

The six thinking hats

- *White hat thinking*. It is computer-like in the way it operates. It is about getting facts, figures and information, to solve a problem, or make a decision. It is a rational, logical, practical and neutral way of thinking. It avoids interpretation, extrapolation, impressions, beliefs, points of view and opinions. A white hat thinker might say, 'Let's establish the facts before we go any further.' Accountants and engineers like logic and facts and thus tend to have a preference for white hat thinking. Similarly, barristers or lawyers use white hat thinking when engaged in cross examination. Judge Judy of TV fame has popularised this approach. People who come before her for judgement must avoid gossip, hearsay and unsupported assumptions and stick to the facts. At any stage during this process you can choose to put your white hat on or take it off, or the chairman may direct everybody to put on their white hat.

- *Red hat thinking*. It is linked to anger; such as seeing red. It is concerned with hunches, feelings, intuition and emotions. The red hat allows you to express your feelings without fear and any need to justify them. It accepts that emotions are part of the thinking and decision making process. It legitimises emotions and feelings as an important aspect of thinking. Red hat thinking gives you the permission to make your emotions visible and to say what you feel. It is almost the exact opposite of factual or white hat thinking. Red hat thinking tries to engage the subconscious mind without the critical interference of the rational conscious mind. A red hat thinker might say. 'I've got a feeling this idea will work,' or 'this is how I feel about the matter.' Creative writers, musicians, designers and artists like to give expression to their emotions, and thus tend to have a preference for red hat thinking. Intuition, feelings or sudden insights are an important aspect of everyday decision making and scientific discoveries. Red hat thinking gives this process some legitimacy by bringing it out into the open and putting it under scrutiny.

- *Yellow hat thinking.* Yellow is the colour of the sun and stands for sunshine and brightness. It is thus linked to a sunny or optimistic disposition. It is for logic, optimism, hope and taking up a positive constructive point of view. The yellow hat encourages you to be expansive, and see the bright side of things. The yellow hat thinker likes to make everybody feel happy, and looks for the benefits of solutions and for ways of making ideas work. It encourages speculation, dreams, visions and hope. It allows you to look to the future for opportunities. At the same time it tries to avoid the Pollyanna type syndrome or being optimistic to the point of foolishness. Optimists have one cognitive flaw in that they look for evidence to confirm their beliefs rather than challenging them. Optimism should not be wishful thinking. Yellow hat thinking is not quite the same as green hat thinking which focuses on creativity and should not be confused with it. A yellow hat thinker might say, 'It's true that this system will take some time to work, but it will improve efficiency and effectiveness, and reduce our costs.' At the early stages of generating ideas we all need to put on our yellow hat thinking to encourage ideas. You can choose to be optimistic and the yellow hat gives you the permission to do so.

- *Black hat thinking*. This is about caution, pessimism, negativity, logic and critical analysis and judgement. It may question assumptions and why one line of argument doesn't automatically follow from another. You become the devil's advocate in action, highlighting things that cannot be done or things that will not work. It is more fun and easier to be destructive rather than constructive. This approach is likely to hinder curiosity, exploration and the generation of ideas, and so yellow hat thinking should precede it. It is useful because it helps people avoid silly costly mistakes, see the downside and consider counter arguments. It points out risks, dangers, shortfalls, disadvantages and potential problems. It evaluates risk by looking at the consequences of your decision. How much money am I risking? What will I lose if I fail? What is the worst case scenario? What is the probability of failure? It may extrapolate ideas into the future to see how they might fail. It prevents people becoming over-committed and over-zealous about their ideas. A black hat thinker might say, "This proposal will never be accepted because the unions will object." We all need to adopt black hat thinking from time to time to see the downside of our proposals. On the other hand, if someone is being very negative about an idea the other person might say: "That is good black hat thinking, but now let's try some yellow hat thinking for a change." The switch in thinking can be made immediately without causing any offense.
- *Green hat thinking*. This is linked to the colour of grass with its possibilities of life, growth and vegetation. It is about new ideas, new concepts, new possibilities and new perceptions. It is about creativity and lateral thinking, the search for

alternatives and moving things forward. With appropriate training most people can become competent at creativity. In real life there is usually more than one solution to a problem. Some alternatives are better, cost less, are more reliable, are more acceptable, and thus easier to implement than others. However, we must consider alternatives if we are to avoid overlooking the simple and obvious solution. Green hat thinking is about provocation, exploring new approaches to problems and risk taking. Provocation forces us out of habitual patterns of perception. When stopped at traffic lights the green light gives you permission to proceed. Similarly, the green hat gives the go-ahead to generate alternatives, and explore new ideas in a meaningful way. It allows you to switch to the creative role. A green hat thinker might say, "We need to develop and explore more alternatives." Green hat thinkers will pick the best of the ideas and push them forward for further consideration and evaluation.

- *Blue hat thinking*. This is linked to the colour of the sky which is blue and cool. This suggests an overview, detachment and being cool and in control. It is about organising; coordinating and managing the thinking process in a sensible way so that it becomes more productive. The blue hat thinker is organised, and likes to manage time and take a considered, thoughtful approach to problems. Business people tend to be blue hat thinkers. The chairperson or facilitator of the meeting usually wears this hat. The blue hat thinker would say, "Let's review where we are before we proceed further." A chairperson has a blue hat function in defining the problem, keeping order, stopping arguments, enforcing discipline and sticking to the agenda, as well as providing overviews, making summaries and arriving at conclusions. Project managers like to follow process, and thus have a preference for blue hat thinking. Similarly, the conductor of an orchestra wears this hat. So blue hat thinking makes sure that the rules of the game are strictly observed and that the objectives are achieved. They carry out a similar function to referees in football games.

"One very important aspect of motivation is the willingness to stop and to look at things that no one else has bothered to look at. This simple process of focusing on things that are normally taken for granted is a powerful source of creativity."

Edward de Bono

The Range of Creativity Paradigms

Academics classify creativity techniques under three headings: paradigm preserving, paradigm stretching and paradigm breaking. A paradigm is a new way of looking or thinking about something. It is a word used frequently in academic, scientific and business worlds. In education the talk and chalk approach is a paradigm. If you suddenly changed to a more participative approach that would be a new paradigm. In business it could mean a new way of marketing, such as using new distribution channels like the internet to reach customers. Finally, there is a paradigm shift in what adds value. Raw materials are becoming less significant in creating wealth particularly in the information and communications technology based industries. The growth of the electronics industry is based on the silicon chip, which is sand with great quantities of knowledge added. Reengineering is the efficient use of existing knowledge (paradigm preserving), while innovation is the creation of new knowledge (paradigm stretching or paradigm breaking).

Paradigm preserving

Paradigm preserving techniques can be used to solve known and more structured problems. In paradigm preserving techniques the boundaries around the problem remain the same. People do not go outside their own perspectives in exploring the situation. Consequently, they develop existing ideas but do not change them significantly. It is a natural incremental progression of idea building on previous knowledge. The fax machine, videocassette recorder, and the high-definition television were invented in the United States. However, they were not taken to the market initially as the costs of making them commercially viable, in the short-term, was prohibitive. On the other hand the Japanese take an incremental approach to creativity. They took the long-term view, improved the technology significantly, and made millions of dollars profit in the process.

Many business techniques such as work study, organisation and methods, operational research, business process reengineering, total quality management and world class manufacturing are paradigm preserving techniques. They borrowed and built incrementally on ideas from previous well-known techniques. For example, organisation and methods are work studies applied to the office. Paradigm-preserving techniques can be useful as they do not require participants to move outside their comfort zones.

Brainstorming and brainwriting (brainstorming on paper) are examples of paradigm-preserving techniques because they do not force group members to view the problem or situation from a different angle. In brainstorming people piggyback on the ideas of others. One idea sparks off another that is similar to the first and so on. Each idea acts as a stimulus for subsequent ideas and each of these ideas is related to the problem under discussion. Ideas produced in a brainstorming session mainly produce incremental improvements rather than revolutionary ones. Cost savings, marginal design improvements, and modifications in products and processes are usual rather than patented ideas or novel products. This approach is therefore a paradigm preserving approach rather than a paradigm stretching, or paradigm-breaking approach.

Paradigm stretching
Paradigm stretching techniques can be used to solve unstructured problems. Paradigm stretching techniques encourage the participants to broaden their existing ways of thinking and looking at something. This can be done by using object stimulation, metaphors and forced association. Object stimulation encourages creativity by using unrelated stimuli and forced association. This encourages people to stretch their existing paradigm by developing ideas that are unrelated to the problem. For example, you can use two unrelated words or ideas to develop new ideas.

The internet was developed by bringing together two unrelated concepts, the telephone and the computer. Similarly, smart televisions combine the television with the internet, giving access to Google, radio and TV channels. It requires imagination and awareness to use this approach effectively. Consequently, a paradigm stretching approach makes some people feel uncomfortable as it pushes them outside their comfort zone.

In his research Alfred Wegener (1880 – 1930) found that fossils of identical plants and animals existed on opposite sides of the Atlantic. Intrigued by this information he found further evidence of similar organisms separated by great oceans. He then noticed the close fit between the coastlines of Africa and South America. Like a jigsaw they could be put back together. This led him to the conclusion that the continents were joined together at one time. This idea was initially ridiculed and took decades to be generally accepted by scientists. Plate tectonics, which explains large-scale geologic changes, is now considered one of the most important geological theories of all time.

Paradigm breaking
Like paradigm stretching techniques, paradigm breaking techniques can also be used to solve unstructured problems.

Paradigm breaking techniques encourage people to look at situations from a number of different perspectives, and so come up with very unique and novel ideas. People produce creative ideas when they bring new elements into the problem situation, by developing new relationships and combinations between existing elements. This technique encourages people to change their perspectives, and break out of existing boundaries. Paradigm breaking techniques overturn rather than add to previous knowledge in the field.

Paradigm-breaking techniques, like paradigm-stretching techniques, use unrelated stimuli and forced associations. In addition, these techniques also tend to rely on modes of expression other than verbal and written, such as drawing, dreaming, fantasising, visioning and role play. This can threaten peoples' sense of security, and therefore these techniques should only be used by groups who have a high degree of confidence, cohesion and trust.

Before 1543, people believed that the sun revolved around the earth. Galileo's discovery, published in 1632, that the sun and not the Earth was the centre of the Universe, is a good example of a paradigm breaking discovery. It confirmed the heliocentric model of the universe that Copernicus had promulgated in his book *On the Revolution of the Celestial Spheres* published in 1543. Copernicus and Galileo moved scientific theory from the Ptolemaic system which claimed that the earth was at the centre of the universe and contributed greatly to the scientific revolution. Galileo is known as the father of observational astronomy. Similarly, Isaac Newton put the tides and the fall of an apple together and came up with the law of gravity. This in turn was superseded by Einstein's theory of relativity and quantum physics.

The French Revolution created a major paradigm shift. A subjugated majority overthrew the ruling elite who often governed with a cruel and callous hand. About 300 years before an obscure monk and professor of theology named Martin Luther challenged the Roman Catholic Church, with his 95 theses and his proclamation of salvation through faith alone. This created a paradigm shift in thinking. Before this few questioned the moral authority of the hierarchy or aristocracy to rule. The mindset was that the aristocracy was born to rule, and the common people to serve. In Plato's time the aristocracy enjoyed democracy, while the enslaved masses did not. Were it not for this monk it would have been unlikely that the French Revolution and indeed the American Revolution would have taken place. Indeed these revolutions triggered off movements for democracy throughout the world lasting to this day. Ordinary people were now prepared to question authority, religious doctrine, societal norms and conventional wisdom.

It was thought for many years that cells communicate predominately by electrical signals. However, in the 1960s and 70s this was overturned when it was discovered that cells communicate predominately by chemical signals. This is dramatic enough to be paradigm breaking. Arvid Carlsson's work on the chemical neurotransmitter dopamine earned him the Nobel Prize for Physiology or Medicine in 2000. Charles Darwin's theory of evolution displaced the biblical story of creation and gave a new understanding of how mankind came into being. In modern music people who pioneered a whole new musical tradition such as jazz, blues and rock and roll achieved similar results.

In art people who pioneered cubism and impressionism were also paradigm breakers. For example, Salvador Dali put dreams and art together and got surrealism. He was one of the most famous artists of the 20th century. Picasso was inspired by the work of Paul Cezanne to produce cubism. Twenty years earlier Cezanne had begun to paint his landscapes and still lives in geometric cubes and cylinders.

Less experienced groups may be happy to use paradigm preserving techniques because these are familiar and comfortable and within their comfort zones. More confident and more experienced groups who trust each other may prefer to use the more adventurous paradigm stretching and breaking techniques. These techniques will encourage group members to produce more creative and novel ideas because they force them to view the problem from new and different perspectives.

> "Creative thinking is not a talent, it is a skill that can be learnt, it empowers people by adding strength to the natural abilities which improves teamwork, productivity and, where appropriate, profits."
>
> Edward de Bono

Brainstorming

Brainstorming is probably one of the best known and most popular techniques for generating ideas. It is easy to understand and use. For best results limit the number of participants to between 6 and 8 people, and ask participants to do some advance work on their own and bring these ideas to the brainstorming session. Keep the session short – about 60 minutes should be sufficient for best results. To conduct the session you need a large, open U-shape where people can interact informally and see each other on an equal basis. Long, narrow boardroom table setups are absolutely the wrong structure for a brainstorming session. Participants are encouraged to build on other people's ideas, and thus do not change them significantly. Just like dancing, brainstorming needs to be done standing up to generate the maximum number of ideas.

A warm up session may be useful to get participants into the mood and to build up rapport. Taking short breaks may also be useful. The need to allow time for the incubations of ideas is supported by research. You can also have interesting conversations with other participants before you return to the problem. For best results you should have a trained facilitator conducting the brainstorming session. The job of the facilitator is to keep the session moving along, relevant and on target. In addition, you should have a note taker whose job is to record the ideas on a flipchart or whiteboard, so that participants can see what's discussed. Typically the outcome of a brainstorming session should be a shortlist of useful ideas to pursue.

The four stages of brainstorming

- *Suspend judgement.* The emphasis is on the generation of ideas, so suspend your critical faculties. Explore ideas fully. Look at them from all angles. Assume anything is possible. Think what you could achieve if you assume that there are no constraints, and that you could not fail. Quieten the voice of the inner critic, and put your critical faculties into neutral gear. Even though you know the idea is very silly, and all the reasons why it won't work, nevertheless, you must keep your opinions to yourself. Also make sure that your body language is neutral, and so doesn't show signs of disapproval. In fact, the 'wildest idea' technique is sometimes used as a way of stimulating ideas by focusing on the outlandish when they are beginning to dry up. As Einstein said: "If at first an idea is not absurd, then there is no hope for it."
- *Freewheel the ideas.* Let them flow, as one idea may trigger off new ideas, combinations of existing ideas or novel relationships. The key thing to remember is not to get hung up on developing or assessing the worth or feasibility of ideas during this stage, as this interrupts the spontaneous flow. Group members should be allowed to communicate an idea, however strange and silly, to the rest of the group. Seemingly strange, stupid and impractical ideas will often contain the germ of a great idea. Many of the great discoveries of history began in this way and attracted disbelief and incredulity until they were proven to be correct. Teams that laugh most easily are more creative and productive than teams who are dour and more formal. Fun, jokes and playfulness relax people and put them into a

collaborative and creative state. Some companies have liberated team thinking by using free-association exercises. For example, at Campbell's Soup Company, a group of product developers began brainstorming by using the randomly chosen word "handle" from a dictionary. Through free association this prompted the word "utensil." This lead to "fork." Then one participant jokingly suggested a soup that could be eaten with a fork. The group then rationalised that a soup could not be eaten with a fork unless it was thick with vegetables and meat. This is how the very successful product – Campbell's Chunky Soups was born. You can use this technique yourself to generate ideas. Open a page at random from a dictionary. Pick a noun. Look for associations with your idea and list them down. This process may trigger off useful ideas just like it did for Campbell's Soups.

- *Generate many ideas.* At this stage you are looking for quantity of ideas rather than quality. The best way to get a great idea is to generate lots of ideas. Outrageous suggestions should be encouraged as these can often trigger off more worthwhile ideas. Piggyback and build upon the ideas of others. Some ideas can be linked, associated or combined with others to give new ideas. The most conducive environment to creativity is one in which people feel supported, non-threatened and relaxed, and where there is fun, humour, spontaneity, and playfulness. Laughter is the best medicine, as it facilitates relaxation, breaks down barriers and promotes creativity. Use irony, exaggeration, word play and absurd association to generate ideas. If ideas begin to dry up you can indulge in reverse brainstorming. With this technique you may discover what others don't do and thus identify a potential gap in the market. A similar idea to reverse brainstorming is Dr. Edward de Bono's provocation

(PO). A PO takes us out of our comfort zone to challenge assumptions.

- *Cross-fertilise.* The different people in the group will cross-fertilise by combining and improving existing ideas causing a variety of new ideas to emerge. Your group could include, inter alia, an accountant, engineer, a marketing person and a human relations manager. A mix of background, personalities and perspectives will help the group to synergise, and consider the problem from many different viewpoints. For example, Sarcos, a technology design and robotics firm brought engineers and biologists together to invent a new way of delivering drugs to the brain and heart. They built a high-tech micro catheter for delivering drugs to difficult-to-reach parts of the brain and heart. Ideas will piggyback on the ideas of others in the group. On the organisational level, companies should look to joint ventures, alliances and networks, to provide alternative ways of coping creatively with competition. Whether undertaken for strategic advantage, or financial gain, these links offer opportunities for cross-fertilisation of ideas and perspectives. It is surprising how outsiders can bring fresh perspectives and new ideas to a problem. For many years physiologists did not understand the purpose of the long loops of small tubes in the kidney. They assumed that the tubes had no function and were a relic of evolution. One day an engineer looked at the loops and realised that they could be part of a counter-current multiplier. This is a well-known device for increasing the concentration of liquids. The fresh perspective from outside solved the problem that had perplexed the experts for a long time. People from the same background will only produce sameness, while diversity facilitates cross-pollination of ideas and creativity. In fact, the best ideas cross disciplinary boundaries. Diversity not only means differences in education, gender, age profile, professional background and function within the company but also different races, cultures and religious beliefs. Diversity changes the way we think and act. It is important to record all the ideas on flipcharts around the room, so that participants have an opportunity to think about their merits and demerits. This should be done by a facilitator who is not involved in generating ideas or recording ideas.

After the flow of ideas has come to a stop, classify the solutions. Rank them from best and most practical to worst and impractical. Have another look at the worst or impractical ideas to ensure that they could not be modified to produce good ideas. This is worth doing as the germ of a good idea is often found in the most unlikely of places. Then have a look at the best and most practical ideas. Critically evaluate these and pick the most feasible. Draw up an implementation plan with a time deadline so that these ideas can be exploited quickly. Make specific people responsible for their implementation and make sure to follow up on their progress.

Summary of ground rules for brainstorming
In summary, for brainstorming sessions the following ground rules may be useful:

- Best to treat the meeting as offsite, and so don't allow email and voicemail access except in the most urgent circumstances.
- Welcome every idea no matter how wild or crazy it may seem. If nothing else it will fire your imagination or someone else's and may trigger some useful ideas.
- Be slow to criticise other people's ideas. In practise we are often too fast to dismiss other people's ideas. Make sure you thoroughly understand another person's idea before you evaluate it.

- Don't underestimate the contribution you can make. You have a unique perspective and unique knowledge and experience. This can make a difference and help solve a given problem.
- Don't be afraid to relax and have fun and adopt a childlike attitude. Playfulness and fantasy can help generate some useful ideas.
- Remember we all have different ways of looking at problems. This is an advantage when trying to come up with alternatives and different perspectives.
- Don't be afraid to make mistakes and allow others to make mistakes as well. See mistakes as an opportunity to learn and start all over again.

> "All work and no play doesn't just make Jill and Jack dull, it kills the potential of discovery, mastery, and openness to change and flexibility and it hinders innovation and invention."
>
> Joline Godfrey

Reverse brainstorming.

This is a negative approach to brainstorming. Instead of asking "In how many ways can we ....?" This technique asks: "In how many ways can this idea fail?" Instead of asking, "How could I solve or prevent this problem?" Ask, "How could I possibly cause the problem?" Instead of asking, "How do I achieve these results?" Ask, "How could I possibly achieve the opposite effect?" It is a good way to tease out problems in advance, so that potential difficulties and solutions can be thought through. Play the devil's advocate with your proposals, and anticipate opposition, counter arguments, unnoticed issues, objections and obstacles. This ensures that you are prepared and rehearsed with the appropriate answers – very useful when you are presenting proposals to your boss for discussion, as a way of anticipating and dealing with flaws and gaps in your argument. Reverse brainstorming can be used to attack a proposal from a competitor's point of view in order to generate defensive strategies.

Challenging your ideas and approach will give you new insights. On a personal basis you can come up with different viewpoints by reversing beliefs, experiences, assumptions, values and people. Reversing your beliefs will give you a different view of the world. Reversing your experiences will give you the opposite viewpoint, and will help you see the world from a new perspective. What if you could turn a failure into a success? Reversing your assumptions will give you the opposite assumptions to what you would normally expect. A change of values might change your ideas or solutions. Seek out people with the opposite viewpoints from yours. How would this affect your thinking? Would it provide new insights?

Alfred Sloan of General Motors used the technique of problem reversal to develop ideas to save the near bankrupt company. At the time it had always been assumed that customers had to pay for their cars in advance before they took possession of them. Sloan reversed the assumption by thinking that customers could pay as they drove the car, thus opening up the idea of hire purchase and instalment payments. In addition, Sloan reversed the idea that all companies had to be managed by one strong individual. He created a divisional structure that delegated decision making while still retaining overall control. 3M was a company with a reputation for sticking things. They challenged this assumption through reverse brainstorming and came up with the idea of making something that doesn't stick – the result was the famous post-it-note. Another company was concerned about its reputation for poor customer service. Instead of asking "How do we improve customer satisfaction?" they reversed the problem statement and asked, "How do we make customers more dissatisfied?" By addressing the sources of dissatisfaction a better customer service was identified and implemented.

Brainwriting versus brainstorming

People may come up with more original thoughts if left to do so alone. This would suggest that brainwriting could be more productive than brainstorming. In brainwriting each participant thinks and records ideas alone. They then pass their ideas around to other participants, so that they can add to them, or use them to trigger off further ideas. After the idea gathering stage is completed, the ideas are read, discussed and evaluated with the help of a facilitator, just like traditional brainstorming.

Writing down ideas instead of speaking them eliminates the problem of production blocking and social loafing. This is because group members don't have to wait their turn to generate ideas and must write them down. It may also reduce conformity since it is independent and anonymous with no necessity for public speaking. The written ideas can be subsequently shared by the group in a round-robin fashion and summarised on a flipchart. It has been found that brainwriting groups produce more and better ideas than brainstorming groups.

Generally, when brainstorming you need to separate the creativity of idea production from the logic of idea evaluation. Both are needed together if you want worthwhile ideas to emerge. Judgement is postponed during brainstorming but not abandoned. Later on the ideas will be subjected to critical analysis, until you are left with the most promising ones. In the meantime, these ideas should be considered starting points for further exploration, rather than finished products. Considerably more time will be needed to develop these ideas into worthwhile commercial projects. This is the 99 per cent perspiration part, rather than the 1 per cent inspiration part that Edison famously referred to in the invention process. Ultimately, the value of a creative idea is determined if it can be applied successfully and profitably in a practical way.

There is some research that brainstorming may not be as useful for creativity as previously thought and that brainwriting is better. This is despite the fact that people enjoy the social interaction of brainstorming. The research suggests that brainstorming meetings may lead people to merely mirror the thoughts of others. Some people may dominate proceedings and take more than their fair share of time. People may not express some ideas because they worry about what people will think. People working alone feel more accountable for producing ideas than in groups. Sometimes people may get distracted and forget their idea, before they have a chance to share it, while listening intently to the ideas of others. These drawbacks of brainstorming can be overcome by using electronic brainstorming via the internet.

Techniques for Stimulating Creativity

In addition to brainstorming there are a wide range of techniques like fantasy, attribute listing, reverse brainstorming, metaphors and SWOT, and creative problem solving (discussed later in this section) for stimulating creativity. These are paradigm stretching and paradigm breaking techniques.

Fantasy

Research has found that creative adults use fantasy for a number of purposes. Fantasy opens up other worlds of experience. In your imagination, you create your own realities unfettered by time and space. Within it you can travel into outer space, journey to exotic places throughout the world, and shrink to the size of an atom to explore microscopic worlds. The idea of becoming miniaturised or something else, in order to understand it better, may be applied to any problem. For example, a pharmaceutical executive discovered a source of contamination by visualising he was a tiny organism, and asking himself how he could get in and cause so much damage. He found the cause was miniscule cracks in the wall of a sterile room.

Writers have discovered that there is a big demand for works of fantasy. *The Lord of the Rings*, a series of three books, by English author J.R.R. Tolkien is the second bestselling novel series ever written with over 150 million copies sold. The Harry Potter series of seven novels by J.K. Rowling has sold 450 million copies (up to July 2013) making it one of the best-selling book series in history, and was converted into the most lucrative films of all time.

You can become anything the mind can think of. Albert Einstein's fantasy of himself riding a beam of sunlight played an important part in the discovery of the theory of relativity. He later expressed these in words and formula. Einstein once remarked that when he examined himself and his methods of thought, he came to the conclusion that the gift of fantasy meant more to him than any talent for abstract positive thinking. Role-play is a type of fantasy used in management training helping people empathise with the role they want to experience, and see things from different perspectives.

Attribute listing

List the main characteristics or attributes of a product, service, object or idea. Attributes are parts, properties, qualities, dimensions, and colour, weight or design elements of the object being examined. Examine each one to see if it can be improved or changed. You can make a new product or design a new process by making combinations or variations on some or all of its attributes. It is a method of exploring business opportunities, rather than solving specific problems.

It is often used in the Research & Development department (R&D) of many companies to come up with new or better products. For example, a product might have several dimensions, such as the design, the material of manufacture, the colour, the package surround, and the distribution system used to bring the product to the customer. Potential applications include, new design, exploring the use of different raw materials in its manufacture, developing different storage, promotion and distribution strategies, changing the colour, determining competitive advantage, and retail location selection.

The Bahco Ergo Screwdriver was developed through a focus on the attributes of its handle both for safety considerations (preventing repetitive strain injury) and that at some point most people want to use a screwdriver with both hands. This meant the handle had to be ergonomically redesigned to make it suitable for ambidextrous use.

You can also look at the attributes of a product, object or idea from different perspectives:

- Physical attributes such as shape, form, colour or texture.
- Social attributes such as responsibilities, taboos, roles or power.
- Process attributes such as selling, marketing, logistics or production.
- Psychological attributes such as wants, needs, motivation or emotions.
- Prices attributes such as cost, discounts, selling price or profit margin.

Metaphors

The Webster New World Dictionary defines a metaphor as: "a figure of speech containing an implied comparison, in which a word or phrase ordinarily and primarily used for one thing is applied to another, e.g. the curtain of night." Metaphors can be drawn from science, technology, nature, industry, sport, literature and history. For example, a revolution is compared to a volcano (a build-up of pressure leading to an explosion), and electric current is compared to water flowing through pipes. Atoms have been, from time to time, thought of as billiard balls, little planetary systems and as waves.

Machinery has been a common metaphor used to understand the workings of modern society. We refer to the machinery of government, re-engineering corporations, and even input-output models for business and educational systems. Managing a company is sometimes compared to running a family. The structure of the human brain has been compared to a telephone system and a computer. We use metaphors in everyday speech as in: "my brain is foggy today."

Einstein believed that the use of metaphors enhanced his creativity. He maintained that if you use a different type of thinking to solve a problem, than the thinking that created the problem, you will be more successful. There are numerous examples of scientists who have employed metaphors as a creative device to generate new inventions. So like Einstein and other scientists, use metaphors and analogies to inspire your creativity. The Greek philosopher Aristotle considered the use of metaphors a sign of true genius. He believed that people, who had the capacity to perceive similarities between two different things, and link them together in a meaningful way, were possessors of a special gift.

Metaphorical thinking is the ability to link two different things by recognising that in some way they share a common trait or principle. Metaphors derive their power by enabling us to see the old and familiar in new and novel ways. Writers use metaphors all the time. A character from one of Shakespeare's plays called the world his oyster. This is his way of saying that the riches of the world are there for the taking. In creativity snowballing is where one idea leads to and builds on another. The metaphor is a snowball which gets bigger and bigger as it rolls down the hill.

Metaphors can be used in business to solve problems. Alan Heeks, a Harvard MBA who worked at Procter & Gamble, uses an organic farm as a model for business life. He runs workshops at a 132 acre farm where analogies run rampant – participants think about harvesting their future development, recycling fertility, and sustainability. He helps participants draw analogies between soil and company staff.

NASA was designing a satellite that needed to be tied to a space station by a thin wire 60 miles long. The designers realised that the motion of reeling in the satellite would make it act like a pendulum with an ever-increasing arc. Stanford scientist Thomas Kane, using the analogy of a yo-yo, discovered that a small electric motor on the satellite would allow it to retrieve the wire back to the space station.

Metaphors have been used successfully in the past to guide new thinking in international relations. The "Munich metaphor" evolved from the failed appeasement between the British prime minister, Neville Chamberlain, and Adolf Hitler of Germany, in 1938 before the start of World War 2. It was agreed that part of Czechoslovakia known as Sudentland could be handed over to Germany. The agreement was broken shortly after, when Adolf Hitler invaded and seized the rest of Czechoslovakia. This served to justify US policy towards the Soviet Union and China after World War 2 that concessionary behaviour doesn't work. The metaphor of the Spaceship Earth, inspired by photographs of the earth taken from space, motivated international diplomats to pursue and find agreement on an ozone depletion protocol in Montreal in 1987.

Metaphors, aphorisms and similes

Some metaphors may become aphorisms. An aphorism is a short pithy instructive statement that is philosophical, witty and wise. Aphorisms are universal truths. Many philosophers, politicians, writers, scientists, inventors, artists, celebrities and sportspeople are remembered for their aphorisms. They embody a general truth or make an astute observation which strikes a chord with all. They can be used as triggers to explore issues and generate creative ideas.

Examples of some well-known aphorisms include:

- "Power tends to corrupt, and absolute power corrupts absolutely."
- "Youth is a blunder; manhood a struggle; old age a regret."
- "The man who removes a mountain begins by carrying away small stones."
- "The journey of a thousand miles begins with a single step."
- "Life's tragedy is that we get old too soon and wise too late."
- "The simplest questions are the hardest to answer."
- "Life is a tale told by an idiot – full of sound and fury, signifying nothing."

- "You never really understand a person, until you walk in their shoes."
- "To err is human, to forgive is divine."
- "Cynicism is an unpleasant way of saying the truth."
- "I find the harder I work, the luckier I get."
- "Hitch your wagon to a star."
- "I disapprove of what you say, but I will defend to the death your right to say it."
- "Lost time is never found again."
- "Nothing great was ever achieved without enthusiasm."
- "A penny saved is a penny earned."
- "Dream as if you'll live forever. Live as if you'll die tomorrow."
- "Always tell the truth. That way you don't have to remember what you said."
- "You made your bed, now lie in it."
- "A stitch in time saves nine."

Similes are specific types of metaphors that use the word "like" or "as". For example: "cute as a kitten," or "as busy as a bee," and "they fought like cats and dogs," and "he slept like a log." Similes can be found in language, literature and music. They can make our language more compelling, descriptive, vivid, understandable, entertaining and enjoyable. Writers, poets and songwriters use similes to make their work more interesting, memorable and emphatic. Similes can be funny, serious, sarcastic or creative. They can be used to make comparisons offering new perspectives and possible novel solutions to problems.

Metaphorical thinking can inspire people to great creative achievements. Alexander Graham Bell (1847-1922) got the inspiration for the telephone from studying the human ear. He was a professor of vocal physiology. The ability to play with ideas and concepts from different areas is basic to problem solving and creativity. Metaphors allow this type of play to occur. They allow your imagination to escape from boundaries and tight conceptual definitions. They encourage you to see things in a new light, where new perspectives and meaning may be discovered. So making comparisons or analogies between problems in business and in nature, biology, science and so on may help to unlock problems and offer solutions.

> "But the fact that some geniuses were laughed at does not imply that all who are laughed at are geniuses. They laughed at Columbus, they laughed at Fulton, and they laughed at the Wright Brothers. But they also laughed at Bozo the Clown."
>
> Carl Sagan

Synectics

Synectics is a creative problem solving process with many similarities to brainstorming but some differences as well. George Prince one of the team who created synectics described brainstorming as "the great breakthrough in creativity techniques; it demonstrated for the first time how much the fear of critical judgement inhibits the expression of ideas."

Synectics widens and deepens the process of suspending judgement in a many ways:

- It extends suspending judgement to the problem definition stage. It accepts the Problem Owner's perception without challenge or questioning.
- It encourages participants to come up with alternative problem statements again without challenge.
- It encourages participants to listen carefully for possible ideas by paying attention to seemingly ridiculous ideas as these may inspire new ideas.
- It actively encourages absurd ideas in line with Einstein's saying "unless at first an idea is absurd, there is no hope for it."

- It uses the excursion as a way of getting ideas from nowhere.

Synectics rely on analogies and metaphors to produce creativity and innovation. These are used to make the familiar strange, or to take the familiar and see it in a totally new light. It is a way of mentally taking things apart, and putting them back together again to furnish new insights to problems. Since creativity involves the combination of things in new ways, every creative thought or action uses synectic thinking.

Buckminister Fuller, the American architect, inventor and visionary, summed up the essence of synectics when he said that all things, regardless of their difference, could somehow be linked together, either in a physical, psychological or a symbolic way. Synectics is a word derived from two Greek words: syn – the coming together of diverse elements, and ectos, from outside. If you want to invent something new, new connections and combinations have to be made. This is more likely to happen if you have a variety of people with a variety of opinions, knowledge, ideas and experiences working on the problem or issue.

The synectics process
The synectics model was created by two members of a successful problem-solving team, George Prince and William Gordon who worked in the Invention Design Group at Arthur D Little in the 1950s. They noticed that sometimes the same group of people worked well together and were successful. At other times they argued fruitlessly and accomplished little. They decided to video the meetings to study and learn from what was happening. They discovered recurring behaviours that always worked and others that didn't work. Based on these observations they developed a process that increased the probability of success. The process has three parts:

1. People need to engage in divergent thinking so that new connections and combinations are made.

2. There needs to be a way of deciding which pieces of divergent thinking are promising and should be worked with.

3. There needs to be a way to take "non-sense," the result of open creative thinking, and use this to "make sense," an idea development process.

The overall flow is from ideas to action. This is so because there is no point in taking the time to be creative if there are no positive outcomes. To achieve success the model needs to establish clear roles, an appropriate climate, and an ability to use the tools effectively.

Three roles in synectics

In addition, there are three roles needed in any synectics meeting:

1. A Problem Owner for any innovations needs to be identified because someone requires to take responsibility for progress, and ultimately for the implementation of the solution. This creates a cooperative win-win approach rather than an adversarial win-lose debate. This person makes the decisions regarding what needs to be done. This is one way synectics differs from brainstorming. In brainstorming all participants have some ownership of the problem. In synectics you have a single problem owner with all other people being there to help that person solve their problem. In addition, the helpers should not know as much about the problem as the problem owner. This encourages "wild ideas" to help trigger other more valid ideas.

2. Resources are people at the meeting who have ideas and opinions but don't make decisions. They may include stakeholders needed to implement decisions, experts who have specific useful knowledge, and non-experts who will find it easier to have new ideas because they are not committed to expected

ways of domain thinking. Experts often find it difficult to think in new ways. This is because they are programmed to think in a particular way by their professional training and expertise.

3. The facilitator acts as a guide by keeping the meeting on track. The facilitator helps the meeting progress from "non-sense" to "make sense" so that a new idea is born. In other words, the facilitator moves the group from problem statement through idea generation, to ideas development and finally to implementation of a solution. The objective is to use analogy and metaphor to create new ways of thinking about the problem, while protecting individuals from criticism for putting forward unconventional ideas.

The facilitator helps people settle down by demonstrating that progress is being made. He shows the Problem Owner and Resource people that there is a route through to the solution and tells people how to get there. The facilitator allows participants to play with connections and share them. He records the results on a flipchart. This provides participants with a visual stimulant to connect the headlined words with their own thoughts, creating a wide variety of perspectives. He thus creates an open supportive climate to facilitate creativity. The facilitator is more effective if he focuses solely on the process of the meeting, rather than putting forward his own ideas. This means that the solution will come solely from the group, and will not be influenced by the facilitator.

In the synectics approach this is called "springboarding," which are take-off points and not normally end points. This consists of headlines expressed as "How to..." or "I wish..." because this is the language of possibility and imagination. These are often abbreviated to H2 and IW. These headlines are then used to generate discussion, making more connections and stimulating more ideas. Springboards should be treated as a series of analogies and metaphors designed to get you thinking about avenues to explore.

If ideas dry up the facilitator can encourage the group to indulge in excursions. Excursions help you think outside the box to consider how you would change particular parameters, features or attributes. They are simply exercises that go up side-roads using different techniques to find potentially useful ideas off the beaten track. It follows that selecting avenues to explore cannot be a logical choice, because there is no knowledge of where the process will lead to. Synectics makes particular use of fantasy, analogies and metaphors, as these give you access to whole new worlds that may lead to many new ideas.

Converting "non-sense" into sense is the purpose of the idea development stage. The Problem Owner reviews the ideas provided by the Resources. The format is a headline – "what you do is..." – followed by an action verb, called specific and actionable ideas. Collect six or seven ideas, and then ask the Problem Owner to review them. He may add information that helps the emerging concept grow, and identify what else is needed to make it more useful. If the process results in a negative outcome then the meeting should go back and choose another springboard.

Synectics is more demanding and more complicated than brainstorming. There are more steps involved requiring more time and effort. The success of the technique depends highly on the skill of a trained facilitator.

Trigger questions

Trigger questions are short simple questions that will help the facilitator provoke new ideas in the group. The acronym TRANSACT will help you remember some of the triggers.

- **T**ake away or subtract. Remove, reduce, abbreviate or simplify.
- **R**epeat. Repeat the shape, colour, form, image or idea.
- **A**dd. Extend, develop or augment.

- **N**ourish fantasy. Trigger surreal, preposterous, outlandish, bizarre thoughts.
- **S**ubstitute. Remove, compress, reduce or simplify.
- **A**nalogise. Draw associations, similarities or differences between things.
- **C**ombine. Link, unify, mix, merge or rearrange.
- **T**ransform or change. Change colour, configuration, shape or structure.

"A man becomes creative, whether he is an artist or scientist, when he finds a new unity in the variety of nature. He does so by finding a likeness between things which were thought alike before."

Jacob Bronowski

Kaizen

Kaizen is a Japanese technique that facilitates little changes and innovations for continuous improvements in products, services and operations. In the 1970s and 1980s, Japanese car companies continuously eroded the market share of US companies. One reason was the successful use of kaizen by the Japanese companies. According to one study, General Motors in the US received less than one suggestion per employee per year, and adopted less than a quarter of the suggestions received. On the other hand, Toyota of Japan generated nearly 18 suggestions per employee and adopted nearly 90% of them.

Kaizen works well when it is managed successfully. The Government of Singapore initiated kaizen in the form of quality circles called Work Improvement Teams (WITs). Hundreds of WITs were started. Each WIT, consisted of the entire work team, a supervisor, and a trained facilitator. Several thousand innovations and improvements were suggested and implemented. These contributed to the administrative efficiency of the Singapore Government.

The Scanlon Plan is a variation on the kaizen approach and is a proven source of numerous small innovations. Gains resulting from the team's work are shared among team members, irrespective of who came up with the idea. While ideas are always welcome it is the implementation of ideas that counts. The team decides on how much each member gets paid as an incentive.

SWOT analysis

This stands for strengths, weaknesses, opportunities and threats. Although developed for corporate strategic planning it can equally be used for personal development. Your strengths might include your education, experience, personality, aptitudes, creativity and initiative. Your weaknesses might include a deficiency in computer skills or lack of assertiveness.

Opportunities might include training courses and possible promotional vacancies arising in the future. Threats might include possible closure of the company you work for due to competitive forces. A threat or weakness, in fact, is often a matter of attitude or perspective. A more positive approach might be to consider how to turn the threat into an opportunity. In other words, treat problems as possible opportunities. Create a mindset in which problems are examined for sources of opportunities and imaginative solutions.

Threats can be classified using a PEST analysis which means political, economic, social and technological. Consider how each of these driving forces can affect your business. Under political you might consider future government policies and laws affecting your business. Abroad you might consider the implications of wars, terrorism and political disputes around the world. Under economic you might consider interest and foreign exchange fluctuations, the growth of global trade, the rise of green issues and how these might impact on your business. Under social you might consider the impact of an ageing population on business, and the changing nature of tastes, fashions and lifestyles. Under technological factors you might consider the rise of information and communications technology, including the internet, iPads, laptops and the smart phone and its ramifications for business.

As you assess your strengths in light of these forces, you may discover new opportunities.

Stretch imaging

Stretch imaging is a technique which encourages you to consider how the world might look at some time in the future. By creating an image of how you think the world will look in the future, you are able to challenge your current thinking and anticipate likely changes. This process helps you to change your current thinking by imagining and rethinking what you need to do to cope with likely future changes. For a company it may help you think of new products and services likely to be in demand in the future. The exercise can be done in groups or individually.

There are three stages in stretch imaging:

1. Imagine that the year is 2030. Consider what the world might look like then. Consider the following questions:
   - What country is likely to be the most economically powerful in the world? China, India and Brazil are currently in the running.
   - Will the trend towards globalisation continue?
   - What are the possible effects of global warming in the future? What effect will a possible increase in sea levels have on low lying countries and coastal cities and towns?
   - How will the world conserve its water resources to best effect?
   - Will conservation issues provide new opportunities for innovation?
   - How long will conventional sources of energy last such as oil and coal? What are the likely sources of alternative energy? What role will wind, wave and solar power play in the future?
   - In early 2014 Google gave the world a glimpse of the future with its driverless car. This will probably take a decade or two to become

commonplace. It is likely to be deeply disruptive on a large economic and social scale, reshaping our cities and impacting entire industries. The taxi, trucking and delivery services are unlikely to survive in their current formats. What is the likely impact of this on employment? Is the self-driving car just the start of a revolution in robotics, and what impacts will this have on our lives?

- How will the world cope with its waste disposal problem? What role will recycling play in the future?
- What type of society will exist in your country?
- How long will the working week be at that stage? In the past the anticipated reduction in the working week due to computerisation never materialised.
- What type of businesses will be the most successful in a competitive and rapidly changing world?
- Will the trend towards diversity in the workplace continue and gain momentum?
- What will the average family look like? The emergence of marriage equality for gay couples and their right to have children will have an impact.
- What kind of an education system is likely? Consider the implications of the internet on education and the trend toward e-learning and lifelong learning.
- Where will information and telecommunications technology have taken us by then? Consider Moore's Law which was formulated in 1965 by the Intel co-founder Gordon Moore, who concluded that computing power, both speed and memory, would double every two years. This law has proved to be phenomenally accurate. Currently cloud computing, in which remote

service will ultimately carry all our software and information, is the next big thing.

Forecasts based on current knowledge should be as well informed as possible and you should state your logic for them to support your view for the changes anticipated.

2. Now that you have developed a vision for 2030, apply this to your own situation. Consider the following questions:
   - What are the social, political, economic and technological issues in the future?
   - Where will the source for World War 3 emerge? The unsettled state of the Muslim world, the rise of terrorism in these countries and the clash of cultures between them and the West is a contender. What effect will all this have on oil supplies?
   - How are these likely to be addressed?
   - What impact will these changes have on your job?

3. Consider what you can do now to meet these challenges in the future. What novel approaches, processes and products will be useful in a rapidly changing world?

Suggestion Schemes

Companies may set up suggestion schemes to encourage employees to make improvements related to their work. These improvements may include making systems and processes better and more cost effective, improving health and safety procedures, and creating ideas for new products or services. The organisation can achieve higher sales, reduced costs and higher profits if the suggestion scheme proves successful. In addition to savings, suggestion schemes provide greater employee involvement with improved motivation and morale. Rates of absenteeism and staff turnover will be improved. Employees feel more engaged with a company if their ideas are listened to and where they feel that they can make a difference.

The scheme should be easy to use, well-run, well-resourced and open to all employees interested in using it. Sometimes managers may publicise current problems and offer prizes for practical implementable solutions saving money. Small money incentives may be awarded for ideas which make worthwhile savings. However, they do not need to offer huge rewards. Recognition and praise are generally more important. A centralised suggestion committee may be set up to adjudicate and make awards. Remember that a suggestion scheme will need continuous senior management support if it is to be successful and live beyond the hype of the launch.

Principles of suggestion schemes
The basic principles of any suggestion scheme should include:

- Suggestion schemes need to be carefully designed to match the culture of the company and the aspirations of the staff. Employees like to feel involved and empowered, and feel their ideas can make a contribution to the success of the company. Steve Proctor, operations director of the professional support network for suggestion schemes said in 2003: "You can change the culture of an organisation by involving people. They feel far more part of things and, as such, become better employees."

- Most companies give financial rewards for implementable ideas achieving worthwhile savings. However, it has been found that recognition and praise can be just as effective. Employees often place more value on the recognition they receive for their efforts. If you start the scheme with financial rewards then it is counterproductive to take them away.

- For continued success, suggestion schemes need senior management support, and the services of a dedicated scheme administrator. Ideas can be sent direct to the administrator, or through the local line manager. Some organisations still rely on the conventional suggestion box.

- It is a good idea to give the scheme a brand so that it is easily recognisable and promotable. For example, Sainsbury's runs a "Tell Justin" scheme, where staff can email the supermarket chain's chief executive Justin King. In addition, training schemes can be used to encourage participation, and ensure that employees understand how the scheme works and the type of input required.

- Ideas should be processed quickly. Employees quickly lose faith in a scheme which takes months to consider ideas, and longer still to implement them. If you want people to be creative you must provide them with prompt feedback about their ideas, and show that you appreciate their efforts. If ideas are not going to be implemented it should be explained why, so that the employee knows for the future what the company is looking for. Feedback demonstrates to employees that the scheme is well run, thus facilitating sustained participation.

- Ideas should be assessed by qualified assessors. This is especially true if a proportion of the savings are awarded to the employee making the suggestion.

- The scheme should be kept fresh and vibrant. This can be done through frequent publicity, constant promotion and imaginative posters. Employees should be asked for ideas on specific areas such as energy reduction, product and process enhancements, or health and safety improvements.

Practical schemes

Steve Proctor is operations director at IdeasUK, a non-profit organisation that promotes staff suggestion schemes. He says: "There are so many benefits to running a staff suggestion scheme. On a financial level, in 2004, our members saved an estimated £90 million as a result of the 120,000 suggestions they received from their employees. And because they engage employees, they can also have a very positive effect on staff morale resulting in a happier and more productive workforce."

Alcoa, an Australian mining company has an employee suggestion scheme, offering financial incentives to those who develop ideas resulting in cost savings. Ideas from refinery and mine site employees have achieved big financial savings and safety, environmental and efficiency gains. Steve Lusted, one of their refinery workers, was awarded $23,000 for his suggestion to transfer simple steam powered pump technology from one part of the refinery to another. This suggestion saved the company $1 million.

Vaillant Group, a UK boiler manufacturer, has a kaizen suggestion scheme that has proved particularly fruitful. In 2009 alone, 380 suggestions were put forward generating an impressive £550,000 in cost savings. Employees are rewarded with prize draws for weekend breaks away.

The winner of the Institute of Management Services Productivity Trophy for 2009 was a power station employee named Nigel Millington, who works in Oldbury power station in the UK. Nigel's idea was an innovative approach to repairing a turbine isolation and emergency stop valve while the turbine was in service. Previously when the valve needed to be repaired, production had to be shut down for several days. His innovative solution allowed service to continue and prevented the need for shut down. The innovation was implemented with savings of £3.5 million.

A bright idea regarding a tool redesign saved the pharmaceutical company Pfizer £70,000 annually. Center Pares achieved £300,000 in savings by implementing energy efficiency measures suggested by staff. Siemens Standard Drives centralised the scanning of serial numbers saving more than £6,000 a year. The company's overall suggestion scheme, which generates 4,000 ideas each year, saves the company about £750,000 annually. Aimia Foods in the UK has saved over £300,000 in one year through innovations generated by its suggestion scheme.

In line with modern technology, some companies have gone on-line with their suggestion schemes. In the UK, technology firm SAP enables staff to send their ideas directly to the managers responsible for implementing them. Employees who submit ideas considered worthwhile will automatically receive a bonus from Human Resources. Ideas successfully implemented will receive a larger reward. The automatic system creates a faster turnover time, and is completely transparent so that staff can see ideas submitted and track their progress. A similar scheme has been installed by British Gas. In the British Gas scheme more than £2 million worth of ideas have been put forward in the course of a few years by employees. In 2005 alone, the value of employee suggestions was about £800,000.

Creative Problem Solving

Many business people complain that their managers and employees have poor problem solving skills. These poor skills were acquired in an educational system that ignored the importance of creative problem solving, and failed to educate students in how to assimilate, manipulate, and synthesise information to solve problems in a creative way. The most common form of creativity is creative problem solving. A good example of creative problem solving is the novel approach to releasing the truck stuck under the tunnel by taking the air out of the tyres.

I have adopted CPS approach to creative problem solving from a technique used in management services called SREDIM, which is an acronym standing for Select, Record, Examine, Develop, Install and Maintain. SREDIM in turn is derived from the scientific approach espoused by Sir Francis

Bacon and other medieval thinkers in the early 1600s. This is a systematic comprehensive step-by-step approach to creative problem solving. Research shows that people trained in this technique are better at creative problem solving than those who have not gone through this training.

The CPS approach helps those trained in it to balance the appropriate amount of divergent and convergent thinking when solving problems. They are more likely to identify the right problem, generate a variety of alternatives and evaluate solutions. They develop a more open minded attitude and acceptance towards the ideas and viewpoints of other people. The creative problem solving approach is not only relevant to business situations, but is also appropriate to solving personal and community issues. Well defined routine problems can be solved by using standard operating procedures. Ill-defined non-routine problems need to be addressed by using CPS.

The SREDIM approach

- Select. This means identifying the problems and opportunities for change or improvement. Discovering problems requires as much creativity as solving them. Too often we rush into developing solutions without determining a good problem statement. The most important point is to find the right problem to work on. Kodak is an example of a company which identified the wrong problem. It focused on making the process of manufacturing and distributing of its chemical-based film more efficient. Instead it should have devoted its efforts to facilitating the change-over to digital photography. In other words, it became better and better at doing the wrong thing. Edwin Land, the inventor of Polaroid said if a problem can be defined it can be solved. After considering alternative problems for study, you should converge on the problem that deserves further consideration, study and exploration. Question the problem thoroughly. A thorough dissection will mean you are addressing the real issues, and not just the symptoms. If you confuse causes and symptoms, because of inadequate fact finding, you may solve the wrong problem. In your quest to solve the problem, consider the following questions. What is the problem or problems? Where does it occur? When does it occur? How does it occur? Whose problem is it? Why does the problem occur? What are the reasons for the problem? How can the problem be overcome? They say that a problem properly defined is a problem half solved. Einstein knew about the importance of properly defining the problem. When he was asked what single event was most helpful in developing his theory of relativity, he replied: "Figuring out how to think about the problem." He also maintained that if he had only one hour to save the world he would spend 55 minutes defining the problem and then five minutes solving it.

- **R**ecord the facts. Collect as much relevant information as possible about the selected problem. Focus on answering the following questions. What facts do I have? What facts do I not have? What facts do I need to solve the problem? How much will it cost, and how difficult is it to get these facts? How urgent is the decision? Can I afford to wait for these facts? In practice, most decisions are made with incomplete information. Researching, recording and gathering information is very time-consuming and expensive. Therefore, you must devise the best and most cost effective method of collecting the facts. At a certain stage, you must make up your mind to go no further, because it is becoming too difficult, time-consuming, less worthwhile, and too costly to continue. Part of the process of recording the facts might be to classify them in a meaningful way. Problems involving systems are best researched by using flowcharts. Flowcharts will help you overview, understand and visualise a system better, and clarify the relationships and sequences between the elements of the system. Flowcharts will highlight inefficiencies and blockages in the system that need to be addressed. When Edison was designing the electric light bulb (to find a suitable long lasting filament) he needed to carefully classify the different types of material that he tested and the results that he found. This systematic approach helped him narrow down the research.

- Examine the facts and interpret. Adopt a critical, questioning and sceptical attitude. Apply common sense principles and make sure that your interpretation of the facts is reasonable, correct and logical. Differentiate between facts, feelings, opinions and assumptions. Disregard opinions completely and treat feelings and assumptions with extreme caution. Be aware of any preconceived biases that you may have, and discount them accordingly. If you've solved similar problems before, the same approach with slight modifications to cater for unique circumstances, might work again. There is no point in reinventing the wheel! Check out and verify the facts, and crosscheck in a rigorous objective manner. If anything you do proves to be incorrect it will undermine your credibility, and may rubbish your findings. Be attentive to the detail, as it may be the detail that discredits your solution in the end.

- Develop alternative solutions. Flexibility of mind and creativity is needed here to generate alternatives. In how many different ways could this problem be solved? If you have no choice you're ineffective, one choice you're a robot, two choices you have a dilemma, three or more choices gives you real choice. Weigh the pros and cons of each alternative including the costs, the time and resources needed to implement them. Some problems may require a new perspective, or a paradigm shift to resolve them. You may need to take a new direction, or form new connections and associations, and even discover unusual patterns or relationships to unravel a solution. You may use some of the paradigm preserving, paradigm stretching, and paradigm breaking techniques, previously discussed, to come up with creative solutions. You can use brainstorming and checklists to generate alternatives. Nobel Prize winner Richard Feynman would think up new thinking strategies whenever he was stuck on a problem. He maintained that the secret to success was to disregard how past thinkers solved problems. The best approach was to think up novel ways of solving the problem. If something didn't work he would consider several different ways until he found one that stirred his imagination. Feynman advocated teaching productive thinking in our schools, rather than reproductive thinking which is rigid thinking. He always felt it better to invent a new way of thinking rather than relying on what is already known.

- **I**mplement your chosen solution. Having considered the alternative solutions, pick the best alternative, or combination of alternatives. Obviously there are many alternative solutions to any problem; therefore, you should rank alternatives in terms of their desirability, suitability, cost effectiveness and acceptability. Accepting and implementing change involves a big selling job to win the hearts and minds of those affected. You can do this by capturing their imagination in a visionary story of how the change will benefit them. Stories make complex issues simple and motivate people to accept the change. People fear change. One of the most solid findings in psychology is the "mere exposure effect." People like most what is familiar to them. The more familiar they become with the status quo, the more they will like it. Thus research indicates that although people may value change because it will bring progress, they often feel uncomfortable with it and hence will initially react negatively to it. People fear that they will have to unlearn the existing ways of doing the work. Draw up an implementation plan. List the types of problems, constraints, obstacles that may be encountered during implementation, and have contingency plans to deal with them. Consider what resources you need to implement the solution. Consider the organisational, interpersonal and political problems you may have to overcome to successfully implement the solution. When will implementation take place? What objections are people likely to have to the change? How can you overcome these objections? How long will implementation take? Who will do it? Where will it happen? How much will it cost?

- **M**onitor and follow up to ensure that the solution is working satisfactorily. The review is an opportunity for feedback, leading to corrective action and improved performance in the future. There is no failure only feedback. Humans learn through trial and error. Look on failure as unintended outcomes or unexpected results. Learn from your mistakes, so that you do not make the same mistakes again. In the business world there is a phenomenon called 'drift.' This idea is similar to the principle of thermodynamics called entropy. Entropy is the idea that everything in the universe eventually moves from order to disorder, and entropy is the measurement of that change. In business it means all things are inclined to revert to their original state unless properly monitored. So it is important to do periodic reviews to see what practical difficulties have arisen, and what modifications are necessary to rectify any difficulties arising, and to put things back on track again. Finally, following a review period if you are satisfied that your solution has worked satisfactorily, then celebrate your success. Savour the feeling of accomplishment and take pride in a job well done.

Skills acquired by people trained in CPS

People trained in the CPS approach acquire the following skills:

- They are more open to ideas and new, unusual approaches to problem solving.
- They defer critical judgement to the appropriate stage, and so spend less time on negative evaluation.
- They realise the importance of researching the issues before coming to a conclusion.
- They produce more and better quality ideas.
- They realise how important it is to understand and define the problem correctly.
- They are less likely to jump to conclusions about a problem.
- They are better skilled at evaluating ideas.

In summary, the creative problem solving approach, if correctly applied, will address all the major difficulties encountered in solving problems. These include:

- Failure to recognise and identify the real problem.
- Failure to collect useful information, interpret it and to apply it appropriately.
- Failure to recognise and question assumptions.
- Failure to generate and evaluate a wide range of alternatives.

- Failure to address implementation issues, and have contingency plans in place to deal with them.
- Failure to monitor and follow up to ensure the solution is working satisfactorily.

> "Creativity comes from a conflict of ideas."
>
> Donatella Versace

TRIZ

TRIZ (pronounced *trees*) is a Russian acronym standing for the **T**heory of **I**nventive **P**roblem **S**olving (TIPS). Genrikh Altshuller, inventor and science fiction writer, developed the technique with his colleagues in the Soviet Union between 1946 and 1985. In 1995 the Altshuller Institute for TRIZ was set up in Boston, USA. TRIZ is a problem-solving, innovation and forecasting tool, developed from world-wide patterns of invention derived from patent literature. Altshuller selected and examined the most effective solutions from this literature – the breakthroughs.

TRIZ can be applied to the formulation of problems, system analysis, failure analysis, and patterns of system evolution. It remained largely unknown outside the USSR until about 20 years ago. Now it's used worldwide, and its popularity is particularly felt in areas such as the Six Sigma processes, project and risk management and in innovation initiatives in organisations.

TRIZ is not just for engineers, chemists, scientists and architects but can be used as effectively by management and business people. In business TRIZ has applications in accounting, marketing, product design, logistics, human relations management, software programming and systems design. Everybody's creativity, including those who consider themselves lacking in creativity, can be dramatically improved by using TRIZ.

There is a difference between brainstorming and TRIZ. Brainstorming is psychology based and is confined to the knowledge of the team in the room. It depends on spontaneous intuition with unpredictable and unrepeatable results. On the other hand, TRIZ is science and logic based, helping you systematically unlock the knowledge in the room and the knowledge of the world. You are almost guaranteed to come out of a problem solving session with several workable solutions. You have a database of knowledge at your fingertips to guide you towards a customised solution.

Like any other technique TRIZ requires practice and experience in its use. However, as you get familiar with the technique your problem solving ability will get faster and better with the passage of time. Having one or two trained TRIZ people in the team will enhance the effectiveness of the group. There are many organisations providing training in TRIZ.

As with other creativity tools it is essential to identify and define the problem clearly. If you formulate the problem clearly then the easier it will be to come up with an appropriate solution. In TRIZ the procedure seeking a solution is replaced by a process of problem reformulation. Through a chain of successive problem reformulations, the problem is transformed from an ill-defined and frequently incorrectly stated problem, to a lucid statement of the problem. A solution either becomes obvious, or it becomes clear that the problem cannot be solved with the current state of technological and scientific knowledge.

Things that TRIZ can do
The following are some of the things that TRIZ can do:

- It can help us think logically and creatively, while solving problems in an innovative way.
- It can help us to be more innovative by developing new products, finding new ways of using and improving existing systems, and using our time more effectively, thereby cutting costs and improving productivity.
- It provides a systematic comprehensive structure for solving difficult problems.

- It can help teams work more effectively together by using the distilled knowledge contained in the TRIZ database.
- TRIZ directs us to the best solutions based on our resources, circumstances and constraints.
- It can help us identify trends in new technologies, new markets and new products. TRIZ is a predictive model. Its underlying premise is that previous inventive solutions can be used to predict future inventive solutions. Past trends in patents may offer future ideas and possibilities. An example of a technical trend was the manufacture of chocolate bars, which went through many evolutionary stages. Originally, when sold they were simple solid sheets. They then became segmented and organised into squares. This was followed by chocolates with holes that eventually were filled with tasty mouth-watering substances.
- It can help you achieve the ideal outcome. Leonardo da Vinci said: "Think of the end before the beginning." In other words, think in terms of outcomes. You should think about what you want rather than what you currently have. Thinking about the outcome will lift constraints by focusing your mind on possibilities rather than limitations and how to achieve them.

Highly innovative companies such as Samsung, Ford, Hitachi, Siemens, NASA, Proctor and Gamble and 3M, among many others, have reported significant success when they applied TRIZ to various parts of their businesses. For example, Samsung claim that TRIZ has helped them become more successful during the past 12 years, and is central to their policy of growth through innovation. A recent article in *Forbes* described how Samsung saved over $100 million in its first few TRIZ projects.

Ford reduced their warranty costs significantly when they used TRIZ to solve a problem with squeaky windshields, costing the motor company several million dollars annually. Previously, they had used TRIZ to reduce idle vibration in a small car by 165 per cent. This helped it progress from one of the worst in its class to 30 per cent better than the best in its class. The principles encourage users to solve problems in more than one way, and it teaches that anybody can be creative and innovative.

Altshuller found that certain common themes are present in inventive patents. The classical form of TRIZ includes a set of 40 principles derived from the study of more than 400,000 patents. It is an algorithm (set of rules) based on logic, structure, data and research and the ingenuity of thousands of engineers, who have solved problems successfully in the past. The codified knowledge base of TRIZ can be taught to people, and provide breakthrough solutions to problems.

Principles of TRIZ
The 40 principles are a list of ideas that provide a different perspective when looking at a problem. The same principles were found to be applicable across many fields, and were the solution to contradictions at the heart of many problems. A list of the 40 Principles of TRIZ Problem Solving can be found at: http://www.triz-journal.com/archives/1997/07/b/index.html.

The following are just a few of the Principles and examples of how they could be used:

- Segmentation (divide an object into independent parts). When applied to cheese the solution was to slice and individually wrap the cheese slices. Local quality (provide different packaging for different uses). The solution was "Adult" editions of Harry Potter books.
- Universality (make an object perform multiple functions). The solution was wine sold in bottles that can be used as candle holders afterwards.
- Nested Doll. The solution in the book retail trade was to have coffee shops in bookstores.

- Another dimension (tilts or re-orients object). The solution was a ketchup bottle that sat on its lid and helps to pour the ketchup.

In addition, to the 40 principles, Altshuller developed the concept of technical contradictions, the concept of the ideal system and the contradiction matrix. It is the combination of all these concepts together, which are the key elements in a process designed to help the inventor to solve problems with purpose and focus. An ideal system is one with fewer elements to consider. In a technical system the fewer the number of parts the easier it will be to add further parts later. The more functions performed, while reducing form, the better.

A motor car is a specific solution to the generic function "move people." Similarly washing powder is a specific solution to the generic function "remove dirt." By classifying knowledge by function, manufacturers of washing powder may examine how other industries have solved the same function of removing dirt. "Solutions change, but functions stay the same," is a key message in the TRIZ methodology. Thus solutions which work in one industry can be applied to another.

Law of Ideality
The Law of Ideality states that systems gradually move towards the ideal by increasing the functions provided, while at the same time reducing the form required. The term "form" is used here loosely to include all the negative things that are required to make the system work. These include size, structure, weight, speed, cost, energy and so on. Taken to the extreme, an ideal solution is one in which function exists without any form – something happens without any apparatus or cost. It sounds like an oxymoron; as Arthur C. Clarke said: "Any sufficiently advanced technology is indistinguishable from magic."

As an example of the Law of Ideality in action, let's consider the evolution of modern cooking which increased function while reducing form. Years ago, wood was burnt in an open fire, making for a smoky, dirty, smelly, energy inefficient and labour intensive kitchen. This evolved into a wood burning stove which used the energy created by the wood more efficiently, considerably cutting down on dirt and smoke emissions. Then the gas stove was developed, reducing the need to store and haul wood around. Then the electric cooker came which eliminated the need for an open flame. Energy was delivered much more efficiently and cleanly with the touch of a switch.

In modern times we have developed the microwave oven, which saves space, reduces the need for time and dedicated cooking utensils, and uses less energy. In each of the cases mentioned, the function (heating food) is similar. However, the negatives associated with cooking and the effort needed is drastically reduced. Demonstrating a modern microwave to a homemaker of the 1930s would exhibit the magic of Clarke's technological progress.

A number of TRIZ-based computer programs have been developed to further assist engineers and inventors in finding innovative solutions more efficiently for technological and other problems. In addition, ARIZ (algorithm of inventive problem solving) has been developed. It is a list of about 85 step-by-step procedures to solve complicated invention problems, where other tools of TRIZ alone are insufficient. ARIZ is the main analytical and problem solving tool of TRIZ.

The three primary findings of the last 65 years of research are:

1. Problems and solutions found in TRIZ are applicable across different industries. The "contradictions" in each problem can be categorised and predict good solutions to that problem.
2. Patterns of evolution tend to be repeated across industries.

3. Creative innovations in one field of scientific endeavour can often be adapted and applied to specific problems in a different field.

TRIZ brings organisations the summarised knowledge, experience and ingenuity of thousands of engineers, to help them solve the challenges of new product development and improved processes and systems. This is needed to maintain profitability, stay in business and keep ahead of the competition. There is nothing new under the sun as most innovation problems have been solved before by somebody else in another context and at another time. All you have to do is find the solution, and adapt it to the problem that you are currently faced with. People working in manufacturing have two types of problem; solving and innovation. Firstly, the process may need to be improved, while at other times you need to produce new products while reinventing the process. TRIZ offers solutions to both types of problems.

Solving contradictions
Altshuller believed that inventive problems arise from contradictions between two or more elements, and the inventor must resolve the contradictions. He said: "Every great invention is the result of solving one or more contradictions." For example, in designing a car, an inventor might want it to be heavy and fuel efficient at the same time. One could look at how people have previously solved the contradiction in general terms and then apply it to a specific problem.

TRIZ recognised two types of contradictions:

1. Technical contradictions known as "trade-offs." The desired state can't be achieved because something prevents you from doing so. In other words, when something gets better, something else gets worse. Classic examples include: when something gets sturdier (good), the weight increases (bad). The

bandwidth for a communications system increases (good), but requires more power (bad). When customer service is increased (good), the system gets more complicated and the cost goes up (bad). When comprehensive off-site training is provided (good), employees are away from their work or assignments (bad).

2. Physical contradictions are known as "inherent." These are situations in which an object or system suffers contradictory, opposite requirements. Examples include: software should be comprehensive (with many features), but flexible and simple to use (easy to learn and move around). Surveillance planes should fly fast (to get to their destination (good), but need to fly slowly when collecting data over the target area (bad). Coffee should be hot and enjoyable, but not too hot (you don't want to burn the customer's mouth). Training takes a long time to be thorough, but ideally should take no time. An example of a physical contradiction is an umbrella – an umbrella needs to be small and large at the same time. The solution was an adjustable umbrella which is neat and portable and is now universally available. Garden chairs need to be strong and sturdy (good) but flexible so that they can be stored easily (bad). The solution was collapsible garden chairs.

A well-known case study, successfully solved by TRIZ, was a dairy farm that could no longer use dry cow manure as fertilizer because of the enormous energy cost of drying it. They were faced with the technical contradiction of dry manure (good) and cost (bad). TRIZ came up with the analogous solution used for the concentration of fruit juice that required no heat.

"Producing something creative is a practical skill that every student can and should develop – just like the ability to read and write."

Jason Ohler

Biomimicry – Creativity Inspired by Nature

The term biomimicry comes from the Greek word bios, meaning life and mimesis, meaning to imitate. Biomimicry is the design and production of materials, structures, and systems modelled on animals and plants. Nature has evolved over 3.8 billion years to solve problems in surprisingly novel and efficient ways. If you have a design problem, scientists are realising that nature is likely to have solved the problem already. With hindsight it has been found that many human inventions appearing to be original have already existed in the natural world for millions of years. The cost and effort of development could be considerably reduced if designers used nature as an inspirational source of ideas in a purposeful way.

Darwin's theory of evolution, and the survival of the fittest through trial and error, would suggest that nature only provides the best, most practical and efficient solutions. Like an unprofitable business those that don't work go to the wall. Biomimicry helps us develop new perspectives or ways at looking at things, while providing us with the means and prototypes to do so.

Biomimicry is the conscious emulation of nature's genius. Products built inspired by natural processes could replace the waste of the first industrial age with cleaner, more elegant, more economical and much more sustainable substitutes. If we can copy the way nature does it, then we can come up with amazing things. Advances in fields like nanotechnology allow engineers to study natural processes at a micro level. Armed with this insight, and motivated by an interest in sustainable design, biologists, engineers and scientists increasingly look outside the laboratory for inspiration.

Over the years, engineers have found that biology has been a rich source of practical parallels. Nature is an enormous and never ending store and source of ideas. Confronted with design problems, mechanical engineers might look for parallel solutions already existing in nature. They might ask: How do birds fly? How do chameleons change their colour to match their environment? Can the secrets of insects, plants, and animals help us solve manufacturing challenges and create new products? What are the similarities between the human eye and a camera? This approach has resulted in the invention of revolutionary glues and coatings, communication tools, improved digital cameras and even devices like carburettors.

Other inventors around the world have created solar panels that mimic leaves and car frames inspired by the way trees handle structural stress. Looking elsewhere, scientists are learning about anticoagulants from leeches, acoustics from dolphins, antibiotics from Komodo dragons, shock absorbers from woodpeckers, and computer networks from slime moulds.

Research carried out on the reading habits of scientists categorised them as innovative, productive and sluggish. The productive scientists read almost exclusively in their field. The innovative scientists, while not as up to date in their technical field as the productive ones, read in a variety of fields. The innovative scientists read everything from science fiction to technical journals, from *Popular Mechanics* to the *National Enquirer*. These scientists had a much richer storehouse of information from which to generate new concepts. The sluggish scientists were neither productive nor innovative.

Bionics
A closely related field to biomimicry is bionics, which is used creatively to mend broken bodies. Major Jack Steel of the US Air Force coined the term bionics in 1960 to describe the interface between natural and synthetic systems. He defined bionics as "the analysis of the ways in which living systems

actually work and having discovered nature's way of solving problems, embodying them in hardware." Bionics was popularised during the 1970s by the popular classic TV series "The Six Million Dollar Man." In the story the main character – astronaut Steve Austin – is horrendously injured in a test flight accident. However, with modern technology they are able to rebuild him.

They claimed "Gentlemen, we can rebuild him. We have the technology. We have the capability to make the world's first bionic man. Steve Austin will be that man. Better than he was before. Better, stronger, faster." His array of upgrades included an eye with zoom and infrared vision, bionic legs which could run at the speed of a car and an arm with the strength of a bulldozer. At the time this sort of stuff sounded like science fiction but it is now coming to pass. Hip and knee surgery using bionic parts is now routine surgery. Artificial robotic arms, hands and legs are available, while stints and battery operated timers to regulate the heart are commonplace.

Retinal implants and cochlear implants are used to restore sight in the blind and hearing in the deaf. Cochlear implants have transformed the lives of deaf children. Artificial heart, lungs, kidneys and other body parts made of plastic, which will not be rejected by the body, are being developed. A new science called "transhumanism" is being developed encompassing everything from robotic limbs to memory enhancing neural implants to gene therapies that slow the ageing process. Ritalin, which was developed as a treatment for attention deficit hyperactivity disorder, is increasingly being used to enhance cognitive performance.

A modern day bionic man is the infamous athlete Oscar Pistorius. On a personal level he has gone from fame to shame because of the suspicion of murdering his girlfriend. When he was 11 months old, both his legs were amputated below the knees. Despite this he has gone on to become a very successful runner when he had a pair of carbon-fibre blades fitted and went on to compete against disabled and able bodied athletes. He has won gold medals in the Paralympics and was the first double amputee to participate in the regular

Olympics, despite persistent objections that his artificial limbs give him an unfair advantage over other competitors. He has given us a glimpse of a "superhuman" future, where Paralympics aided by bionics may set hitherto unimaginable sporting records. In the future prosthetic limbs will be inside our bodies, rather than being outside or replacements. Athletes will be able to use 3D printing to create new limbs perfectly tailored to their bodies, or grow replacement body parts when the old ones wear out.

Evan Reynolds, a sports biology student at the University of the West of England in Bristol, is one of the first people in the UK to be fitted with the i-LIMB technology. The 19 year old rugby player lost his left hand in a car accident. His bionic hand is controlled by electronic muscle signals from the remainder of his limb. Touch Bionics, the manufacturer of the device, has won many awards. In the US, American soldiers who have been injured in action have also benefited from the device. Reynolds was the second Briton to be fitted with the hand. Bionic hands with a sense of touch have now been developed. Andrew Garthwaite, a British soldier whose arm was blown off by a rocket-propelled grenade in Afghanistan, has become the first person to master a prosthetic limb controlled by thought.

Anthony Atala, a professor of regenerative medicine some years ago worked out how to engineer human tissue with a desktop inkjet printer using cells instead of ink. He is now using these machines to make actual human organs, which have been successfully implanted into people. One of these people is Luke Massella who was born with spina bifida. At the age of 10 he suffered kidney and bladder failure. Today he is a fit and healthy college student. In the sea, crabs have extremely tough outer skeletons to protect them. This has given rise to the invention of exoskeletons which are used to help support paralysed people to walk, or provide supersonic strength to able people. Superhuman hearing could eventually be available to everyone. Researchers from Princeton have made ears that capture sounds over a frequency range much broader than that perceived by human ears.

Inventions inspired by nature

The creativity and innovation of people has been inspired by birdlife, fish, plants, insects and humans/animals. Nature has evolved over billions of years and has already solved most problems that humans are likely to be confronted with. Copy what nature does so well; there is a vast source of inspiration that we can use. The following are practical examples of how these sources of nature have influenced human creativity and innovation.

Inspiration from birds

One of the earliest examples of biomimicry was the Archimedes screw, a type of water pump that is still used today. The concept was taken from the spiral and put to practical use. A later example of biomimicry was the study of birds to enable human flight. Leonardo da Vinci (1452-1519) drew sketches of flying machines inspired by his observation of bird's flight. He also designed a helicopter, and conceived a functioning parachute. He was the original Renaissance man. The invention of the modern aeroplane depended on scientific analysis of bird flight combined with the invention of the internal combustion engine.

The Wright brothers succeeded in flying the first heavier than air aircraft in 1903, by being inspired from observations of pigeons in flight. They also created stabilisers for their aeroplanes by analysing how a turkey vulture uses its body to reduce turbulence. All of this combined with the invention of the internal combustion engine around that time contributed to their success.

In modern times, scientists have started finding ways to mimic the mechanics of bird flight through various robotic ornithopters - aircraft that fly with flapping wings. Fixed wing airplanes and rotary-wing helicopters haven't the manoeuvrability and flexibility of pigeons that can flap their wings to swoop, dive, glide, and alight on perches. Aircraft based on laboratory experiments could soon be used in military or search-and-rescue missions. One of the most impressive of the new flock is Smart Bird, a prototype flier made by Festo, a German-based automation technology company. The remote controlled aircraft has intrigued audiences on a worldwide tour as it uncannily flies like its avian inspiration - a herring gull.

Paul MacCready invented the first human powered aircraft. He was inspired by watching hawks and vultures in flight. On 23 August 1977 MacCready's *Gossamer Condor* made history when it flew a figure-eight course over a distance of 1.15 miles. It became the first human-powered plane to achieve sustainable manoeuvrable flight. On 12 June 1979 his aircraft called *Gossamer Albatross* crossed the channel from France to England a distance of more than 22 miles. In 1985, the Smithsonian Institute commissioned Macready to build a life size, flying replica of the pterodactyl, a prehistoric flying reptile with a 36 foot wingspan. The remote controlled flying model can be seen in the IMAX film *On the Wing*. This film traces the art of flying in all its various forms exploring the relationship between natural and mechanical flight.

Japan's bullet train was able to travel faster, use less energy and make less noise after its nose was rebuilt to mimic the beak of the kingfisher bird that can dive into water without making a splash. When first designed they made a thunder like noise going through tunnels because of the change in air pressure. The new design solved the problem and in addition was more aerodynamic. Radar was inspired by studying the way bats used reflected sound waves.

Even everyday devices may benefit from nature inspired improvements. We all have experienced the difficulty of seeing the screens on digital cameras and laptops in bright sunlight. The solution could lie in peacock feathers. Their iridescent blues and greens do not come from pigments. They come from repeating microstructures on the feather that reflect certain wavelengths in perfect synchrony, intensifying a given hue. Using the same principle, a company named Qualcomm is designing a display that uses adjustable microstructure just behind the screen's surface to create colour. Because its brightness depends on ambient light, rather than illumination from within, the colours actually intensify outdoors and require less power.

Inspiration from the sea

Over millennia evolution has determined the ideal characteristics for survival in an aquatic environment. This includes a streamlined shape, fins instead of limbs, and a fin near the tail for stability. Sharks and other sea animals glide effortlessly through water without a boost from an energy source such as gasoline. The shape of sharks could be replicated in boats and airplanes to reduce drag and increase fuel efficiency. Inspired by this, German scientists developed a special paint that, when applied to the hull of a ship mimics the water-repellent design of sharkskin and reduces drag by 3%. This results in savings of 2000 tons of fuel per ship, per year. Similar studies are being carried out to reduce the drag on aircraft. The paint contains nanoparticles, which ensure that it can withstand ultra-violet radiation and changing temperature, particularly important for aircraft. Scientists say that if you painted every aircraft in the world with this paint it could save 4.48 million tonnes of fuel annually.

Boeing and Airbus have both tested the use of sharkskin-inspired technology and found it has the potential to reduce drag by 3%. This would translate into an equal reduction in fuel costs. Max O Kramer's anti-turbulence linings for submarine devices imitate the skin structure of dolphins. The cargo doors on airplanes were a variation of the way a clam opens its shell.

Fiona Fairhurst and her design team, at the swimwear company Speedo, were faced with a difficult challenge. They needed to design suits that would reduce drag, and thus improve the performance of competitive swimmers. For inspiration, they looked at the animal kingdom, and in particular sharks, who have no problem swimming fast despite the shape of their bodies. They analysed samples of sharkskin, and found that it had tiny structures on its surface called denticles that kept water molecules from sticking to it. The team created a fabric that mimicked the denticles, and designed full-body swimsuits with it. Soon after the new Fastskin swimsuit was introduced, world records were broken. It is a testimony to the success of this swimwear that at the Sydney Olympics in 2000, 28 of 33 Olympic Gold Medal winners wore this type of swimwear.

The body of mobile phones incorporates principles derived from the tough protective shells of crustaceans (crabs, lobsters and shrimps). Seaweed has inspired a new way to generate electricity from ocean waves – a source of renewable energy. Timothy Finnigan, an engineer and founder of BioPower Systems in Australia, wanted to create a better way to harness wave power and based his design on seaweed.

Mussels make glue that lets them anchor themselves firmly to a rock and remain there despite being buffeted by the ocean's waves. A new kind of plywood is being manufactured with a material that mimics the proteins that allow blue mussels to maintain their grip on rock, rather than using formaldehyde-based adhesive. It is hoped the mussel-inspired glue will one day be used to repair shattered bones.

The mother-of-pearl coating inside an abalone shell (a type of shellfish found in warm seas) is twice as strong as industrial ceramics, which require enormous kilns to manufacture. Not only are abalone shells difficult to fracture, but once cracked can heal themselves – a trick no ceramic tiles can do. IBM designers analysed the way abalone shells form by merging microscopic particles of calcium carbonate chalk in a process called "self-assembly." They're now applying the same principles to the development of a series of processors. While still experimental, results reduce energy consumption by 35%. NASA supported researchers at Princeton are analysing the remarkable strength of abalone shells to help make impact-resistant coatings for thermal tiles used on spacecraft.

Bell Labs brought in an outside speaker to one of their meetings whose talk on how whales communicate with each other led to an idea for new technology. Roger Payne, a world expert in whale communication, described to the group his major finding that whales sing to each other to communicate, but they change their language patterns each year. This contrasted with birds, which stick to the same pattern year after year. Halfway through the presentation, a scientist suddenly left the room with an idea on how to improve communications between submarines. The talk triggered a solution to a problem he was trying to resolve in another context.

Bell Laboratories are studying a tropical deep sea sponge, and a relative of the starfish called a brittle star, hoping for technological breakthroughs for future voice and data systems. The two sea creatures have remarkable properties, surpassing anything that human technology has achieved so far. The five arms of the brittle star are covered with thousands of microscopic lenses. These can focus light 10 times more sharply than the finest man-made lens.

These function like one big eye enabling the brittle star to spot predators and find places to hide in the shallow Caribbean waters where it lives.

The sponge, called a Venus' flower basket, has a body made of natural glass fibres. The body transmits light and can be tied into knots without cracking. This contrasts to the costly high temperature manufacturing that man-made fibres required to prevent cracking. Joan Aizenberg, Bell Labs researcher says: "Nobody could have imagined that something like this could have existed in nature for millions of years. What's most rewarding about this work is the study of the absolutely incredible world around us and everything we can learn to improve our technology."

The Kingfisher has the super sight to see through the glare of water to catch fish. This revelation from nature inspired a camera which is able to detect humpback whales in the sea. The same technology is now used to help find bodies in water during rescue and search and find operations. Cuttlefish change colour, shape and texture in response to changes in their environment. It has light sensitive cells all over its body. This inspired a way to camouflage army tanks by attaching panels to change the appearance of the tank in line with the environment. The tank can even be made invisible. An ultra-sonic cane for blind people was inspired by bats.

Mercedes Benz wanted to create an aerodynamically efficient compact car without sacrificing safety or spaciousness. Their concept car (DCX) is based on the counterintuitively shaped boxfish. After studying its streamlined bony skin structure, they designed the body of their bionic concept car with hexagonal plates, resulting in door panelling one third lighter than conventional panelling, but just as strong. They claim that the DCX is fuel efficient and gets 70 – 84 mpg. Another company wanted to lessen the noise generated by turbines and improve their reliability during periods of low wind. The large, irregular bumps on the leading edge of humpback whale flippers gave the aptly named WhalePower a model for its turbine blades. They reduce turbulence across the surface, increasing the angle of attack and decreasing drag.

Inspiration from plants
Plants have been the source of many of the chemicals used for pharmaceuticals. Many drugs are inspired by molecules found in nature, such as the cancer drug Taxol derived from the bark and needles of the yew tree. Plants are inherently more complex than the synthetic drugs and better at targeting the sources of disease. Hundreds of thousands of years of natural selection have made them better and more compatible to our genetic makeup. It is now known that the building bricks of plants, trees, animals and humans are similar.

One of the most iconic stories happened in 1948 when George de Mestral, a Swiss engineer, was out walking one day and came back with cockleburs stuck to his jacket. Rather than treating them as a nuisance his curiosity was aroused. When he examined one under his microscope, he found that thin fins with hooks on the end, were responsible for them sticking to his jacket. Over thousands of years many other people must have noticed the same phenomenon, but nobody saw its significance or commercial potential. George immediately recognised the potential of his discovery for a practical new fastener, now widely used on shoes, coats and bags. Discovery is one thing, but practical application and marketing exploitation is another. It took 8 years to perfect the invention, and thus the modern Velcro was born.

Ignazio and Igo Etrich built the first tailless glider. Their design was based on observations of the spread of anemophilous plants (pollinated by the wind), whose seeds, transported by the wind, are able to cover considerable distances. The shape of the rhubarb leaf inspired the Kingsgate footbridge in Durham England designed by Ove Arup.

The South American water lily, Victoria Regia, inspired 19th century architect Sir Joseph Paxton's design of the Chrystal Palace in Hyde Park, London. This plant floats on delicate leaves up to two metres in diameter. Despite this it is able to support a weight of 90 kg. The underside of the leaf has a system of hollow ribs giving it both strength and buoyancy. Paxton maintained that nature was the real engineer. Nature provided the leaf with horizontal and traverse girders and supports. All he had to do was copy nature to design his building.

Many products on the market today, such as self-cleaning windows and exterior paints, were inspired by the leaves of the lotus plant. It remains clean even in muddy river deltas, its natural habitat, without the use of harsh cleaning agents. Inspired by the lotus leaves, Pilkington Activ Self-Cleaning Glass uses natural daylight and rain to break down organic material, reducing the need for window cleaning. Because the glass is hydrophilic, water spreads over the glass instead of forming droplets just like lotus leaves.

Columbia Forest Products, the team who developed Pringles stacked potato chips, was inspired by the idea of pressing tree leaves into uniform shapes between the pages of books. They realised that leaves are not pressed when they are dry but when they are wet. So they packed potato chips in stacks, moist enough not to crumble, but dry enough to be nearly flat. The result was Pringles.

Pax Scientific, based in San Rafael, California, has produced a line of impellers, pumps and fans whose basic shapes are inspired by nature. As a result they require up to 30% less energy and produce less noise and heat than parts made by giants like General Electric, using traditional engineering techniques. Harman, the owner of the company, has an intuitive understanding that nature reduces drag and turbulence by swirling things towards their destination like water rotating down a sink or bathtub drain. He maintains: "If we look at what nature can do and reproduce it faithfully, I think we can solve just about any problem on earth."

A pharmacist may look to botany for inspiration to solve the problem of haemophilia – the vascular systems of plants may spark off insights about bleeding in humans and help come up with a blood-clotting drug. The combination of knowledge from disparate fields may offer a solution to the problem. This is why it is so advantageous to be widely read across disciplines when trying to solve problems creatively. It is often a question of combining knowledge from different sources.

Inspiration from insects
In 2005, Ford's Volvo Division developed an anti-collision system based on the way locusts swarm without crashing into one another. They studied the neurology that governs how locusts fly in groups, and designed a system that can sense an impending crash while simultaneously warning drivers. Known as the Accident Avoidance System, it's now available on Volvo's high-end vehicles.

Jewel beetles, which lay their eggs in freshly burned trees, can detect fires. Inspired by this, the defence industry is studying the beetles for clues to designing new low-cost, military grade infrared detectors. The honeycomb structure of bee's nests offers a perfect template for light, stable and pressure-resistant constructions for aircraft wings and honeycomb walls and doors.

Fabrics, paints, and cosmetics are being developed emulating the way butterflies create colour on their wings.

Teijin Ltd of Japan used the idea of structural colour in morpho butterflies to create coloured fabric without using dyes.

Spiders create silk, at room temperature, that weight for weight is five time stronger than steel, without the need for the dirty and energy-intensive smelting process. Scientists are now studying spider silk that they produce when making their webs for possible commercial application. It is remarkable material, very strong though thinner than hair, and its possible applications are limitless. However, its secrets still remain elusive. The wings of the morpho butterfly inspired a new type of screen for mobile phones, computers and e-readers.

An office building in Zimbabwe, designed by architect Mick Pearce in collaboration with Arup Associates, features a cooling system modelled after termite hills, which maintain a constant internal temperature of 31 degrees Celsius despite changes in the external environment from 3 to 42 degrees. The building is self-regulating, needs no air conditioning and consequently uses less energy. Some reports claim that it uses only 10% of the energy consumed by traditional buildings, significantly lowering operating costs.

Inspiration from humans/animals

Scientists and engineers have identified the similarities between the human eye and cameras. They have gone on to use this knowledge to improve digital cameras, surveillance equipment, robotics and microscopy. Engineers at a Swiss company called inLabs are applying lessons from biology in an effort to build a more efficient digital camera inspired by the human retina. The new camera is named the Dynamic Vision Sensor (DVS). The camera is inspired by how the human eye interacts with the brain. It has been used in several research projects including one that recorded traffic and another that tracked particles in a fluid. The next goal is to add colour sensitivity and to enlarge the camera's retina from its current resolution of 240x180.

In further research, another company, Georgia Tech, has replicated the muscle motion of the human eye to control camera systems in robotic equipment. The new muscle like action could help make robotic tools safer and more effective in MRI guided surgery and industrial robotic systems.

The elephant's flexible trunk inspired a German company called Festo to make a bendable robotic arm.

In the 1920s it was very difficult and dangerous to drive on dark roads. The only light available to guide a driver was from the moon, and then only when the sky was clear. Percy Shaw, a young British road contractor, was determined to find a solution to the dangers of driving in the dark. One night as he was driving home his headlights caught a cat on a fence and its eyes lit up. He immediately got the idea that markers on the road could guide a driver on its way and set out to mimic the effect of the cat's eyes.

In 1933, at 23 years of age, after much trial and error he had designed a suitable self-cleaning reflector and patented it in 1934. He set up his own company and eventually became a multi-millionaire. Transport officials were slow to take up his invention. However, in 1947 the post-war Labour government implemented a plan to introduce cat's eyes all over Britain's roads. The basic design is still in use today. In 1990, *The SolarLite* was invented by Martin Dicks with 10 times the visibility of the cat's eyes and lasts far longer. The invention of the cat's eyes has contributed significantly to safety on our road.

Biomimicry design portal
A biomimicry design portal has been put on-line for those interested in the possibilities of biomimicry. This is a free, open-source, wiki-like data base enabling anyone to read and contribute examples of nature's solutions to industrial problems. Entries will be cross-referenced so users searching for information can find it easily. For instance, those interested in adhesive mechanisms can find articles on species that create glues, their commercial properties as well as biographical notes of the prominent scientists working in the field. Submissions will be rigorously peer-reviewed similar to the standards of academic publishing. The portal site will be a

practical guide for scientists, engineers, chemists, industrialists and designers as well as students and interested readers.

Living nature is a rich source of inspiration supplying lots of interesting solutions for solving technical problems for engineers, biologists, scientists and designers. Researchers hope one day to develop synthetic equivalents of the best that nature has to offer.

> "The most remarkable discovery made by scientists is science itself. The discovery must be compared in importance with the invention of cave-painting and of writing. Like these earlier human creations, science is an attempt to control our surroundings by entering into them and understanding them from inside. And like them, science has surely made a critical step in human development which cannot be reversed. We cannot conceive a future society without science."
>
> Jacob Bronowski

Summary of Chapter 4

The creative process can be broken down into five stages namely: preparation, effort, incubation, insight and evaluation. These are stages that people go through when being creative.

Practical creativity can be triggered by the acronym CAMPERS. This stands for combine, adapt, modify, put to other uses, eliminate unnecessary parts, rearrange and simplify. This acronym is the cornerstone of creativity.

In many organisations ideas are killed before they ever get off the ground. Selling killers include "It won't sell" and "We tried that before and were unsuccessful." Pessimism killers include "It's impossible" and "There are too many difficulties." Business killers include "It's against company policy" and the "Not invented here" syndrome.

Different creative perspectives can be engaged through the six thinking hats. These are white hat thinking, red hat thinking, yellow hat thinking, black hat thinking, green hat thinking and blue hat thinking. This is a practical technique of creative problem solving widely used in organisations.

The range of creativity paradigms are paradigm preserving, paradigm stretching and paradigm breaking. A paradigm is a way of looking at something. Paradigm preserving approaches are used to solve known and structured problems. Paradigm stretching approaches are used to solve unstructured problems. Paradigm breaking approaches break new ground by going out of existing boundaries and solving problems in new and unique ways.

Brainstorming is probably one of the best known and most popular techniques for generating ideas. Other techniques include fantasy, metaphors, synectics, kaizen, swot analysis, and stretch imaging. Companies may set up formal suggestion schemes to encourage employees to make improvements related to their work.

Creative Problem Solving (CPS) is a major technique for generating ideas and solving problems. TRIZ is the Theory of Inventive Problem Solving. It is a problem solving, innovation and forecasting tool, developed from world-wide patterns of invention derived from patent literature.

Biomimicry is the design and production of materials, structures, and systems that are modelled on animals, plants and insects. Nature has evolved over 3.8 billion years to solve problems in surprisingly efficient and novel ways. It is an unlimited source of inspiration for creativity and innovation.

5
Where Does Creativity Take Place?

Introduction

Creativity starts in the brain. Both sides of the brain are needed for creativity. The entire creative process engages different regions of the brain. The neocortex is the part of the brain that distinguishes us from the other mammals. Thanks to the neocortex humans can perform extraordinary, creative and complex tasks. These include writing a book, composing a symphony, painting a landscape or building a computer. Creative people tend to lose themselves in the creative process. This is known as a state of flow.

Exercise, sleep and meditation are good for your creativity. Creativity can happen at home or in work. Creativity is needed in our personal lives to solve everyday problems. These could include household budgeting, interior design and carrying out do-it-yourself projects.

In the workplace there are numerous opportunities to exercise creativity. Simple everyday changes and improvements may reap major benefits in productivity. Responding in a creative way to a customer's request, or solving a crisis requiring a quick response, is an everyday occurrence in most businesses. In addition, people can develop new products and services.

Universities are designed to encourage the flow of ideas between disciplines within and outside the university. Pure research is conducted in universities rather than development. The fruits of this research benefits industry.

Western and eastern countries differ to the extent that they are creative. Originality, initiative, fluidity and flexibility are highly regarded and respected in the west. On the other hand, eastern cultures emphasise the importance of the group over the individual, and the need for conformity and social harmony.

Major cities are creative hubs. The average inhabitant of a city is three times more creative than someone living in a small town. Globalised cities such as New York and London now trade in creativity, ideas, knowledge and innovation.

Creativity in the Brain

The research of Roger W. Sperry, who was awarded the Nobel Prize in 1981, came up with the right brain, left brain theory. He discovered that cutting the corpus callosum could eliminate or reduce seizures during epilepsy. He also found that patients who underwent this procedure seemed to be operating from two different and independent brains. This in turn led to the conclusion that different activities were controlled by either side of the brain.

Language and logic is from the left, and creativity and imagination from the right. The left brain is verbal and sequential, and looks at the pieces first before putting them together. The right side is visual and processes information in an intuitive and simultaneous way, looking first at the whole picture and then the details. The left side is linked to planning and organisation, analytical thinking and deduction. The right side is associated with imagination, emotions, feelings and artistic creativity.

Later research suggests that both sides of the brain are not as separate and distinct as previously thought. For example, abilities in subjects such as mathematics are actually strongest when both halves of the brain work together. Today, neuroscientists know that both sides of the brain work together when involved in creative problem solving such as generating and evaluating ideas, and that both halves cooperate and communicate through the corpus callosum. There is clear evidence of interaction between distant regions in both the left and right sides of the brain when the electrical activity is measured.

The conventional wisdom was that creativity is mostly located in the right side of the brain. This side of the brain was considered the more creative or emotional side. The left side was considered the analytical and judgemental side. It is now thought that this division of the brain is not as rigid as was once thought. Many brain functions are not confined to certain fixed locations. In fact, they are much more distributed and interactive across both sides and all brain regions. Even though the major areas for language are located in the left side of the brain, the right side has language capabilities that can be used (through speech training) to overcome loss of speaking ability in stroke victims.

Both sides of the brain are connected by the corpus callosum which is involved in creatively linking both sides. Information is passed from the left side to the right side and vice versa. This is important as the two sides perform different tasks, and need to communicate with each other efficiently and extremely quickly.

Both sides of the brain are needed for creativity. The right side of the brain is needed for generating ideas and arriving at an insight, and the left side for evaluation and implementation. The entire creative process – from preparation to incubation to illumination to verification – consists of many different brain processes and emotions. Depending on the stage of the creative process, different regions of the brain are needed to handle the task. Researchers using functional MRI have found that all parts of the brain are involved in creativity including imagination, memory and emotions. Imagination is the cornerstone of creativity. It would be impossible for anyone to be creative without having a rich imagination.

Imagination, in turn, is highly dependent on memory and experience. Without the storehouse of memory you could not feed your imagination with information, knowledge and experience. For example, brain imaging has shown that the hippocampus, a memory structure deep in the brain, is active at the moment people use insight to solve riddles. A large working memory correlates with increased creativity. The more information you have stored in your memory, the more likely you are to make creative connections. In addition, emotions are intimately involved in our creativity. Intense desire and interest drive our creativity.

Neuroplasticity means that the brain changes through action and experience by laying down new neural pathways and connections. Areas of the brain that are used intensely increase in size. While we are born with a complete set of neurons, the connections between them are determined and strengthened in major part by learning, experience and using the brain creatively.

Neocortex and relaxation

The neocortex is the most human part of the nervous system and is situated just behind the forehead. This is the part of the brain that distinguishes humans from other mammals. During human evolution it went through a dramatic expansion so that it now represents one-third of the brain. It is not fully developed until we are in our early twenties. Thanks to the neocortex, humans can perform extraordinary and complex tasks. These include writing a book, composing a symphony, painting the Mona Lisa, or inventing the computer. The neocortex is the control centre for the brain. If it decides to turn on the right side of the brain, then we might end up with an insight. On the other hand, if it decides to restrict the search to the left side of the brain then it will probably arrive at an incremental logical solution.

The neocortex needs to be relaxed to seek out the more remote associations in the right side of the brain to provide insight. The relaxation phase is crucial. That's why so many insights occur when out walking, taking a shower, travelling abroad, or visiting a museum or exhibition. Letting the mind wander is good for insights. The big idea often comes when people are thinking of something else, or doing something that has nothing to do with their research.

Consider the history of science and how frequently this has happened. For example, in 1990 a team of NASA scientists were trying to fix the distorted lenses in the Hubble telescope. An expert in optics suggested that tiny inversely distorted mirrors could solve the problem. However, nobody could figure out how to fit them into the confined space inside the Hubble telescope. One of the engineers, while taking a shower in a German hotel, noticed the European style showerhead mounted on adjustable rods. He realised that this was the solution to the problem. The mirrors could be mounted on similar folding arms.

In 2001, researchers at Washington University identified regions of the brain that are active when people are not doing anything in particular. These are called "the default network." These regions were found to be responsible for introspective thought and our ability to imagine past and future events or even different realities. In other words, the parts of our brains that are active when we are doing nothing are important to our creativity and our ability to think about things differently. This suggests that we need time for relaxation and recreation to rest our minds and facilitate creativity.

Another ideal time for insights is early in the morning just when we wake up. The drowsy brain is disorganised and open to all sorts of unconventional ideas. The right side of the brain is also unusually active during this time. EEG monitors show alpha wave activity at this time in the frontal brain region with a diffuse and widespread pattern throughout the brain. Alpha waves typically correlate with a state of relaxation and has been linked to inspiration, originality and creativity. You are more likely to associate and combine ideas when you are relaxed as alpha waves increase synchronisation between the two sides of the brain. Just before the "aha" or "eureka" moment, the brain fires off alpha waves. In an alpha state it is easier to form new concepts. On the other hand, trying to force an insight can be counterproductive. The harder you try to do it the more difficult it becomes.

Flow and Creativity

Flow is achieved when you lose all sense of time and self while being fully engaged and responding to a challenge. It is also known as being in the zone. It is a state of complete, intense concentration and absorption, where time seems to move very slowly or stand still. Children, more so than adults, can easily enter a state of flow, where they become completely absorbed in their work and time does not matter. Adults are more conscious of the passage of time.

Or, the opposite may happen, where time seems to stretch out. In a state of flow we are only aware of the here and now. Creative people tend to lose themselves in the creative process. If a musician thinks about health or tax problems while playing they are likely to get distracted and play a wrong note. The secret to happiness is to learn to get flow from everything we do including everyday activities such as work and family life. We will enjoy things much more if we consider that everything is worth doing for its own sake.

States of flow are usually associated with world class athletes who perform great sporting feats when in a state of flow, even though it can happen to anybody in any domain. It happens when your skills perfectly match the situation so that all feelings of self-consciousness disappear. If your skills are not up to the challenge you will experience anxiety. On the other hand, if your skills are too great for the task you will experience boredom. Playing tennis or chess against a much better opponent leads to frustration; against a much inferior opponent, to boredom. In flow the players are evenly matched in order to create challenge, uncertainty and excitement.

Neurological studies of flow show that people expend less energy when in flow. The reason for this appears to be that the parts of the brain most relevant for the tasks are most active and those that are irrelevant are relatively inactive. By contrast, when one is in an anxious or confused state there is no distinction in activity levels between parts of the brain. You can train your brain to get into a state of flow by doing activities that you are passionate about and really enjoy, and thinking of how to make other tasks more fun and challenging. When a job is enjoyable it also has clear goals and constant feedback.

In flow there is a need for an immediate feedback to one's actions. A musician hears straight away whether she has played the right note. A mountain climber knows the last move was correct because he hasn't fallen off the mountain. If we can't get feedback from others we should provide it for ourselves. Some research scientists drift away from pure science because they haven't the patience to tolerate the long cycles of insecurity before reviewer and editors evaluate their work. The ones that stay internalise the field's criteria of judgement and provide their own feedback.

When we are in flow we are too involved to be concerned with failure. We know what we have done and our skills are up to the challenge. Failure is not an issue. In addition, when we are in flow our self-consciousness disappears. In flow we are too involved in what we are doing to be concerned about what others think. Afterwards we may emerge with a stronger self-concept and sense of self-efficacy. This is because we know we have succeeded in overcoming a difficult challenge.

Interviews with prominent creative people, such as engineers and chemists, writers and musicians, historians and architects, artists and photographers, sociologists and physicists, confirm that they all do what they do primarily because they are passionate about their work, rather than any monetary reward involved. Most of them say that they are lucky to get paid for doing what they love! In particular, people love designing or discovering something new. It seems evolution has programmed humans for work, challenges, creativity and discovery.

Exercise, Sleep and Mediation

Exercise, such as walking, cycling or swimming is good for getting your creative juices flowing as it releases a peptide that helps produce serotonin. Exercise also increases oxygen and glucose in the bloodstream and helps the brain release feel-good endorphins. Serotonin levels tend to be highest in the morning, making this time the ideal period for brainstorming sessions. If you have brainstorming sessions in the afternoon take a brisk walk beforehand to build up your serotonin levels.

Serotonin and dopamine are needed for your best creative work. Increases in the stress hormones such as cortisol will counteract the creativity boosting effects of serotonin. The appropriate combination of both will produce a condition in which you are calm but energised. When you are in a good mood parts of the brain that have dopamine receptors are activated, and these are the regions responsible for creativity, problem solving and decision making.

We spend a third of our lives asleep and this activity is just as important to us as our waking hours. As we sleep, our brain processes what we've seen and learned during the day and helps to consolidate our memories and experiences. When you're tired you lack alertness, you have poor memory, you have poor creativity, you are inclined to be impulsive, are more likely to be stressed and exercise poor judgement. Sustained stress is associated with lack of sleep and eventually leads to poor health.

Stress has a negative effect on creativity. People under stress are likely to stick with the familiar when under too much pressure. Getting insufficient sleep has also a negative effect on creativity. Most people need up to 8 hours sleep a night including 2 hours of deep, non-REM (rapid eye movement) sleep for the brain to restore proper levels of serotonin. Research from the University of California, San Diego School of Medicine shows that REM sleep enhances creative problem solving. It appears that REM sleep lets the brain make new and useful associations between unrelated ideas. Deep sleep accounts for less than 30% of the average person's sleep, but it can be lessened by sleep interruptions as well as alcohol and caffeine consumption.

It has been known for years that meditation calms the mind and is good for creativity. Meditation puts you in touch with your subconscious enabling you to explore possibilities. Practising silence for a few minutes each day can unlock your creative juices because stillness and quietness slows down our thoughts and clears our minds. Even sitting on a park bench during a summer's day leisurely watching the world go by can be very relaxing and do wonders for our creativity.

You may have quiet creative oases such as a beach, lakeside or scenic location where you find peace and solitude that you can use as a retreat for creative thinking. Bob Dylan used his isolated log cabin retreat when he wrote his bestselling song "Like a Rolling Stone." It is known that Steve Jobs practised Zen Buddhism. He was very focused which had been honed by his Zen training, and was able to filter out distractions. He also had an ability to simplify things by concentrating on the essence of things and eliminating unnecessary components and complexity.

> "If you stuff yourself full of poems, essays, plays, stories, novels, films, comic strips, magazines, music, you automatically explode every morning like old faithful. I have never had a dry spell in my life, mainly because I feed myself well, to the point of bursting."
>
> Ray Bradbury.

Creativity in the Home

Some people think that creativity is restricted to great inventions and works of art. In fact, creativity can happen in any area of our personal and work lives. We tend to think of creativity as the realm of geniuses like famous artists, sculptors, musicians, songwriters, novelists and poets. However, creativity is not just about creating a masterpiece but about creating something new and useful that we can apply advantageously to enrich our lives. Everything around us in our homes was conceived as an idea and developed by practical people to make all our lives easier and more comfortable.

Seek out and embrace change and novelty in your personal life to boost your creativity. Creativity is needed in our personal lives to solve everyday problems, such as doing more with a shrinking household budget, like seeking out cheaper sources to buy our weekly groceries, or carrying out on-going repairs and maintenance to our homes instead of relying exclusively on tradespeople.

If I can improvise a costume for a school play, then this is being creative. If I can better organise my day, write letters and reports in more effective ways, or make more interesting presentations, then this is being creative. This everyday creativity plays a vital role in our learning and personal development as well as boosting our confidence and self-esteem. One way to spark creativity and leave a legacy for your children and grandchildren is to write an autobiography of your life.

Many people find a creative outlet for interior design when they are furnishing, painting and decorating their homes. Others can develop their creative skills by designing lighting effects, colour schemes, rearranging the furniture in their home, landscaping the garden, or experimenting with new cooking recipes. You don't have to be a master chef to be creative; all you need to do is to create something new. More important is to adjust your mental attitude so that you approach life experiences with an open mind, and cultivate a belief that possibilities and solutions are always within reach. This means that you are equipped to handle any challenge that comes your way with confidence and flair.

Parents can encourage or suppress the natural creativity in the home environment by their actions. Most children at preschool kindergarten or crèche level love going to school. They are excited about exploring, experimenting and learning. This continues into the first grade of formal education. However, by the time they are in the third and fourth grades they have lost much of this natural curiosity and creativity. They lose the facility to revel in imaginary play and ask outlandish questions, unless they have a supportive teacher who tolerates unconventional questions. Without this support they tend to underperform and drop out of school.

The childhood of Stanley Mason (1921-2006), an inventor and holder of many patents illustrates the negative impact of some educational systems. He grew up to be a prolific inventor of such useful everyday things as disposable nappies, granola bars and microwave cookware. In relation to the diaper he said: "My wife asked me to put the diaper on the baby. I held up the cloth diaper, and it was square. I looked at the baby, and it was round. I knew there was an engineering problem."

One day while in 3rd grade Stanley was locked into the principal's room because he would not colour between lines. But in art classes outside school he learned how to visualise and his work in the library as a teenager exposed him to diverse ideas. Until the 9th grade he got poor grades because of his daydreaming and lack of focused attention in class. However, his 9th grade maths teacher recognised his potential and turned him into an honours student. One can only imagine how many inventors were never discovered because the educational system didn't nurture their creativity, and would not allow them the freedom to colour outside the lines.

Why children lose their creativity
Psychologist Teresa Amabile in her research has identified the reasons why children lose their creativity as they grow up. These reasons can be recalled by the mnemonic SCOPE:

- Surveillance. This means continually looking over children's shoulders. This makes them feel that they are constantly being watched and policed while they're working. This inhibits freedom of expression, initiative and creativity.
- Competition. Putting children in win/lose situations, where only one person can win. A child should be encouraged to progress at their own rate. They should compete against themselves, rather than worry what others think about their work. They

should be encouraged to become the best they can be, rather than be continually comparing themselves with others. Encouraging cooperation rather than competition should be the approach adopted.

- **O**ver control. Telling children exactly how to do things rather than encouraging them to explore, experiment, use their own initiative and find things out for themselves. Children perform best when given a good degree of freedom.
- **P**ressure. Establishing expectations that are over-ambitious for a child's performance. This approach can backfire and cause a lifelong aversion for the subject being taught. Creativity flourishes when things are done for fun, entertainment and enjoyment, rather than perfection.
- **E**valuation. Making children worry about other children's judgement about what they are doing. In a research study, participants who did not know that they were being evaluated made the most creative works. They were just enjoying themselves and were not concerned about other people's opinions, judgements or rewards. In tasks that require creativity, new insights, or learning, we do better when we are not being evaluated. On the other hand, in routine tasks we do better if evaluated.

Just like adults, children need all the praise that they can get. A study of students showed that it took four praises to one criticism to keep students motivated, and a ratio of 8 to 1 to change behaviour. The same study found that teachers' most common methods for changing behaviour were fear, humiliation and embarrassment. If this approach is common in classrooms we can see why conformity rather than creativity is the outcome of our educational systems.

Psychologists have discovered that the birth position may affect creativity as can family size, the age gap between siblings and the number of siblings and family values. It seems that children born later are more likely to be creative and pursue a vocation in the arts. Research shows that middle born children frequently develop into rebellious and non-conformist adults. Creativity can also be influenced by the availability of mentors and role models.

Creative adults tend to grow up in families with professional occupations that provide stable homes with clear rules and boundaries, but where the parents encouraged uniqueness. These families were highly sensitive to children's needs, yet challenged them to develop skills, be different, be imaginative and be adaptable. On the other hand, there are exceptional cases where highly creative adults grew up with hardship and in the most trying and unlikely circumstances. Hardship by itself doesn't lead to creativity, but expediency forces children to become more flexible, inventive and imaginative in dealing with problems in straitened circumstances, and flexibility helps with creativity.

Play

Apparently the games children play in early childhood help them to grow into creative adults. Neurology shows that play is now considered crucial to brain development. In laboratory experiments, animals that lived in an "enriched environment" grew bigger brains. An enriched environment is one characterised by frequent changes of toys and interactions with other animals. Children have an innate desire to experiment and explore - to try out new things. Pre-schoolers who spend more time in role play tend to be more creative. Similarly, involvement in stage plays is a great way for children to develop their creative talents. Ideally plays should be written by the children themselves to bring out their creativity, and to ensure understanding and compatibility with their world.

Preparing for the play and the process of acting is inherently rewarding for the children irrespective of the approval received from parents or teachers. Acting out someone else's point of view, helps develop the child's ability to analyse situations, empathise with others and see things from different perspectives. It also helps them to experience situations that life so far has not made available to them. Even when playing alone they can act out strong negative emotions such as anger, sadness and hostility, in a safe experimental environment. One of the functions of play in childhood is to stimulate brain development. Play also helps build their character and develop them into responsible adults.

A child can sit astride a stick and imagine they are cowboys riding a horse. A little girl plays with a doll and imagines she is a mother. She dresses up as a nurse or doctor and imagines she is caring for the needs of patients. A girl dresses up in her mother's clothes and imagines she is a model or a film star. A boy puts on a soldier's uniform and imagines that he is involved in a war. In his games he can become a soldier, a sailor or a pirate – all within the space of a few minutes. He uses a make-believe microphone and imagines he is a pop star.

Children have no problem impersonating animals, superheroes, and creatures that they invent themselves. Most children have imaginary friends they play with at some stage in their lives. All of these are examples of role play and authentic creativity. The role play is not merely a reproduction of the child's experience, but a creative reconstruction of the impressions he has acquired Children's ability to draw and make up stories are other examples of creativity at play.

Children have great imaginations which should be encouraged and developed. Telling children stories, myths, legends and fairy tales and exposing them to different life experiences will fire up their little fertile imaginations. The more knowledge and experience a child has, including wide reading, adventure holidays, visits to the playground, zoo and circus, the more productive his imagination. Through reading a child can imagine another's experience without actually going through the same physical process. A child can read books and read about thousands of events that they have not directly experienced and imagine them in their minds. If a child studies geography and history they can visit far away countries in their imaginations, and see things from other's perspectives without leaving the comfort of their own homes.

It is well known that in early childhood, especially during the pre-school period, children go through a drawing stage. During this period they draw eagerly, if primitively; sometimes even without the encouragement of an adult. It is important that we unconditionally praise their efforts during this phase. However, when they reach school age the love of drawing begins to diminish. In some it disappears completely. After 11 years of age a child's drawing improves, so that we get real conventional drawing. Similarly verbal or literary creativity takes over especially during puberty.

Developing writing skills in children

Literary skills are helped by increased knowledge through reading and personal experience, including an understanding of how people relate to each other, which helps the child to express themselves in writing. A child of early school age is unable to do this because of their limited knowledge and experience of the world, and because their brain is still developing.

A child's literary skills are developed if they are encouraged to write about topics that interest them, and that they understand and emotionally want to write about. Writing is a great outlet for heartfelt feelings. The opposite happens if they are compelled to write about things they have little knowledge, understanding or interest in. Encourage children to take a strong interest in the world around them, so that they can build up a database of knowledge to draw on and write about. Encourage children to ask questions as they have a natural ability to be inquisitive and are unafraid of being judged by others. Edward De Bono maintains that the natural creativity of children is a part of their innocence. If you do not know the usual way of doing things, the usual solution to problems, you are more likely to come up with original ideas.

Hobbies and holiday vacations can be a great source and inspiration for ideas. Encourage children to write about what they know well and have thought about deeply. Leo Tolstoy, the great Russian author, believed that the true task of education was not to prematurely inculcate adult language in children, but rather to help them develop and shape their own natural literary style. Just like an adult, when a child has something to write about, he writes with great conviction. In addition, writing helps them master language and express their thoughts and feelings in a creative way.

Some experts have categorised three stages of verbal expression in children. The first stage is oral language and lasts from about 3 to 7 years of age. The second stage is literacy and lasts from 7 to adolescence. Finally, the literary stage lasts from the end of puberty to young childhood. This is in line with reality as we know that the development of oral language is always ahead of the development of written language. Even afterwards childrens' words are often more expressive and picturesque than their writing.

Emotions affect our ability to see and feel. Experiencing fear or happiness will colour the way we see and experience things. In the half-dark the vivid imagination of a child may see clothes hanging on a clothes line in the kitchen as a strange man or a robber who has broken into the house. The image of the robber is not real but the emotions of fear and terror experienced by the child are.

Some artists are able to regress into their childlike imagination to reproduce great artwork displaying this sense of fear. Such work can induce a strong emotional effect on viewers of the art subconsciously. Similarly, music experienced in our childhood in a particular context when heard again can evoke a whole complex world of experiences and feelings to the person listening to the music, and bring back childhood memories and emotions. These fantasy experiences from childhood can help us become more creative. Some writers have exploited this facility to help them recall childhood experiences and write great works of literature.

> "There's really no secret to our approach. We keep moving forward – opening up new doors and doing new things because we're curious. And curiosity keeps leading us down new paths."
>
> Walt Disney

Creativity in the Workplace

In the workplace there are numerous opportunities for creativity to flourish. We spend a significant proportion of our waking hours at work, and it is one of the most important places to express our creativity. Unfortunately most of us have not been encouraged to be creative at work. Nevertheless, creative thinking has contributed to the rise and continued success of countless companies, from start-ups like Facebook, Twitter and Google, to long-established companies like Microsoft, Procter & Gamble, 3M and General Electric.

Contrary to conventional wisdom, a time of recession is often an opportune time in which to set up a company. Companies such as Burger King, Microsoft, CNN and FedEx were all set up during a recession. Steve Jobs released his iPad during 2001 when the economy was in a recession. A recession forces a company to think in an innovative fashion, while overcoming problems and seeking out opportunities. They are forced to undertake cost reduction strategies to eliminate waste and run an efficient company. Unnecessary sources of cost are ruthlessly taken out of the system.

Creativity can take place in any area of an organisation, and not just in research and development (R&D), design, marketing and advertising. Inventiveness and creativity have become even important in spheres such as computer programming. The routine work of testing, maintaining and upgrading software has been outsourced to low cost countries. Engineers in developed countries who are able to develop new software products are highly regarded and remunerated. Once new software products have been invented they need to be launched in the market and taught, explained and maintained to customers. Training manuals need to be developed, and users trained in the new systems. Ongoing innovation within companies may take the form of the development of new products, services and processes. At a more routine level, incremental innovation takes place all the time with the continuous improvement of products, services and processes.

You don't need to come up with anything spectacular to be creative in the workplace. Simple everyday changes and improvements may reap major benefits in productivity. Responding in a creative way to a customer request, or solving a crisis requiring a quick response, is an everyday occurrence in most businesses. In marketing creative approaches to pricing, identifying niche markets, advertising, packaging and distribution are examples of creativity in action. Marketing managers also need to identify new and profitable product-market opportunities that appeal to customers' wants and needs.

Improving a purchasing procedure or a reporting procedure by eliminating unnecessary paperwork and by combining operations is creativity in action. The best way of doing this is by mapping the process through flow charts. Flow charts will help you visualise the complete process. You can then break the process down into individual stages so that you can readily see how it can be improved by eliminating unnecessary steps.

Structures can be rationalised and systems made more efficient. Moving a desk or a filing cabinet so that the work flows smother may result in a significant saving of time and effort. We may redesign a job so that the same tasks are combined and given to one person thereby increasing efficiency and productivity. In a factory, unnecessary operations, movements and congestion points can be eliminated to improve work flow, produce faster cycle times, while at the same time reducing work-related stress. You can discover how to reduce the wear on a cutting tool or diagnose an intermittent fault on a complex piece of machinery.

In logistics you can discover a clever way to move a product more efficiently to a customer or improve its design for greater customer satisfaction. In industrial relations you can figure out how to use more empathetic and precise language to favourably influence behaviour. In human resource management you may want to design remuneration packages that get skilled staff to stay with the company without paying them excessive salaries.

Maybe the reporting procedure in your company could be improved, the sales territory redesigned or the purchasing procedures simplified, all resulting in significant savings. Forms can be simplified and combined and analysed to ensure that all information requested on the form is necessary, and that the form is user friendly to fill up. Credit control and invoicing systems can be improved.

Managers may make relatively novel changes in problem solving, decision making or implementation. They may simplify control procedures and coordination and thereby improve efficiency. They may introduce better staff motivation systems and improve accountability. They may introduce better and more streamlined organisation structures, including communication channels, and implement better planning and budgetary procedures.

Creativity can even occur in accounting. I'm not referring to creative accounting here! Over the past couple of decades, there have been many innovations in accounting that are extremely profound and ethical, such as activity based costing, and zero based budgeting. Accountants can also advise when outsourcing is the more profitable course of action rather than doing it yourself. They can demonstrate through investment appraisal studies when further investment through capital expenditure is the wisest and most profitable course of action.

The most creative ideas often come from front line employees working closest to the customer, because they understand the customer, and know the operational problems that they face on a daily basis. Creative ideas should solve pressing problems that customers have. For example, in a restaurant the best ideas may come from the waitresses and waiters, rather than the management. They may have ideas about new additions or deletions to the menu, more efficient ways of paying the bill, improvements to the décor and layout of the restaurant, and ways to attract more customers into the restaurant.

Company culture and creativity

Organisational culture is the underlying values, beliefs, attitudes, behaviours, and principles that a company operates, that encourage, supports and reinforce a culture of innovation. The culture is supported by the company's mission and vision that sets the tone for the organisation. The creative organisation believes in flexibility, adaptability and involvement, implemented by a policy of empowering and developing their employees. Employees are more likely to generate and offer ideas if they are empowered, work in teams and given every opportunity to develop their talents through training and development. The culture of innovation should be supported by a system of incentives, and the appointment of champions to encourage innovative thinking. Champions help break down the barriers of resistance to new ideas while bolstering the culture of creativity and innovation in the company.

Innovative organisations are adaptable and able to respond rapidly to the changes going on around them. They have an outward focus and quickly respond to the needs of customers and competitors. They encourage risk-taking and produce innovations that customers need and value. They have a clear vision of what they want to do, and the way the organisation should advance. For example, Apple has been largely driven by a strong vision, rather than customer ideas. Innovative organisations invest in their employee training and development, promote empowerment and facilitate teamwork. They create an environment that encourages the exchange of knowledge, encourages constructive confrontation, initiative, and independent thinking to stimulate creativity. General George Patton said: "Never tell people how to do things. Tell them what to do and they will surprise you with their ingenuity."

Creativity may be easier to achieve within the smaller firm where flexibility is a key factor when addressing business opportunities. Creativity flourishes in a culture, where it is supported, valued, celebrated and recognised. Obviously if you work in a stultifying environment, where conformity and mediocrity are rewarded, you are unlikely to be creative. People like the opportunity to engage deeply in their work and make real progress. Organisations conducive to creativity are more informal than formal, and allow people to participate, network and experiment.

Innovation doesn't always work. When Coca-Cola introduced New Coke in April 1985 to replace Classic Coke, they expected a major success story. Instead the launch of the New Coke was a public disaster with overwhelming negative reaction. Their customers, who weren't consulted about the change, preferred Classic Coke. Even global companies make mistakes – there is no such thing as being right all the time. Coca-Cola probably spent large sums of money on research, such as focus groups and taste testing, before they launched New Coke but still failed. Failure is part and parcel of innovation and employees must be allowed to fail in order to successfully innovate.

Creating an innovative corporate culture

There are six critical rules to guide innovative culture in an organisation:

1. Develop passion in the workplace to provide a sense of purpose, promoting collaboration and having fun.
2. Celebrate employee ideas through praise, recognition, career opportunities and encouraging employees to enjoy their work.
3. Foster autonomy by reducing the number of obstacles employees must go through to get their work done.
4. Applaud courage by telling employees to say what they think, even if it is controversial, and to

question actions inconsistent with company values and ethical standards.

5.   Fail forward by learning from experiments that didn't succeed, and taking risks that will lead one step closer to the ideal solution.

6.   Maximise diversity in the workplace to understand customers better, and see the world from their perspective.

Companies need to be continually creative to differentiate their products from competitors in the market. They may do this through innovative pricing strategies, improved packaging and design, and better and more efficient distribution channels. In marketing you may develop new markets for your existing products or produce new products for new markets.

Practical examples of companies with a creative culture
Generally, employees in 3M are allowed to spend 15% of their time on projects of their own choosing. This time is generally unstructured and is given to creative thinking, trying new products, and reading up on new ideas and processes that could help employees be more creative. Specifically, 3M, engineers are rotated to a new division every few years. Sometimes these rotations bring big payoffs. 3M realised they had a problem with their laptop battery life because the screen used up too much energy. The engineers applied their knowledge of see-through adhesives to create an optical film that focuses light outward, producing a screen that was 40% more efficient.

It is part of the culture of Microsoft that people will fail as part of the process of finding better solutions. This is acceptable provided people learn from their mistakes. At Google, engineers are encouraged to work on "20% projects." Basically they can spend up to a fifth of their time on ideas that interest them. For Google this approach has created new services like Google Scholar. Twitter has a similar concept called Hack Week, described in a company blog as "a full week to work with people from other teams, explore new ideas, experiment with different projects and let our creativity run wild."

Executives at Walt Disney Company know that good movie ideas can come from anybody within the company, and not just from executives. There times a year they hold a "Gong Show," in which everyone in the company, including janitors, secretaries and mailroom staff get to share their ideas with the top executives.

Kodak has a humour room for people to unwind, play games, or watch funny videos. IDEO designers describe brainstorming sessions as one of the most fun things that they do.

Some companies introduce "casual Fridays" where people can dress casually. The idea is that the informality in dress will eliminate status and encourage creativity. Formal dress codes are a part of bureaucracy and a barrier to creativity. The change in atmosphere, signalled by the change in dress, will hopefully free up communication, engender trust, encourage people to network, and improve interpersonal relationships. People work best when they are relaxed, and care and have mutual respect for each other.

Milliard Dexler is chairman and chief executive of J. Crew Group Inc. a speciality clothing retailer. He maintains that creativity is letting people think outside of the box. He says most companies don't listen to their employees and have ineffective leaders. He has organised his offices to encourage cross-pollination of ideas. The space has no enclosed offices - the goal is to facilitate active collaboration and interdisciplinary learning. He believes walled off spaces hinder creativity.

Employees can also be inspired by training events such as training courses, workshops, sabbaticals, and visits to museums. Hallmark, each year, brings into its Kansas City HQ outside speakers from various artistic backgrounds. The sole purpose is to provide stimulation to the world's largest corporate creative staff of artists, designers, writers, editors and photographers who generate thousands of original designs for their cards and related products each year. At Mazda

Motor Manufacturing USA, a combination of creativity skills, training in teamwork, and constantly improving process methods was used successfully to improve overall output and efficiency.

Sometimes people can be inspired by attending overseas exhibitions. Starbucks was originally set up to sell coffee equipment and coffee by the bag. Howard Schulz, the director of retail operations and marketing, was attending an international housewares show in Milan. On the way back to the hotel he noticed an espresso bar and decided to investigate. He had his first cafe latte and realised that Starbucks was in the wrong business. Coffee was meant to be a social experience. The revelation prompted Schultz to take Starbucks down a new path, resulting in the profitable worldwide business it is today.

The SAS Institute is a US based developer of analytic software. It is one of the world's largest private software companies, and has the largest market share in analytic software. As it grew it added more divisions, instead of layers of management, so that it has a very simple and flat organisational structure. SAS believe in the training and development of their employees, and send them to conferences and training courses to hone their skills, and keep up to date with cutting-edge technologies. They help their employees do their best creative work, and keep intellectually engaged by removing workplace barriers, and creating a stress free environment. They believe that challenging work is a key source of motivation rather than salary or bonuses. The most fitting reward for a job well done is an even more challenging project. There is no penalty for making mistakes in the pursuit of better products. Experimentation is crucial for breakthroughs, and some paths are bound to be fruitless. They engage with customers as creative partners so that they can deliver superior products. They listen to their complaints and suggestions and use this feedback to produce better products.

Steve Jobs invested in Pixar, a company involved in the production of cartoons, and made it into the creative force it is today. Pixar displayed great creativity in Toy Story which went on to be a huge box office success. It has gone on to win 26 Academy Awards, 5 Golden Globes and 3 Grammys. This is very impressive when you consider that in 1991, Pixar was a computer hardware company with only 42 employees, on the brink of bankruptcy. Jobs believed that good teams produce good movies. He believed if you bring a diversity of talent together they learn from each other.

He designed the Pixar studio to facilitate social exchange and lively discussion with employees randomly bumping into each other. His brief to the architect was to design headquarters that promoted encounters and unplanned collaborations. The atrium or centre of the building houses focal points like the café, foosball tables, and a fitness centre. As we know random conversations often lead to creative breakthroughs. The more people you talk to the more ideas you are going to have. He exploited the findings of the Allen Curve, claiming that people are more likely to talk to neighbours at a nearby desk, rather than somebody who sits more than 50 metres away.

W.L. Gore & Associates is a private company located in Newark, Delaware, USA. It specialises in products derived from fluoropolymers. Its medical products include heart patches and synthetic blood patches. Its cutting edge fabrics are worn by astronauts, soldiers and North and South Pole trekkers. It is one of the most innovative companies in the USA. The company's ability to innovate does not come from huge research in R&D, but springs from its culture where creativity is encouraged, resourced and celebrated. Employees are free to pursue ideas on their own, communicate with each other, and collaborate out of self-motivation rather than a sense of duty.

The company has a flat organisational structure where employees are known as associates. There are neither chains of command nor predetermined channels of communications. Associates spend about 10% of their time pursuing speculative new ideas. Anyone is free to launch a project and be a leader provided they can win followers by their passion and ideas. This approach to business is based on founder Bill

Gore's experience with task force teams while working at the DuPont Company. These multidisciplinary teams attack problems on an ad hoc basis, and typically operate for a short period outside the formal management hierarchy.

Bell Laboratories was one of the most famous and productive creative and innovate centres in the world. It invented radar, lasers, fibre optics, mobile phones, and satellite communications, and produced 13 Nobel Prize winners. It designed the transistor and the first silicon solar cells. It developed Unix and the C programming language.

The driving force behind Bell Labs was Mervin Kelly (1894-1971) whose greatest contribution was in creative technical management. He believed leaders or managers should be technologically trained and technologically competent. He designed a work environment where engineers, physicists, chemists, material scientists and mathematicians would inevitably interact. He fostered an open, cooperative, and interdisciplinary environment. He believed in the value of training. He gave his researchers plenty of scope to pursue whatever they believed would be beneficial and profitable to the company. He promoted ability and conversely was impatient with mediocrity and didn't tolerate incompetence. He took a long-term view and often supported pure scientific research even where an immediate payoff was unlikely. He accepted that failure was a necessary part of the process of making technological breakthroughs. Despite the importance of teamwork he believed that the individual's role in creativity was still paramount. He once said: "It is in the mind of a single person that creative ideas and concepts are born."

Kelly believed that the formula for innovation had three ingredients:

- Bring together a multi-disciplinary team of clever creative people. The building was designed with this in mind to increase the chance of serendipitous encounters.

- Give them practical problems to solve. One of their famous innovations was replacing vacuum tubes with transistors.
- Provide them with the best resources and adequate funding.

In a company there is a positive correlation between investment in R&D and sales growth. Investment in R&D is an important element in creating a culture of innovation in a company. However, it is important that R&D is focused on the needs and objectives of the company, so products that customers actually need are created, and sales and profits grow as a result. There is no point in producing products that nobody wants to buy.

Nurturing Creativity at Work

Individually employees can become more creative by getting involved in opportunities, such as foreign assignments, cross-functional projects teams, job rotation, or being involved in a crisis situation where their abilities and skills are stretched to the limit. A static environment in the same old office with the same old desk, doing the same routines, and working with the same old colleagues can be stifling.

If managers want to encourage creativity and innovation they must simplify bureaucracy, and reward new ideas and risk taking. If you delegate work to staff you should give them the freedom to exercise their initiative to decide how to tackle the work. In all environments you get what you reward. Rules should be designed to reward initiative and creativity. Incentives should be aligned with the goal of creativity.

Jobs should be enriched and enlarged and workers empowered to make changes concerning their immediate work. After all, they know more about their work than anybody else, and so are in a greater position to improve it by constructively engaging their initiative and creativity. Organisations should encourage employees who have skills outside the job to develop them further. For example some employees might be amateur photographers or artists. The creative mindsets involved in these skills can be transferred to on-the-job situations. For example, innovation often occurs when two separate realms are combined together.

Structures influence the level of creativity, or lack of creativity in an organisation. Centralised structures and control generally encourage rigidity and bureaucratic thinking, whereas decentralised structures and delegation facilitate creativity, innovative thinking, and empowerment. Creativity suffers greatly during a restructuring or downsizing. It is even worse coming up towards the downsizing as people's fear of the unknown causes them to lose interest and disengage from the work. Communication, trust and collaboration decline significantly as does people's sense of motivation, morale, freedom and autonomy.

A blame culture should be avoided and people should be encouraged to use their initiative, and treat their mistakes as learning opportunities. This point is illustrated by a story told about the Ford Motor Company. One of Henry Ford's Vice Presidents made a huge inventory error that cost the company in excess of $1million; a lot of money back in 1920. The VP assumed he would be fired and handed in his resignation. Ford declined to accept the resignation pointing out that he had just invested $1million in the VP's education.

There is a global creativity gap according to a survey carried out by the Adobe (Nasdag: ADBE) benchmark study in 2012. Five thousand adults across the US, UK, Germany, France and Japan took part in the survey. The research shows 8 to 10 people feel that unlocking creativity is critical to economic growth. Two-thirds felt that creativity is valuable to society, but only 1 in 4 people believe they are living up to their own creative potential. The study revealed a workplace creativity gap, where 75% of respondents said they are under growing pressure to be productive rather than creative, despite the fact that they are increasingly expected to be creative on the job.

Across all five countries surveyed, respondents said they spent only 25% of their time at work being creative. Lack of time is seen as the biggest barrier to creativity. Four in ten people believe that they do not have access to the tools or training to be creative, which are seen as the biggest driver to increase creativity. Technology is seen in a positive light as it helps people overcome creative limitations. The study reveals that lack of education and training is draining people of their creative abilities, producing a workforce conditioned to prioritise conformity over creativity. In the study generational and gender differences were marginal, reinforcing the idea that everyone has the potential to be creative.

Surveys show only 30% of companies do anything substantial such as training about creativity. The most creative companies are in agriculture, arts, leisure and the media. Most employees feel they are not encouraged to be creative and many feel they are actively discouraged to be so. On the other hand, most senior managers are more positive about creativity in their companies than their staff. Google, Twitter and Microsoft actively encourage their employees to be creative – they give their staff time off during working hours to devote to personal creative jobs. Google recruits employees with diverse interests and encourage them to think freely.

Maintaining company creativity
Companies can create and maintain creativity in their organisations by:

- Keeping organisational structures as simple as possible. The command and control structures popular in the last century were not conducive to creativity and have been replaced by the more progressive divisional and decentralised structures.
- Hire employees from varied backgrounds. This will encourage diverse ideas and interdisciplinary inputs to problem solving. On an ongoing basis encourage employees to learn additional skills. Encourage employees to take on difficult or novel tasks.

- Encourage creativity through creative leadership. Leaders should communicate a vision conducive to creativity. At all levels of the organisation creativity should be encouraged and contrary influences eliminated. Mistakes should be treated as learning opportunities. Managers and supervisors should be role models for creativity. The Pygmalion effect suggests that if leaders expect their followers to be creative, then it is more likely that they will live up to their expectations. It becomes a self-fulfilling prophecy.
- Creative people should not be treated differently from others. Their uniqueness, independence of mind and non-conformity should be appreciated. Their creativity should be celebrated and it should be emphasised to others how it will benefit the company. Creative energies should be channelled into creating innovative products, services and processes that are profitable for the company and create competitive advantage.
- Collaboration rather than competition between employees should be encouraged. Such an atmosphere encourages people to exchange creative ideas and help each other.
- Communication channels should be maximised across departmental and hierarchical boundaries.
- Create a stress free environment as far as possible as a stressful environment is likely to impair creativity.

Nurturing Creativity in Teams

Creative individuals within organisations contribute to overall competitive advantage and organisational innovation, while teams or groups of creative individuals increase this advantage further. It is essential that the right leaders are appointed so that creativity is nurtured and supported. A culture within the company of openness to innovation, and acceptance of new ideas should be encouraged.

Transformation leadership, in particular, stimulates creativity and innovation. They lead by example, are honest, convey a strong vision, show consideration for others, are creative themselves and inspire others to be likewise. Employees like to work in a company where creativity is supported, valued, recognised and celebrated. This results in lower employee turnover and greater customer satisfaction with significant growth in revenues.

People are more creative in work groups that have different experiences, cultures, gender mix, age profiles, expertise, perspectives and world views. The more diverse the group, the more likely they are to come up with breakthrough ideas. For example, the best ideas for Disney theme park adventures have come from older people in their 60s, 70s and 80s. So don't neglect the older generation, while at the same time giving the younger generation opportunities to develop and grow! In addition, work groups that collaborate rather than compete are more creative.

Steve Jobs was a firm believer in groups with multi-disciplinary backgrounds. He once said: "I think part of what made the Macintosh great was that the people working on it were musicians, poets, artists, zoologists, and historians who also happened to be the best computer scientists in the world."

Interactive versus nominal groups
Researchers have found that interactive groups are less effective than nominal groups (single individuals) at producing novel ideas. This is because of social loafing, evaluation apprehension, production blocking and participant domination. Social loafing or free-riding occurs when a member in a group sits back and lets the other members come up with the ideas. This might be because they feel they are not accountable or that their contributions are not needed. Interactive groups can stymie creativity if members of the group withhold ideas because they are frightened of negative criticism. In an effort to reduce evaluation apprehension many

idea generation techniques suspend judgement until after the idea-generation phase.

Production blocking occurs in an interactive group because only one member can communicate at a time. Because they are so intent on listening, group members may suppress or even forget their own ideas. Participant dominance occurs when some extroverted group members exercise undue influence, or monopolise time in an unproductive manner at the expense of the shy or introverted ones. A nominal group is one where individuals generate ideas alone, before pooling their results with the rest of the group and so avoid evaluation apprehension, production blocking and participant domination.

Groups that change membership are more creative than those whose membership remains the same. They generate more ideas and different kinds of ideas than those groups who remain intact. Groups that stay together without any change get into a rut. New blood introduces new ideas into the group. They may also motivate existing members to revisit problems and develop new and improved ways of finding solutions. In addition, teams that experience membership change are more task-oriented. They like to get the job done quickly because of the transitory nature of the group.

A trained facilitator should be appointed to steer and motivate the team. The facilitator will be good at handling groups, and use strategies to avoid conformity within the group while challenging them to be creative. He will be aware of and follow the rules of brainstorming. He will keep the team on track, keep the process moving, and ensure that social loafing, evaluation apprehension, production blocking and participant domination do not occur. He will encourage the shy members to come forward with their ideas and support all who offer ideas. Sarcasm, criticism and put-downs are not allowed.

The most creative teams are those that have the confidence to share and debate ideas. They bring different perspective to problems, encourage individual contributions, and respect the different thinking styles of members. They resolve conflicts diplomatically, and provide positive feedback for ideas. They create a positive playful environment to enhance creativity.

Teams high on shared goals and tasks that engage in participative problem solving, within a climate supportive of creativity, are more creative.

Teams that socialise inside and outside of work break down barriers quickly facilitating creativity. Teams that are open and transparent, and that are made up of diverse personalities, such as introverts and extraverts, are generally more creative. On the other hand, when people compete for recognition, they stop sharing information. Such destructive behaviour means that nobody in an organisation has all the information required to put all the pieces of the puzzle together. This means that sub-standard decisions and solutions to problems are made.

"Curiosity about life in all of its aspects, I think, is still the secret of great people."

Leo Burnett

Universities and R&D

Universities are designed to encourage the flow of ideas between disciplines within the university, and outside the university through links such as joint ventures with industry. They are more concerned with pure research rather than development. Development is more the concern of companies as they want specific marketing results and profitable products. University Research & Development (R&D) are interested primarily in the advancement of knowledge, and sometimes make many major breakthroughs. Joint research projects are often undertaken with government and industry and the outcomes shared. Students in universities are drawn from different countries with different cultures, so that universities become a hothouse for creative ideas. Universities produce PhD's for employment in research and development departments within companies and government research agencies.

The internet means that universities throughout the world can be in instant contact with each other. Researchers in one university can work as closely with their colleagues in other universities throughout the world, as they do with their colleagues in their own research departments sharing information and research results. This means that they are constantly up to date in their particular speciality. This is why it pays for industrial R&D to keep in touch with what is happening in the Universities. R&D departments focus on interdisciplinary or cross-functional learning which enhances learning, and the creation of innovations. The leadership provided in the management of R&D departments plays a vital role in their effectiveness.

An important aspect of R&D is monitoring and scanning the external environment for new knowledge, so that you know what research and breakthroughs are happening elsewhere. This includes keeping track of new patents and breakthroughs published in professional journals. A gatekeeper may be appointed to perform this role possessing the set of skills needed. The importance of scanning the external environment is confirmed by the view of one R&D director, who maintains that it is often faster and cheaper to look outside for the relevant technology than to develop it in house. Expertise can also be bought in through the purchase of patents and mergers and acquisitions. New advances can come from anywhere in the world.

R&D departments routinely exchange know-how and technologies with other R&D departments, through strategic alliances and professional networks of scientists and engineers. For example, Procter & Gamble can create cheaper and better products faster through collaboration with others. It collaborates with suppliers, competitors, scientists, entrepreneurs, and others; systematically scanning the world for proven technologies, packages and products that they can adapt. This means improving, scaling up and marketing them on their own or in partnership with other companies. To do this a company needs additional skills such as negotiation and project management and evaluation. Just like manufacturing and services, R&D can be performed in house or outsourced to others at home or abroad.

No longer is basic research centralised near the corporate headquarters of companies, as was largely the case in the 1970s. The trend to decentralise R&D was evident by the early 1990s. Studies found that the share of foreign R&D sites increased from 45% in 1975 to 66% in 2004. Units abroad have evolved from listening posts and product development for the local market, to more significant R&D departments. For example, new product development tasks in laptop computer production, including design, prototypes, and pilot production are relocating to China. Concept and production planning remain in the US and Japan. The separation of research (R) from development (D) is becoming more common. It is still the case that research is less dispersed than development. Research is concentrated in a few regions worldwide, while development is more widely decentralised. Basic research remains largely in a firm's home country, usually situated near the headquarters of the company.

R&D departments, when decentralised, tend to locate in places where the best conditions for success are found, both for research and for the transfer of results into viable profitable products. This means that R&D clusters are usually found in major cities with access to cutting-edge research in universities and government laboratories. The academic and industrial labour markets overlap in postdoctoral research and doctoral students. R&D clusters also need a good local infrastructure, such as airports and telecommunications, to facilitate communication and knowledge exchange.

International collaboration
Globalisation has intensified the amount of collaboration between research agencies around the world. The Human Genome Project, the International Space Station, the Large Hadron Collider at CERN near Geneva, and ITER (formerly the International Thermonuclear Experimental Reactor) in

France, are only a few examples of international collaboration in science. The Human Genome Project was an international research effort to sequence and map all the genes in the human body. It was completed in April 2003 and gave us the complete blueprint for building a human being.

The International Space Station is mainly financed by the US and Russia but other countries are involved as well. ITER is an international nuclear fusion research and engineering project. The project is run and funded by seven member states including the EU, India, Japan, China, Russia, South Korea and the US. CERN, the European Organisation for Nuclear Research, employ physicists and engineers from all over the world to probe the fundamental structure of the universe. It was one of Europe's first joint ventures and now has 21 member states. The globalisation of science has provided many tangible benefits for humanity, including greater cooperation between nations, and an unprecedented opportunity for a cross fertilisation of ideas leading to creative problem solving.

"A business's ability to innovate is vital to global competitiveness. It is only by continually developing new products, processes and services that businesses can gain the competitive edge necessary for the increasingly global economy. R&D is a key component of this, helping to generate the advances that lead to new value-added products and enabling people and capital to be more effective."

Lord Sainsbury

Western Verses Eastern Cultures

The western world encourages individualism, independence of thought and freedom of expression. Originality, initiative, fluidity, and flexibility are highly regarded and respected. It is very supportive of competition, productivity and variety. The whole western society is built on capitalism, consumerism and choice. Private enterprise and the work ethic is very much part of western culture. It has a philosophy of building for the future and material progress. It believes individuals can improve their standard of living by working hard. This means that creativity, innovation and continuous improvement is very much part of everyday business life.

The rise of the US economy has been built on its openness to new ideas, allowing it to mobilise and harness the creativity of its people. Freedom of expression has encouraged new technologies and culture to emerge – from biotechnology in science, to rock and roll in music. The influx of talent since the 1930s from Europe, fleeing from fascist and communist regimes, has contributed in no small way to the success of the US economy.

During the 1980s and 1990s, thanks to a more liberal immigration policy, talent has poured into the United States from every corner of the globe. For example, the cofounder of Google is Sergey Brin who was born in Moscow and Hotmail confounder is Sabeer Bhatia, who grew up in Bangalore. In 2004 the foreign born population of the US was in excess of 30 million or about 11% of the total population. Vinod Khosla, the cofounder of Sun Microsystems was born in India. These people set up creative industries that have been the inspiration for numerous offshoots as well.

On the other hand, eastern cultures emphasise the importance of the group rather than the individual, and the need for conformity and social harmony. It engenders respect for collective endeavour, tradition, culture, authority, seniority and age. It deemphasises the importance of the individual and competition in achieving results. For example, Chinese people are socialised since childhood to revere their elders and respect authority, and be concerned with the opinions of others. They are worried how others regard, receive and perceive them especially by family members and clan. Negotiations between people from western and eastern cultures often run into trouble because each misunderstands the other's point of view. Eastern cultures perceive people in the west as brash, loud, aggressive and pushy, while westerners see people from the east as respectful, shy, diffident and slow to make decisions.

Muslim cultures ban the representation of religious icons in their mosques. On the other hand, religious icons are prized in most Christian churches and cultures, and this gave rise to the renaissance in art and sculpture during the 15th and 16th centuries. Muslim culture also views the worst excesses of consumerism in the west as evil. So we see that a particular cultural view may hinder freedom of expression, economic development and creativity.

An historical perspective

Historical studies of art and literature show many great breakthroughs in China and Japan throughout the centuries. Many of the great inventions in history such as gunpowder, paper, printing and the compass were first discovered in China despite claims to the contrary. History reveals equally impressive ancient accomplishments in astronomy, botany, seismology, and other scientific fields. Chinese astronomers have been gazing at the heavens for hundreds of years, and are credited with the discovery of sunspots long before the Europeans.

According to the historian Ian Morris, up until about 1700 China was 'the richest, strongest and most inventive place on earth.' Over the next few hundred years the west has raced ahead economically and technologically. The Chinese authorities weren't interested in exploring the knowledge and technologies of the west, because they were perfectly happy with their lot. They preferred to look inwards to their ancient and rich traditions and were uninterested in what was happening outside the country. Today they realise the error of their ways, and are now beginning to catch up at a fast pace.

Evidence suggests that the Renaissance and the Enlightenment in Europe were highly influenced by the exposure of European culture to Asian influences in the middle ages, through the Silk Road and Indian Ocean trade routes. In addition, contemporary historical research concludes that the key reason why the industrial revolution broke out in Manchester first rather than in Shanghai or Tokyo was not culture but geographical, with the availability of the right kind of coal.

If you use Nobel prizes as a measurement of creativity, then the east comes out poorly. The tally of Nobel laureates isn't high for Asian creativity, especially in science, as countries with a lesser population such as the US, UK and Germany outpaces all of Asia. The comparative difference in wealth may account for some of the difference.

Even Japan, which is a wealthy country, lags behind small nations such as Switzerland and the Netherlands. In fact, Japan seems to be better at making incremental improvements rather than breakthrough innovations. It was incremental improvements that accounted for Japan's success in the late 20th century in the automobile, electronics and other high technological industries. This zeal for improvement has prompted some researchers to suggest that East Asian culture fosters incremental improvement, while Western culture fosters breakthrough innovation. The open ended basic research practised in the West has given rise to numerous serendipitous inventions such as Viagra.

Human resource procedures are different in Western and Eastern countries, and mirror the cultural tendencies for breakthrough innovation versus incremental improvement. In the West we favour a more participatory and decentralised approach to management, whereas in the east a more top down autocratic approach is favoured. It is known that participatory leadership styles and empowerment policies facilitate employee creativity. Breakthrough innovation is fostered by cross-pollination of engineers and scientists from universities and other companies. Incremental improvements are fostered by long-term employment where employees have been rotated through different jobs, and are able to use their accumulated experience. The Eastern philosophy seems to prefer usefulness rather than novelty.

Some psychologists maintain that the academic approach in Asian cultures stunts scientific creativity. It is thought that ideographic languages such as Chinese do not exercise abstract thinking, unlike the alphabetic languages. In addition, Asian education emphasises holistic thinking rather than analytic thinking. A more positive sign is the number of basic research investments in recent years by companies such as Microsoft, Pfizer, and Exxon in the labs of East Asia.

The world's scientific community has become less dependent on the US and the West. Fifteen years ago the US published more than 10 times as many scientific papers as China. In 2010 China ranked second in the world in published papers and is now ready to overtake the US. A Thomson Reuters report showed that China surpassed the US and Japan in new patent applications last year. During the past decade, China, India and Brazil more than doubled their expenditure on research and development. Their contribution to world R&D spending increased from 17% to 24%.

Cities as Creative Hubs

A large proportion of the world's output is now produced in large cities with a population in excess of 1 million. In 2013 it was estimated that half of the world's population lives in urban areas, and this is likely to grow in the future. Vibrant cities act like magnets to people who want to improve their lives. The average inhabitant of a city is three times more creative than someone living in a town. They are also likely to earn a higher income and generally have a higher standard of living.

Innovation is a prime driver of economic growth in a city or region. Cities provide the infrastructure for individuals to network, be creative and learn from each other. Physical proximity is an important factor in creativity, and in cities a lot of people share the same space. When people spontaneously interact, often serendipitously, it facilitates the exchange of knowledge, ideas and innovation, and is the reason why cities have produced most of our great political and social ideas, books, inventions, works of art and economic wealth. In addition, the closer one is to research laboratories, universities, institutes, government departments, journals and conference facilities, the greater the chance of being creative.

In ancient Greece, Athens became a hub for philosophers such as Socrates, Plato and Aristotle giving rise to the birth of democracy and Western Civilisation. In the Renaissance, creative people moved between Milan, Venice, Florence and Rome. Florence in particular became a magnet for creative artists such as Michelangelo, Leonardo da Vinci and Donatello. Today our creative talents move easily between Silicon Valley, Shanghai, London, Paris, Tokyo, New York and other major cities.

Fostering creativity is the reason why in 2000 the European Council set the goal of making the European Union (EU) the "most innovative and dynamic knowledge based economy in the world. Innovation is achieved when firms and individuals in close proximity in a particular city swap information and expertise. In the Adobe (Nasdag: ADBE) 2012 survey Tokyo ranked as the most creative city with New York second. Outside of Japan, national pride in each country is evident, with the UK, Germany and France ranking their countries and cities next in line after Japan.

The attraction of cities

The most important creative resource in cities is people. Creative people are attracted to cities with strong art, musical, social, cultural and economic infrastructures. Globalisation means that these people can come from anywhere in the world as well as from the local economy. Immigrants from different countries bring their own cultures and unique perspectives and thus add to a city's vibrancy and creativity.

Creative people like to live in places that provide them with a good lifestyle, with access to cultural outlets such as museums, libraries, art galleries, craft workshops, theatres, and cinemas. They are attracted by social outlets where they can meet other people in a vibrant downtown; bookshops, coffee shops, restaurants, parks, playgrounds, pubs, race meetings and sports facilities. They also like to meet other professionals through professional associations and conferences to network and exchange knowledge and expertise. The internet facilitates social networking through Facebook, Skype and Twitter, even though the internet is still a poor substitute for meeting face to face.

Cultural and artistic facilities also encourage tourists to visit a city creating employment in service industries such as retail shops, hotels and restaurants, which adds further to the vibrancy and attraction of cities. Some cities try to establish a unique selling point by running literature, art, film, music and other festivals to attract tourists to visit. Many cities provide financial assistance through grants for creative and artistic people, interested in setting up small enterprises.

Because of the variety of opportunities in creative and diversified cities people have great job mobility. They can easily move between different jobs bringing their unique skills and expertise with them, doing so without having to relocate their families, or lose their friends or social networks. This facilitates the transfer of knowledge and learning between firms in the same and different industries which fosters creativity. Many administrative and manufacturing processes are generic in nature, and so can be applied in different contexts within different companies fairly easily. They do this by adapting specific know-how they have acquired in previous employments to other lines of work they encounter in their new jobs.

The facilities and energy of cities in turn attract industries and businesses such as multinational companies and financial services centres. They are attracted because of advantages such as a developed research infrastructure, information and communication technology infrastructure, a highly qualified and educated workforce, and an innovative culture. Big cities tend to have universities and government agencies with research facilities and companies who like to tap into these. They also have the services that companies need such as management consultancy, accounting, advertising, banking and law. In addition they have good airports, rail, roads and broadband facilities linking them to other major cities and town.

In April 2013 Booz & Co published a report which concluded that all growth in the creative industries is underpinned by digital technology. This involves improving upload and download speeds and educating people in digital technology. A good physical and digital infrastructure provides people with the choice to communicate and share information with each other face to face, or on the internet. In the modern world all of the factors mentioned previously are more important than natural resources.

Firms in similar or related industries tend to locate in particular places. The economic benefits that firms enjoy when located near each other include networking, shared infrastructure, suppliers and customers. This is the reason why Silicon Valley, near San Francisco in California, USA became attractive and world famous as a hub for information and communications technology. The term Silicon Valley originally referred to the regions large number of small silicon chip innovators and manufactures in the area, but now includes the high-tech industries in the area. These firms and industries in turn created spin-offs when employees left and set up their own firms. Silicon Valley continues to be a leading hub for high-tech innovation and development, accounting for one-third of all the venture capital investment in the United States. It has attracted firms like Intel, Apple, Cisco, Oracle, Sun Microsystems, Netscape, Google, Netflix and Facebook. Science parks have been set up in major cities throughout the world modelled on Silicon Valley.

Globalised cities

When industries, individuals, professions and occupations gather together in close proximity in cities, this creates an environment in which ideas can flow quickly from one person to another. These interactions between people can help them to be creative and innovative. Creativity, knowledge and information are now the key factors in economic growth. Some researchers have categorised New York and London as "learning and knowledge intensive cities" because of the marvellous social, cultural, education and economic resources in these major cities. The same can be said for other major cities throughout the world.

Globalised cities in the developed world now trade in creativity, ideas, knowledge and innovation. Jobs that can be made routine gravitate towards countries where labour costs are cheap, meaning that manufacturing is now mostly done in poor countries. On the other hand, developed economies are concentrating on the design, development and marketing of increasingly complex products and systems.

New York is a leading global city and a major centre in the US for finance, insurance, real estate, media and the arts. It has a strong competitive advantage in creative industries, such as new media, advertising, fashion, design and architecture. Its television and film industry is the second largest in the US outside of Hollywood. It always has been considered a major place for the music industry, from the development of modern jazz in the late forties and early fifties, right through to the creation of rap music and hip-hop in the mid-seventies. In addition, high-tech industries such as biotechnology, software development, game design and internet services are also important to the New York economy.

The scientist and entrepreneur Ralph Landau, maintained that the success of his small R&D organisation was because it was located in the Greater New York City area. This allowed his employees to benefit from the cosmopolitan perspective, vibrancy and creativity that only a large city can offer.

London is a global city, the capital city of England, and the biggest city in the EU. It generates about one-fifth of the UK's Gross Domestic Product (GDP). More than half of the UK's top FTSE listed companies and over 100 of Europe's 300 largest companies have their headquarters in central London. Moreover, 75% of Fortune 500 companies have offices in London. It is one of the major financial services centres in the world. It is also a thriving centre for creative writing, plays, novels, musicals, and cinema. Any service or facility that a person desires is available in London.

Creativity is now seen as an engine for economic growth. It is the driving force behind a wide variety of innovations, such as service and marketing innovations, as well as engineering and technological ones. It generates wealth and employment through business, cultural and artistic innovation. Globalised cities tend to attract creative people and creative industries. The creative industries include publishing, film, television, multimedia, electronic publishing, design, advertising, marketing, software and research and development. These industries in turn attract the highly educated people needed to run these businesses, including university professors, scientists, engineers, PhD holders, novelists, entertainers, artists, actors, designers, non-fiction writers, journalists, editors and other opinion makers. These are highly educated and talented people, and are particularly good at inventing new jobs through their entrepreneurial skills and setting up small businesses.

The number of patents awarded to inventors in a city is a rough indicator of how inventive the people in that city are. Other indicators of innovativeness in a city are the rate at which it attracts inward investment in research and development. Studies show there is a positive relationship between investment in research and development and the number of patents awarded.

"To live a creative life, we must lose our fear of being wrong."

Joseph Chilton Pearce

Summary of Chapter 5

Without the human brain it would be impossible to be creative. Both sides of the brain are needed for creativity. It is the neocortex that separates us from other mammals. This is the part of the brain that enables us to carry out extraordinary creative and complex tasks. People who are creative and fully engaged in what they are doing are said to be in a state of flow. Exercise, sleep, meditation and relaxation facilitate creativity.

People can be creative at home and at work. Creativity is needed at home to solve everyday problems. Creativity is needed at work to improve systems, procedures, and processes and to come up with new products and services. Japan has built its reputation on continuous improvement rather than invention.

Universities engage in creative pursuits through their research and inter-disciplinary collaboration. They tend to do pure research rather than development. The internet enables them to collaborate with and keep up to date on the research activities of other universities at home and abroad.

Western countries, because of their culture tend to be more creative than eastern countries. Western countries encourage initiative and creativity. On the other hand, eastern countries encourage conformity and respect for tradition.

The major cities of the world act as creative hubs. Vibrant cities are like magnets drawing creative people into their midst. Innovation is a prime driver of economic growth in cities and regions. Globalised cities such as New York and London trade in creativity, ideas and knowledge.

6
Who Is Creative?

Introduction

Most people are creative. Everybody is creative in one way or another. The average person underestimates how creative they are. Creativity can be expressed in our lifestyle, in the way we dress, in the way we speak, in how we interact with others and in the way we cook. However, certain people like artists, sculptors, designers, entertainers, film makers, musicians, comedians, management consultants, advertisers, journalists, writers, poets, landscapers, chefs, architects, engineers and scientists are especially so.

Creative people are often seen to be very independent minded, and because of their creativity, difficult to manage. Psychologists have identified the characteristics of creative people. These include playfulness, resilience, imagination, novel ideas, curiosity and energy. These traits are well worth developing.

There is a dark side to creativity. Many famous creative people show symptoms of extreme personality disorders such as schizoid, histrionic, narcissistic and manic depressive. The DISC Personal Profile System attempts to develop a creativity quotient (CQ) similar to the intelligence quotient (IQ). However, it has not earned the same wide scale acceptance as IQ tests. There are general thinking style preferences such as the inventive style, the implementing style and the evaluating style. Optimistic and confident people tend to be more creative. Men and women are equally creative.

Creativity lasts a lifetime despite the fact that some people consider themselves too old to be creative. Creativity is a highly desirable skill at any age even though it may vary over a person's lifespan. Scientists, artists, politicians, entertainers and writers can remain creative throughout their lives. The four creativity stages in later life are the re-evaluation phase, the liberation phase, the summing-up phase and the encore phase.

The diffusion of innovation curve tracks the creativity of consumers from a marketing perspective. Some people adopt innovations quickly while others adopt a wait and see approach. Education plays a critical role in creativity. Creative people need a store of knowledge to fall back on. Entrepreneurs need to be knowledgeable and creative if their business is to survive.

Traits of Creative People

Use the acronym **PRINCE** to recall the traits of creative people:

- *Playfulness.* Creative people are extroverted and quite happy to play about with ideas that others might find childish. Creative people have a well-developed sense of humour. If you can think like a 7 year old you will be more creative. Children of this age are not self-conscious; enjoy the freedom to take risks, and the opportunity to explore alternatives. Being happy, rather than anxious, means that they are more likely to be creative and solve problems. During the 1930s and 1940s, laughter was a disciplinary offence at the Ford Motor Company's River Rouge plant in Michigan USA. Today, many organisations actually encourage their employees to enjoy their work with opportunities for fun, humour and playfulness. Management should embrace the flexibility of playfulness that allows creativity to flourish. Both Isaac Newton and Albert Einstein believed that having fun and being playful was an essential part of creativity. Richard Feynman (1918-1988) got the inspiration for his Nobel Prize in Physics while watching students playfully spinning plates in the cafeteria of Cornell University. He loved having fun while playing with problems in physics. He related the mathematics of this behaviour to an unsolved problem in quantum physics. Playfulness, laughter and humour can also be useful in providing new perspectives and stimulating ideas, while creating an enjoyable and relaxing atmosphere.

- *Resilient.* Creative people are driven by a need to create and are not put off by obstacles and setbacks. They are not too worried about ideas that do not seem to work, but just get on with the job of producing better ideas. They have an unrelenting work ethic enabling them to turn mistakes into successes and problems into opportunities. They know that creativity depends on difficulties, constraints, ambiguity and learning from failures. Physicist Ernst Mach wrote that many accidental events 'were seen hundreds of times by others before they were noticed.' Most 'overnight success' stories are made after many years' hard work and struggle with a seemingly insurmountable problem. Even before this you must have acquired the appropriate expertise through study and experience in the field. It takes at least 10 years of constant study and practise to become an expert in a subject. This is so irrespective of the discipline, whether music, art, science or sport. For example, Mozart, perhaps the most precocious and most prolific of composers, took ten years before he produced his first masterpiece in 1777. Therefore, you should always consider learning as a work in progress, rather than a chore or a fait accompli.

- Imagination. Creative people have vivid imaginations, above average intelligence and a facility to come up with new ideas. It is not logic, but imagination that gives birth to new ideas. Imagination is like a muscle that strengthens with use. Expect to be creative and you are more likely to be so. Creative people have above average intelligence, are good at using imagination and fantasy, and are open to new experiences. They have the ability to visualise problems and come up with new ideas. Imagination gives you the ability to explore options and see situations from different perspectives. Imagination helps you explore the past and visualise the future. We use our imagination when we give directions, describe an event, tell a story, or bake a cake. We need imagination to design a house, paint a picture, organise a party, or write a book. When executives use their imagination it is called vision. The novelist uses imagination to create characters, locations, a plot and a storyline. Chemists imagine molecules interacting to anticipate and understand how chemicals will behave when combined. Inventors use their imaginations to come up with useful products to improve our lives.

- **N**ovel ideas. Creative people are capable of coming up with unusual ideas. It is this facility that makes them stand out from others. They are often non-conformists, and happy to stick with their viewpoints despite lack of popular support. They dislike routines. They are often difficult to get on with, and employers should bear this in mind when hiring creative people. They are reluctant to follow a consensus group view. They frequently appear to be preoccupied and waste time. They are chronically dissatisfied with the status quo. They are comfortable with change and have a tolerance for ambiguity. They often lack business acumen and are prepared to leave the development and exploitation of their ideas to others. They can be more interested in producing ideas, rather than exploiting them commercially, and consequently many who didn't bother to take out patents to protect their inventions finished up bankrupt. Dick Fosbury won the gold medal for the high jump for the USA at the 1968 Olympics in Mexico City. He is the creator of the novel and famous "Fosbury Flop," which is now the most popular high jumping technique.

- Curiosity. Curiosity is an internal motivator of exploratory behaviour, which leads to learning, or increased knowledge. Curiosity is a natural personality trait, stronger in some people than in others. Creative people have broad interests and specific interests, and are innately curious. Their broad interest motivates them to seek out various sources of novelty, challenge and information. Their specific interest motivates them to increase the depth of their specialist knowledge and experience. Creative people, whether they are artists, inventors, or scientists, share some common traits such as openness to experience. In addition, they like to question the purpose of everything and see things from a new perspective. They bombard others with "whys" and "why nots." They like to ask "what if?" Their need to question things may irritate others with a more practical bent of mind. James Watt invented the steam engine, and asked the question why? After noticing the power of steam to lift the lid off a kettle. Newton is said to have formulated the law of gravity, after being hit on the head by an apple falling from a tree. Curiosity about their discovery raised questions to be answered in their minds, and spurred them on to great achievements.

- Energy. Creative people have high energy levels with great staying power, and are driven by an innate need to produce creative work. They believe they must put in the effort if they are to be successful in whatever they undertake. Creative people create more ideas, come up with more possibilities, and generate more schemes. They make more attempts, make more mistakes than others, and endure more setbacks. They treat mistakes as experiments to learn from. They know that if they don't make mistakes they fail to learn, let alone do anything unusual or innovative.

> "Creativity comes from a conflict of ideas."
>
> Donatella Versace

The Dark Side of Creativity

Many famous creative people show symptoms of extreme personality disorders such as schizoid, histrionic, narcissistic and manic depressive. These traits seemed to help rather than hinder their creativity.

- A person with schizoid personality disorder is marked by withdrawal and an inability to form close relationships. People with this personality disorder tend to be detached, aloof, and appear to be cold, detached and disinterested. They are obsessive about their work and neglect interpersonal relationships. They spent long hours in solitude working on their complex, abstract problems. Well-known examples were Albert Einstein, Isaac Newton and Nikola Tesla. Einstein spent long hours thinking about his proposed theories, and preferred this approach to physical experimentation. During these long periods of time he wasn't interested in social discourse. Like Einstein, Newton was a loner and found it difficult to relate to other people. He never married and spent his life in conflict with the famous scientific personalities of the day. Similarly, Tesla never married because he believed it would interfere with his work. He preferred to work long hours in his laboratory.

- Histrionic relates to acting. People who are histrionic are like actors because they love to be the centre of attention. They are extroverted, exhibitionistic, dramatic and imaginative. Their constant need for attention and to be in the limelight encourages them to be flamboyant and creative. They love to dress in a colourful, showy, outrageous fashion to attract attention. They often exploit sexual themes to further their careers. Actors, singers and dancers would be good examples. People with histrionic personality disorder tend to be creative and include Liberace, David Bowie, Elton John and Madonna. One of the most famous histrionic performers in the world was Liberace. He was an accomplished pianist, who gave concerts dressed in flamboyant colourful costumes with ornate pianos and candelabra. His over-the-top showmanship won him the fame and attention that he craved for. David Bowie is a rock star, song writer and actor. Bowie dressed in outrageous costumes, and was known as a musical chameleon because of his ever-changing styles and colourful appearance. Elton John is a singer, pianist and composer. He was known for dressing in fabulous, over-the-top costumes, and outsized glasses for his elaborate staged concerts. Because he wasn't handsome or a sex symbol like David Bowie, he decided he was going to attract attention, and compel people to look at him. Madonna is an exhibitionist and uses sexual innuendo in her performances to further her career.

- Narcissistic people are obsessed with themselves and particularly with their looks. The word narcissistic is related to the Greek myth of Narcissus. He was a boy known for his good looks who fell in love with his own reflection in a pool. He wasted away, too fascinated with his own image to look after himself. People with narcissistic personality disorder like to manipulate and exploit others for their own ends. They use others ruthlessly and selfishly to meet their ambitious goals. They are independent, self-sufficient, have a superiority complex and be imaginative. They tend to be arrogant and hold deep secret feelings of contempt for others. Narcissists are not only found in the entertainment world but politics attract them as well. Napoleon Bonaparte, Adolph Hitler and Joseph Stalin are good examples from the political world. Napoleon was preoccupied with power, prestige, vanity and grandiose thinking. Napoleonic Complex is named after the French Emperor, who overcompensated for his small stature by his overweening ambition to become Emperor of France. Like Napoleon, Hitler was obsessive, self-centred, preoccupied with power, prestige and grandiose thinking. Picasso is a good example from the artistic world. Picasso wrecked several lives that he came in contact with - more than one of his closest companions committed suicide. Stalin was so obsessed with hanging onto power that anyone who disagreed with him was jailed. When he thought that Leon Trotsky was a threat he sent his henchmen to Mexico to kill him.

- Manic depressive. They suffer from a disorder characterised by alternating extreme mood swings of mania and depression. Many creative people have suffered from manic depression. When they are manic they become energetic, ruthless and self-obsessed. In this phase they tend to be full of energy and highly creative. When they are depressed they become despondent, listless and dependent. Michelangelo, Edgar Allen Poe, Abraham Lincoln, Winston Churchill and Ludwig Von Beethoven are examples. Michelangelo was a manic-depressive for most of his adult life. He was known to binge drink for weeks on end. Edgar Allen Poe suffered from depression and attempted suicide during his short lifetime. Abraham Lincoln suffered from depression most of his life. One of his friends said he was the most depressed person he ever met. Like Lincoln, Churchill suffered from manic depression all of his life. He complained to his friends that he suffered from the "black dog of depression." When he was in his mild manic phases he was personable, but his moods could change quickly and unpredictably. However, his periods of high mania were highly creative and productive. He would stay up all night, eventually producing 43 books in addition to his political career. Beethoven suffered from manic depression most of his life. When he was on a high he could compose numerous works all at the same time. It was during his low periods that many of his most famous works were produced. It was also during one of these low periods that he contemplated suicide.

The DISC Personal Profile System

There have been numerous attempts to develop a Creativity Quotient (CQ) similar to the Intelligence Quotient (IQ), but none have been scientifically proven. The DISC system is one of the most popular. DISC is based on the theory of human behaviour by psychologist William Marston and was developed into an assessment tool by industrial psychologist Walter Clarke in 1940. His theory claimed that people express their emotions using four behaviour types called **D**ominance, **I**nfluence, **S**teadiness and **C**onscientiousness. Hence the acronym DISC. He argued that these behavioural types came from peoples' sense of self and their interaction with the environment.

The distributors of this creativity profile maintain it is the oldest, most validated personal assessment measure, and has been used by more than 50 million people. It enables people to understand their personality traits in relation to leadership, teamwork, communication and creativity. The behaviours reflect how people tend to react to their environment, either actively or passively, depending on the individuals perception of their power.

People with dominance traits are confident, direct, outspoken and like to solve problems and accomplish results. They see the big picture and like to accept challenges. They can be blunt as they like to get straight to the point. People with influence traits are open, friendly, outgoing and like to influence and persuade others. Hence, they tend to be good at interpersonal relationships. They are optimistic, enthusiastic and like to collaborate with others. People with steadiness traits are patient, consistent, sincere, cooperative and dependable. They like to keep the peace and maintain the status quo. They are humble, calm and supportive and don't like to be rushed. People with conscientious traits are competent and like accuracy and quality. They are independent, organised, methodical, and logical and like to pay attention to detail. They tend to be perfectionists.

Dominance and influence traits are active in those people who see themselves as more powerful than their environment. They are therefore, more likely to be creative and work actively to shape and change it. These people are comfortable with change and may work effectively to implement change. People strong in steadiness and conscientiousness see the environment as something stronger than themselves. They are therefore, more likely to be uncreative and passive - adapting and preserving the environment.

People with dominance and conscientiousness traits tend to see the environment as unfavourable, and consequently are task oriented, and ignore rather than confront people issues. On the other hand, people high in influence and steadiness see the environment as favourable and prioritise people issues ahead of tasks.

> "Every child is an artist; the problem is staying an artist when you grow up."
>
> Pablo Picasso

Thinking Styles Preferences

People have a characteristic style, or way of doing things. There are three such styles; inventing, implementing and evaluating.

- Some like to do things their own way. This is known as the inventing style.
- Some like to follow established procedures. This is known as the implementing style. They prefer to follow the procedures of others rather than inventing their own.
- Other people prefer to sit back and watch others do things while analysing and criticising their efforts. These have an evaluating style. They typically act as critics, judges or evaluators, rather than doing it themselves.

We all possess all styles to one degree or another. What differentiates one person from another is the preference they have for exercising one particular style.

To be creative, a person must prefer the inventing style and so like thinking up novel or unusual ways of doing things. We all have the ability to be creative, but some of us choose not to exercise it or develop it. If we choose not to practise our creativity we will not become good at it. If a person habitually criticises the ideas of others, without practising generating and developing his own ideas, his analytical ability will become sharp and precise, but his inventing ability will become dull from lack of use.

Psychometric tests can be used by Human Relations specialists to identify the people likely to have personality traits facilitating creativity. These tests purport to measure originality (novel ideas), fluency (number of ideas) and flexibility (different perspectives). These tests, though popular, have questionable scientific validity. The difficulties of validating these tests are many and include the following:

- There is still no agreed standardised definition of creativity.
- The traits of creativity differ from one test to another.
- Motivation and culture are almost impossible to measure.
- It is impossible to test and control behaviour in laboratory like conditions, so that similar results could be reproduced elsewhere.
- Creativity differs from one person to another.

Optimism and creativity
Optimistic and confident people think more positively, flexibly and creatively. With an optimistic attitude you have a belief that things will work out well, despite adverse circumstances, and that all you have to do is to figure out how. This attitude helps you to come up with innovative solutions, while pessimism may have the opposite effect. Inventors tend to be more confident and optimistic than the general population. They spend more time on their projects, even after receiving negative feedback that it is time to quit.

There is the widespread idea that fear and sadness is a spur to creativity. On the contrary, creativity is positively associated with joy, love and happiness, and negatively associated with anger, fear and anxiety. People are happiest when they come up with a creative idea, but they are more likely to do so if they experience happiness beforehand.

Empowered people, or people with control over their lives, are more likely to be creative than people who believe they cannot influence the circumstances under which they live. Such people believe their lives are controlled by others, and therefore have little incentive to be creative, or learn new things.

Even though some people think that they are far more creative when working under time constraints, the opposite, in fact, is true. Creativity requires an incubation period as previously discussed; people need time to soak in a problem, and let the ideas emerge. Time pressures stifle creativity, because people haven't the time to deeply engage with and think about the problem. John Cleese, the actor and comedian, talks about how beneficial it can be to "sleep on a problem." He recalls observing a dramatic change in his approach to a creative problem, when he decided to leave it aside and concentrate on other things. This approach eventually resulted in a solution to his problem. Engaging our conscious minds on other tasks, like sleeping, walking, driving or taking a shower, allows our subconscious to work on the problem using the information we've gathered to-date.

However, people may become more innovative with the challenge of recessionary times, more competition, tighter budgets, and deadlines. When your back is to the wall you are often forced to come up with more effective, efficient, smarter and less costly ways of living. The pressures and demands of wartime often give rise to an increase in useful inventions and ideas for everyday living and survival.

> "If you would be more creative, stay in part a child with the creativity and invention that characterises children before they are deformed by adult society."
>
> Jean Piaget

Gender and Creativity

There is no doubt that men and women have the capacity to be equally creative. Similarly, few would contest the assertion that men and women have equal brainpower or intelligence. Despite this it is a fact that most significant inventions have been made by men. Patents submitted by men far exceed those submitted by women. Since it was established the Nobel Prize has been awarded 807 times to men and only 44 times to women.

Fifteen women have won the Nobel Prize for Peace, twelve have won it in Literature, ten have won it in Physiology or Medicine, and four have won it in Chemistry, two in Physics and one in Economic Science. In other areas women are also scarce on the ground. Consider professions like visual artists, top class chefs, musicians, mathematicians, composers, artists, designers, sculptors, film directors, playwrights, business directors and architects. What is the reason for this?

There are in fact numerous reasons. Over thousands of years women have been brainwashed, dominated, suppressed, stereotyped and discriminated against by men and by society generally. For many years the education of women was actively discouraged, and they were seen as the property of men. It was not until the turn of the last century that women were allowed to vote. In some Muslim countries this situation has not changed with violence being used against women who dare venture outside their culturally expected roles. The role of women in society was confined to being a good wife, mother and nurturer of children.

This meant that their husbands had the time to pursue and develop their own creative interests from a supported, secure and safe home base, at the expense of women. Because of their domestic workload women had little time or incentive to pursue or develop any creative interests or inclinations of their own. They would have little energy left after fulfilling their household duties of caring for two or more children, doing housework, laundry, cleaning and looking after the needs of a husband. It seems women's creativity is channelled elsewhere as it takes a lot of creativity to rear children, prepare meals, decorate a home, wash clothes and run a household successfully.

Creative work requires long periods of concentrated and dedicated effort and time. This opportunity is not available to women during their peak work and childbearing years, which also coincides with their most creative period of life. Take the case of Marie Mileva Einstein, Albert's first wife. She was a gifted mathematician in her own right. She ultimately sacrificed her own promising career for her husband's. After marrying and having children her life changed drastically. She spent all day cleaning, cooking and caring for the children. During the evening she would proofread her husband's work and do mathematical calculations to help him.

It is only in relatively recent times that women have been actively encouraged to pursue careers outside of the home in areas like business, law, politics, science and medicine. Even today despite the rise of feminism and much equality legislation, the position of women hasn't changed as much as they would like. They still only hold a small percentage of significant jobs in business, academia, politics and science. The number of women on boards of directors is still much too few. The number of female professors in relation to male professors is small. The same holds for science and politics.

A disproportionate amount of family responsibilities, household chores and childcare still falls on the woman even if she is pursuing a career. A study published in 2013 in the magazine *American Scientist* found that a woman's career in science compared favourably to a man's before they had children. However, the challenges of childcare and the demands of running a research lab are often seen as incompatible. The authors of the study found that women who plan to have children drop out of the academic research race at twice the rate of men. Balancing childcare and career pursuits is difficult in any profession especially if you are expected to carry a disproportionate share of the childcare burden.

Older people have some advantages when it comes to innovation. They have a greater capacity for empathy because empathy is improved and refined as we age. Empathy is critical in design, as people need to understand the needs of the people they are designing for. Generally, older people can decipher patterns more easily, and see the big picture. They have more knowledge and experience, so that they have a rich and greater resource to draw on when coming up with ideas and making decisions. Combining knowledge is what creativity is all about.

Older people are unlikely to be distracted by the fads and temptations of modern life that often trap the young. As we age we are better able to anticipate problems, and reason things out than when we were young and inexperienced. Older people tend to be more mindful and live more in the present, because they are aware that their future is finite. This sense of urgency to get things done contributes to creativity. They have a greater self-knowledge and are more aware of their environment leading to new useful ideas. They have the tenacity, willpower, and persistence needed for creative tasks needing long-term commitment. They often bring better powers of concentration, interest and motivation, to bear on a task.

Many younger people have short attention spans, and are preoccupied with status and personal advancement rather than self-fulfilment. They sometimes don't know what has been tried before, and thus have a tendency to reinvent the wheel. Those who don't know history are prone to repeat it.

Family influences
Parental values are passed on to children. Males and females within families are often treated differently and they absorb the cultural expectations of their roles from parents from an early age. This is often traditionally expressed in different colour schemes when decorating a girl's and a boy's room – pink for a girl and blue for a boy. It is reinforced by the way parents dress their female and male children. Gender appropriate toys are bought for girls and boys – dolls and prams for girls and cars and Meccano for boys. Advanced games and toys and challenging educational experiences are more likely to be provided for boys.

Girls are prepared for a nurturing role while boys are taught to be more competitive and aggressive. Generally girls are not supported or encouraged to pursue creative occupations unlike boys, and they often lack appropriate role models and mentors to do so. In school, girls are often steered away from science based careers even if they excel at maths. Dance, drama, art and music is more often thought to be appropriate for girls, while getting good grades in science and mathematics are expectations for boys. Professions like nursing and teaching are considered more appropriate for girls, while boys are encouraged to be engineers and scientists.

Parents' expectations for female children are for them to get an appropriate education, become financially secure, get married and have children. Girls are often taught to be more modest, mannerly, polite, ladylike and less assertive than their brothers. Girls learn early on to be modest about their achievements and intelligence, and to downplay it in relation to their male friends, to win the acceptance of attractive males, while at the same time not upsetting their male egos. They thus grow up to be less competitive, and to be more concerned with social relationships and friendships than individual achievement and status. This means they are reared to be more interested in people than things.

These imbued behaviours passed on to girls are the opposite of what is necessary to be creative - the ability to challenge convention, question authority, take risks, pursue goals with passion and determination, and speak out for change. On the other hand, boys are encouraged, usually by their fathers, to be more mechanically minded and find out how things work. They also expect their boys to be more physically active, and take part in competitive sport such as football and rugby. This gives boys a valuable head start in the physical manipulation of objects – a skill necessary for science and engineering class projects. Being part of teams also helps boys to develop valuable networking skills from an early age. In later life they use these networks and contacts to help further their careers. Girls don't seem to do so to the same extent.

Famous Creative People

People have been creative from the beginning of human history. We have built on the shoulders of giants to get to our present state of sophisticated civilisation and comfortable lifestyles. Evolution is just as applicable to science as it is to biology. Scientific discoveries are built on previous scientific breakthroughs. Every inventor is a product of his time, his culture, education and environment.

It is unlikely that the creativity of Mozart, Einstein, or Picasso would have happened if they were born in a different culture or time. Inventions cannot happen without the materials, technology, intellectual atmosphere, sociological and psychological conditions necessary for them to occur have appeared. They must also fulfil a need or purpose. The middle classes produced a disproportionate number of inventors because they had the education, wealth and time to devote to their work.

Creation is a historical incremental process. Leonardo da Vinci conceptualised tanks and helicopters but the technology was not there to produce them. Similarly Charles Babbage designed a computer 100 years before the electronic one, but the technology was not there to support it. These inventors were visionaries who foresaw what the world would eventually become.

I have taken a few inspirational figures from history and from more modern times. These demonstrate the significant effect people can have on our lives, either working alone, or in teams. We can model our behaviour on these people and learn from their achievements. Be inspired by their enthusiasm, great powers of observation, concentration, curiosity and hard work.

Historical creative figures

Many discoveries were made by people, obsessed by and totally immersed in their subjects, after much patient, research and experimentation over a long period of time. Isaac Newton, when asked about how he discovered the law of gravity, said he thought of it all the time. It seems if you are not actively looking for new discoveries, and clued in for relevancy, you will overlook them when they happen. Many people saw the apple fall but none except Newton understood its significance. By the way, the story about the apple is probably apocryphal. It also plays down the 20 years of hard work and sacrifice that Newton spent thinking about and developing his theory of gravity.

The development of the theory of evolution offers a good lesson in creative problem solving in science. The idea that all animal species were related had been around for many years. However, the mechanism of evolution, through natural selection of the survival of the fittest, went unnoticed.

Both Charles Darwin and naturalist Alfred Wallace coincidently arrived at the solution to the evolution puzzle by the same route and around the same time. Each had stepped back from the immediate problem, and noticed how relevant the ideas of Thomas Malthus were to the evolution puzzle. He had described the struggle for existence of increasing populations and reducing food supplies. This was the eureka moment and the analogy that Darwin and Wallace needed to solve the conundrum of evolution.

Creative geniuses such as Benjamin Franklin, Nikola Tesla, and Leonardo da Vinci did not simply create great things, they created things of value, highly desired and useful to people. Franklin invented bifocal glasses, Tesla invented the alternating current and the electric motor that made the generation, transmission and distribution of electricity possible and revolutionised our lives. Leonardo da Vinci painted the Mona Lisa. All of these things have enriched and have had a great impact on our lives.

Modern inventors

Dean Kamen is best known as the inventor of the Segway – the two wheeled human transporter which has been taken up by police services throughout the world – but he's far from a one hit wonder. The US entrepreneur has created many inventions, from an all-terrain wheelchair, to a water purification system for Third World villages. His obsession with innovation came gradually. He wasn't inventive as a child, but he did have one standard trait: an insatiable curiosity about the natural world. He derived great pleasure in finding unexpected uses for existing technology, such as making tiny portable pumps for diabetics.

He thinks that the public have the mistaken perception that inventors have great ideas, get the parts, and make the product. However, he points out the process of inventing is not like that – it's not a linear, straightforward process. You have to be willing to adapt your ideas quickly, no matter how passionate you are about them, and just keep working patiently away until you have a worthwhile product.

Esther Takeuchi is an engineer at the State University of New York, who has turned her talent for figuring out how things work into a very successful career. She holds over 120 patents – more than any other woman alive – and has received many awards for her work. She developed the Lilliputian battery that powers implantable cardiac defibrillators, a device that has improved the lives of thousands of heart patients. Perfecting her most famous invention took many years of hard work. She doesn't discount the importance of split-second inspiration, but emphasises that innovators need to have an extensive background of knowledge before they arrived at the eureka moment. She highlights the importance of spending sufficient time exploring and thinking about the problem, and reading extensively around it. Sometimes she sets the problem aside, and finds that she arrives at the solution in the most unexpected manner, often when doing something else.

Tim Berners-Lee, who was born in England in 1955, is the inventor of the World Wide Web which came into existence in 1989. It has revolutionised information and communications technology with an impact on the world as great as Gutenberg's printing press. The World Wide Web is quite distinct from the internet. The internet is the physical infrastructure through which data can be transmitted. On the other hand, the World Wide Web was the first means through which the world gained access to and the ability to share information across the internet. These days you can do anything on the web, from buying a car, to researching an essay, to listening to the TV or radio, to getting a weather report, among thousands of other things. Thirty years ago this was impossible.

> "Creativity involves breaking out of established patterns in order to look at things in a different way."
>
> Edward de Bono

Creativity over the Lifespan

Creativity is an ability that develops over the course of the human life span, despite the fact that some people might consider themselves too old to be creative. It is true that certain abilities decline with age. Fluid intelligence, which involves working memory, computational speed and the ability to hold numerous ideas in the mind at the same time, does deteriorate with age. This type of intelligence is innate and is little affected by learning. Its various components peak early – in a person's teens, twenties or thirties. Later decades show some deterioration in these skills, and after 70 years of age, the decline may be severe in some people. In addition, with age your reflexes slow down and your hearing, eyesight and energy levels decline.

The second type of intelligence is known as crystallised intelligence. It is more dependent on learning than innate skills. It involves making judgements, seeing similarities and differences between things, using deduction and logical reasoning. These abilities depend more on reflection than quick reaction. Thus they usually improve with the passage of time, at least up to the age of sixty and sometimes beyond. Creative people depend more on crystallised intelligence.

So age is not a barrier to creativity provided you keep healthy and reasonably fit. We are hardwired for creativity, and so can exploit our creativity from cradle to grave. Creativity is a state of mind rather than a number indicating age. You don't want to come to the end of your years and regret not having done something you always wanted to do. Many famous people did not reach the heights of their creativity until they were past middle or indeed into old age. They spent their lives continually reinventing themselves with new challenges and new opportunities. Their mental prowess rises above their physical limitations which they adapt into their style.

The old model of the aging brain was negative. It was believed that all the neurons of the brain were in place by the age of two. From that age on it was thought to be all downhill, neurons dying off at an alarming rate particularly in middle and old age. Once lost, it was believed these neurons were irreplaceable and gone for ever. However, in the past decade a new model of the aging brain has now gained acceptance.

The word "plasticity" currently characterises our latest understanding of the human brain. The brain is flexible well into old age. Even people after suffering strokes can be trained, so that part of their brain can take over and compensate for the functions that have been damaged. In fact, if you keep your brain challenged, the number of dendrites, or connections between brain cells grow, and new contact points called synapses increase. This means that your mental capacity improves. This phenomenon is known as "neurogenesis."

Research has found that dendrites grow to their greatest length in humans from their early 50s to their late 70s. Creativity helps neurons in the brain to add insulating fat layers, in a process called myelination helping the brain to run smoothly. Previously, it was thought this only happened in our 20s – hence the reason why some scientists and mathematicians peaked at this time. However, recent research suggests this process may continue into our 50s and even 60s provided we continue to engage in creative activities. In any event, even if it is true that myelination is less efficient as we grow older, connectivity in the brain may loosen up associations allowing ideas to move more freely, and help combine familiar information in an unusual way. This means that older people may generate more ideas rather than just have one great idea – the difference between the great inventor who comes up with a once-off amazing invention, and the jazz musician who improvises all the time, or the artist who improves incrementally over a lifetime.

There is no better way to keep your brain challenged than by continually exercising your powers of creativity. Become a lifelong learner, be willing to do new things, develop strong social networks, observe what is going on in the world, and don't be afraid to move out of your comfort zone. As you get older take up a new hobby, travel to new places, develop a new interest, and learn to play a musical instrument, challenge yourself with word games and crossword puzzles, and seek out unique experiences. Change newspapers occasionally as reading the same newspapers will not challenge your views. Hobbies can provide a source of information, and analogies not generally available to others, which can be applied in your work and used profitably in creative problem solving.

Challenge your assumptions, become comfortable with ambiguity, and be prepared to take calculated risks, listen to different points of view, and develop your ability to accept differences. There is even evidence that creativity has an anti-aging effect on the mind and body. Dr Gene Cohen in a study sponsored by the US National Endowment for the Arts found that those engaged in painting, jewellery making, or singing in a choir had better overall physical health, made fewer visits to the doctor, used less medication, and had less medical problems than a control group.

Examples of Lifespan creativity
The following are examples of lifespan creativity in science, art, politics, entertainment and writing.

Science
Creativity is a highly desirable skill at any age even though it may vary over the aging process. Some research maintains that creativity can be divided into two types: conceptual and experimental.

- Conceptual thinkers like Einstein come up with their best ideas when young but often remain productive into old age.
- Experimental thinkers often peak when relatively old. Their ideas are incremental, often improvements on existing or previous ideas. They are uncertain about their goals, and thus proceed more gradually and cautiously than their conceptual counterparts. These can take decades, so that their best work comes late in life.

Alfred Hitchcock directed his best and most creative films between the ages of 54 and 61. Edison, one of the most prolific inventors of all time built on the ideas of others and continued productively right into old age. Although Edison is credited with the invention of the electric light bulb, it was actually Joseph Swan who invented it. However, his refinement of the light bulb ushered in the age of electricity. In fact, most of his inventions were incremental improvements of existing ones. He had an amazing capacity to make things practical and commercially viable and useful, so that they could be mass produced. Thus he created an electricity distribution system in New York for those who wished to use his electric light bulb.

The opposite case can also be made. It is known that the more education and life experiences novelists and philosophers have the greater their capacity to write. It is also known that the best novelists are the most avid readers. Similarly, scientists can peak at any age, and many don't make their major impact until quite mature. However, scientists are often quite young when they make radical conceptual breakthroughs. Others take longer improving incrementally with experience, whilst learning from mistakes.

Einstein believed if you didn't do any major work by 30, you wouldn't do any. This is no longer accepted. Take for example the number of PhD holders who are advanced in years when they eventually win the coveted Nobel Prize.

Many composers change their musical styles as they mature and often peak in old age. Similarly, many artists change their artistic style as they mature, and often peak in middle or old age.

Frank Lloyd Wright, the renowned architect, designed the Guggenheim Museum in New York City at 76. Benjamin Franklin invented bifocal lens at the age of 78. Graham Bell perfected his telephone at 58, and was over 70 when he solved the problem of stabilising aircraft balance. John Ericsson designed and built the revolutionary new warship USS Monitor in 1862. It changed the course of the American Civil War.

Artists

Politicians, artists, scientists, entertainers, writers, chief executives, prime ministers, judges, diplomats and medical specialists are all considered very young at 50, and are often considered only in their creative prime when well into their 60s and 70s. In the artistic field, Picasso produced some of his best work during the later stages of his life, and reinvented the conventions of painting. Claude Monet, the French impressionist, painted well into his 80s, and created masterpieces in the last decade of his life. He continued painting up to the final months of his life, and stopped when he was physically unable to do so.

Cezanne, a contemporary of Monet, produced his best work in his 60s. They both believed in continuous improvement through practise of their trade. Michelangelo was appointed architect of St. Peter's in Rome when he was 72. Grandma Moses didn't start painting until the age of 76 after arthritis forced her to give up embroidery. She had no formal art training, and yet when she died at 101 her paintings were featured in many prominent museums throughout the world.

A striking example of someone who became more creative as they advanced into old age is the sculptor Louise Bourgeois. She is regarded as one of the greatest female artists of the 20th century. Her most renowned work was produced in the first half of her 80s. Some art historians judge that the most important work of her career was made in her ninth decade. It is no surprise that Bourgeois believes that artists improve with age. She said: "I am a long-distance runner. It takes me years and years and years to produce what I do."

In 1909 Monet similarly declared that he became better with the passage of time: "I have half a century of experience, and soon I shall have passed my sixty-ninth year, but my sensitivity, far from diminishing, has been sharpened with age, which holds no fears for me as long as unbroken communication with the outside world continues to fuel my curiosity, so long as my hand remains a ready and faithful interpreter of my perception." Research has found that artists who are at their most creative late in life are invariably experimental innovators. They believe that they constantly learn through experience and experimentation, and change their style gradually over the years.

Politicians
Nelson Mandela, de Gaulle, Churchill and Regan are some of the politicians that made it late in life. Nelson Mandela, after spending 26 years in prison, for his opposition to the apartheid policies of South Africa, was elected deputy president of the African National Congress at the age of 72. He was almost 74 when he was elected President of South Africa. Charles de Gaulle was in his 70s when he was president of France.

Winston Churchill was in his late 70s when he became Prime Minister of Great Britain in 1951. He was also a great writer and won the Nobel Prize for literature in 1953. He played a significant role in the defeat of Germany in World War 11. Similarly, George C Marshall became Chief of Staff of the US Army at 59. He is credited with bringing about the victory over the Nazis and then spearheading the Marshall Plan. Bernard Baruch became the US representative on the Atomic Energy Commission of the UN at 76, and formulated the Baruch Proposals for international control of atomic energy.

Ronald Reagan became the oldest President of the USA, when he was elected the 40th President of the USA. He served two terms from 1981 to 1989 retiring in his late 70s. During a presidential debate he whimsically said that he would not hold his opponent's youth against him. Even when politicians retire they often find scope for their considerable creativity such as negotiation talents, diplomacy skills and political savvy. These skills are highly reliant on creativity and experience. For example, many make their names as peace negotiators in trouble spots around the world such as Northern Ireland, Eastern Europe and the Middle East.

Many of the rest of us thrive in our retirement years accomplishing things we could only previously dream about, but hadn't the time to devote to. We then push ourselves to do things we never thought possible. Some of us even turn hobbies such as photography into worthwhile pursuits when we retire, discovering dormant abilities that we never knew we had.

Justice Oliver Wendell Holmes began studying Greek at 92, because he hadn't the time to take it up previously. He had resigned from the US Supreme Court due to ill health in 1932 at the age of 90. Except in circumstances of poor health or dementia evidence suggests there is little or no decline in creativity and intellectual ability until advanced old age. This is provided you keep on challenging yourself through lifelong learning and novel experiences.

While some old people become more conservative as they get older, others become more liberal and radical than they were in their middle years, often supporting radical causes. A case in point would be the former British Labour Minister and MP – Tony Benn. If anything he became more radical and more committed to his principles of social justice as he matured and progressed into old age. Having rid themselves of the responsibilities of middle age they feel a sense of liberation.

Entertainers

In the entertainment business, Frank Sinatra, Tony Bennett, Andy Williams, Perry Como and Tom Jones all performed successfully until very late in life. As they got older they reinvented themselves, and adapted their styles and interpretations of songs to the demands of the modern audience. Frank Sinatra enchanted millions with new material right up to his death at the age of 82. Andy Williams of TV and recording fame continued to play live into his 80s. During a 2007 tour of the UK he maintained that performing kept him well. He died aged 84 in 2011. Tony Bennett's career continued into his 80s. His most recent recording was made in 2012.

Over a fifty year span Perry Como had a very successful recording and TV career. He died at the age of 88 and performed right into his 80s. Tom Jones is still going strong in his 70s and is as popular as ever. He still appears on many TV shows and gives live performances. George Burns, the famous US comedian, was active right into his 90s. He didn't believe in retirement. He wrote two autobiographical books when he was 92. He died when he reached 100. In classical music Verdi, a composer of tragic, sombre romantic operas, wrote Falstaff as his last opera when he was nearly 80. In education, it is not uncommon for people in their 50s, 60s and 70s to complete third-level and postgraduate qualifications.

We now know as far as creativity is concerned that people peak at different ages. Some peak when quite young while others bloom late in life. For example poets, chess players, computer experts, fashion designers, scientists and mathematicians peak early in their careers while philosophers, historians, lawyers, psychologists, and novelists peak later. Orson Welles was only 26 when he made *Citizen Kane*. The film was released in 1941 and is considered the best movie of all time. When asked at 45 how he did it, he replied "Ignorance, ignorance, sheer ignorance – you know there's no confidence to equal it." This suggests that our originality and creativity is often held back by experience and others people's ideas.

Writers

The following writers demonstrate that there is no time limit on creativity. Some writers even claim that their creativity can be spurred on by their keen sense of mortality. They realise just how short life is. They want to leave a legacy in the form of published work. Valerie Trueblood, who did not publish her novel *Seven Loves* and two short story collections until in her 60s, maintains age can bring greater urgency to the creative process.

Peter Mark Roget got the first edition of his famous Thesaurus published when he was 73, and he oversaw subsequent editions until he died at 90. He had managed to produce the most enduring and iconic reference book in his retirement years. Noah Webster wrote his famous and monumental dictionary at 70. Canadian short story writer, Alice Munro won the Nobel Prize for literature at 82 after a prodigious lifetime of writing. She had won the Booker Prize at 78. She said that she intends to retire in June 2013, although she has recently hinted she may go on for another while.

Goethe finished writing Faust at 82 years of age. George Bernard Shaw was still active in his 70s. Adam Smith remains a towering figure in the history of economics. He was 53 years old when The Wealth of Nations was published, which is the age that many people are now contemplating early retirement. Mary Wesley, a bestselling author, was 70 when her first book was published. She went on to write a further nine novels and regularly appeared in the bestseller lists.

Elizabeth Jolley had her first novel published at the age of 57. In one year alone she got 39 rejection slips. Despite this she went on to have 15 novels and four short story collections published to much acclaim. Lorna Page got her first book titled *A Dangerous Weakness* published when she was 93. Millard Kaufman's first novel *Bowl of Cherries* was published in 2007 when Kaufman was 90 years of age. He was 86 when he began working on the novel.

Doris Lessing, the Nobel Prize winner, who died at the age of 94 in 2013, was prolific most of her life. Her books covered a broad range of themes including racism, colonialism, politics, feminism and communism. When she won the Noble Prize in literature at 88 years of age, she was the oldest author, and the 11th woman to win the Nobel Prize in literature.

Learning from the example of others

Peter Drucker (1909-2005) was a quintessential renaissance man. He was a writer, professor, management consultant and self-described "social ecologist." He was hailed by Business Week as "the man who invented management." He wrote articles for business management magazines right into his 90s. He wrote 39 books and even wrote a novel. He invented the term "knowledge management" and was a proponent of lifelong learning. He emphasised the important role knowledge would play in the future, as a basic resources for problem solving, decision making and innovation. During his life he set himself the task of learning the rudiments of a new area or discipline every three years, mainly in the arts, humanities and the social sciences. He did this for 60 years or more and thus built up an extraordinary store of knowledge. He used this knowledge to inform his writings in management.

As a young man Drucker was inspired by Verdi who wrote the opera Falstaff at the age of 80. Verdi is known to have remarked that despite his best efforts, perfection had always eluded him as a musician, and he therefore felt obligated to make another try. Verdi's work ethic and striving for perfection became Drucker's ideal and modus operandi. Drucker said:"I then resolved that if I ever reached an advanced age, I would not give up, but would keep on. In the meantime, I would strive for perfection even though, as I well knew, it would surely, always elude me." He wrote business articles up to the end, even though old age and poor health diminished his prodigious energy. He believed that your first career is but a preparation for creativity in old age. When asked by his students for the source of his original ideas, his answer was extremely modest. He retorted that all he had done was to take ideas from the universe around him and adapt them to solve business problems.

We should be prepared to learn from the examples above of artists, writers, politicians and scientists that we can remain creative all through our lives and into ripe old age. We should strive to develop our talents, and pursue perfection as we age wherever possible. Famous creative people were passionate about what they did, developed their talents, worked hard and were persistent in the face of obstacles. Just like the rest of us they had their ups and downs going through life. Some suffered from bad health, relationship difficulties, ridicule and opposition to their ideas, past failures and other challenges that could have derailed them, but didn't. Instead they reflected on them, learned from them and found renewed sources of energy to carry on.

> "Grow old along with me
>   The best is yet to come,
>   The last of life, for which the first was made."
>
>   Robert Browning

The four creativity stages in later life

Dr Gene Cohen in his book *The Creative Age*, after thirty years of research has classified four creativity stages that older people go through

1. ***Re-evaluation Phase****.* This happens when people are in their 40s and 50s. When people enter their 40s they think about how much time is left rather than how much time has passed. In some this triggers off a mid-life crisis. However, in a much larger group it triggers a constructive mid-life re-evaluation of life. It triggers off questions such as: Where have I been? Where am I? Where am I going? What am I going to do with the rest of my life? Some people may have regrets about how the first half of their life has panned out and are determined that the second half will be better and

more in tune with what they really want. So they decide to change careers or undertake new challenges before it's too late.

2. **Liberation Phase**. This stage is reached when people are in their 60s. At this stage people are not concerned with what others think of them. This gives them the permission to do things that they have never done. They may be financially secure with a pension, giving them the scope to pursue interests they had no time to do before. People in their 60s are more socially creative having acquired good interpersonal relationship, empathy, diplomacy, facilitation and negotiation skills. They are better at controlling their emotions, less prone to anger and come up with better solutions to conflict. That is why retired politicians are sent to trouble spots throughout the world to solve conflict problems. They have nothing to lose in doing what's right rather than what's expedient. Senator George Mitchell is admired for the major contribution he made to the peace process of Northern Ireland in 1998. When most other people of his age are thinking of retirement he selflessly devoted his time to bringing about the peace process. His considerable patience, tact and facilitation skills won the day.

3. **Summing-up Phase.** At this stage people are in their 70s, 80s or even beyond. People at this stage like to reflect back on their lives and tell their life story. They consider what they have achieved and gained in life, and want to give something back. They may do this through volunteering and philanthropy. They may also attend to unfinished business, or to what remains undone. This is why some people in advanced old age achieve creative success through art, music or writing.

4. **Encore Phase.** This is the end stage. George Abbott the American playwright, screenwriter and film

director is a good example of the encore phase. He was a vigorous man who remained active past his 100th birthday. His *New York Times* obituary read: "Mrs Abbott said a week and a half before his death at age 107 he was dictating revisions to the second act of *Pajama Game* with a revival in mind, in addition to working on a revival of *Damn Yankees*." At the age of 106, he walked down the aisle on the opening night of the Damn Yankees revival and got a standing ovation.

> "If you take all the experience and judgement of men over fifty out of the world, there wouldn't be enough left to run it."
> Henry Ford

Diffusion of Innovation Curve

This is a predictive tool used in marketing suggesting how fast different types of consumers adopt a new product. Some consumers adopt a product as soon as it comes on the market. These are the creative risk takers. Others are amongst the last to adopt a new product. The successful diffusion of an innovation within an organisation is a two-step process. First it is taken up by early adopters and opinion leaders and then subsequently adopted by a larger population. The model provides a useful tool for marketing managers when targeting likely buyers for their new products. Obviously the laggards should never be targeted initially for their new products. The new product adoption process can be modelled in the form of a bell-shaped diffusion curve. The diffusion curve shows that 2.5 per cent of people are innovators, 13.5 per cent are early adopters, 34 per cent are the early majority, 34 per cent are the late majority and 16 per cent are laggards.

In more detail these groups of people can be defined as follows:

- *Innovators.* These are well-informed risk-takers who are not afraid to try out a new unproven product. They either have a pressing need, or are rich enough not to worry too much if the product doesn't live up to expectations. They are likely to be knowledgeable and self-confident and may be people that others look up to. They are venturesome with the ability to apply complex technical knowledge. They act as gatekeepers to the flow of new products. The innovator plays a critical role in the diffusion process. They initiate new ideas by introducing innovation from outside into the organisation.

- *Early adopters.* These people do not buy until they get positive feedback from innovators. They will check out the product with the innovator. Early adopters tend to be educated and technically competent opinion leaders who are prepared to try out new ideas, but in a careful and studious way. They are respected by peers for their discrete use of products, and serve as role models for other people. They decrease uncertainty about the usefulness of a new product through their practical example by adopting it. Their faith in the product is then passed on to others implicitly or explicitly through social networking.

- *Early majority.* These are careful, thoughtful consumers who are cautious about new ideas, and tend to avoid risk. They adopt the product out of economic necessity, and as a result of peer pressure. They wait until the product has been proven by the early adopters. They rely on recommendations or endorsements from others who have experienced the product. Despite their caution they are prepared to accept change faster than the average consumer. The early majority are the largest category representing about one third of the total.

- *Late majority*. These are extremely sceptical and cautious consumers, who acquire a product only after it has been widely accepted and used successfully by others. Late majority buyers are more likely to welcome simplicity and reliability, rather than hi-tech gadgetry. Like the early majority the late majority represent about one third of the total, making them also a significant category of consumers. They are motivated to buy through necessity, by the volume of uptake already achieved and by the growing impact of peer pressure.
- *Laggards*. These consumers avoid change and do not trust new inventions. They are set in their ways and stick to the old ways of doing things. They desire to retain the status quo and live by tradition. Their financial resources tend to be limited. They may not adopt a new product until traditional alternatives are no longer available. Socially their friends are other laggards holding similar opinions on innovation. By the time they adopt an innovation it may have been overtaken by a new product already adopted by innovators.

"Creativity is contagious, pass it on."

Albert Einstein

Education and Creativity

Having an appropriate education provides a firm foundation for creativity. Knowledge is acquired through formal education. An individual must have knowledge of a specific field of study to engage in problem solving related to that field, and make a creative contribution to that domain. Some experts now maintain that a MA in fine arts is the new MBA for business.

A broad liberal arts education is suggested that includes literature, philosophy, and history, as well as technology and science. Through a liberal arts education people are trained to gain personal insight, and to challenge their assumptions by studying other cultures or disciplines for ideas and diverse perspectives. In addition, their powers of observation are enhanced. In business this helps people see the company in the context of its environment and the world. It helps people make sense of groups, societies, cultures and technologies and to see patterns and relationships between them. It provides them with a holistic view. In seeing the entire system they will be able to make unique connections that weren't made before. This is what creativity is all about.

Research in 2001 found the accuracy of diagnoses made by medical students in Yale University was improved after taking an art history course. The study concluded that the medical students became better diagnosticians because the art history class improved their observation skills. Art teachers tell their students that in order to draw they must see.

To be a good novelist you must be a keen observer of people. Inventors will tell you that to invent you must observe what is going on around you. Even in football the best players are those who observe, anticipate and react quickly to what is going on in the playing field. The importance of keen observation to enhance creativity has been known for a long time. In the Renaissance, artists such as Leonardo da Vinci relied heavily on observation of the natural world to see possibilities beyond themselves. Like in art, managers can improve their understanding of problems through better observation before searching for solutions.

Entrepreneurs

Innovation means coming up with practical products or services that have a good chance of succeeding in the marketplace. Innovation is a core responsibility for any business that wants to grow. Entrepreneurs are creative and innovative in that they exploit business opportunities for competitive advantage when they establish a new business.

This is despite the fact that most businesses fail, and only a tiny minority are successful. They would never undertake risky business projects, if they did not believe that their one is the one that is going to defy the odds, and be successful. They provide the basis for innovation and business growth, as well as meeting the needs of customers and investors.

They also create employment opportunities for others, while generating revenue through taxation for the government. This is why governments encourage entrepreneurship through mentoring and financial incentives, such as taxation allowances and grants. Optimism motivates them to work hard, while protecting them against the ever present risk of failure.

Entrepreneurs tend to be proactive rather than reactive and be risk-takers and innovators. Being proactive means making things happen through hard work, persistence and adaptability while at the same time solving problems in a non-conformist way. Risk-taking means committing money and other resources to your business in the firm belief that you will succeed, despite the fact that most start-ups actually fail.

Entrepreneurs should not be afraid to fail. In Silicon Valley, venture capitalists encourage entrepreneurs to "fail fast," "bounce back," and learn from their failures. Sometimes failure may not be your fault, but was caused by unpredictable market conditions. Failing fast means that you will make mistakes that you will learn from and never repeat again. The attitude is if you are not failing often you are not trying hard enough. Every failure gets you one step closer to success. You have to keep trying until you get it right. When true entrepreneurs fail, they identify and learn from their mistakes, dust themselves off and start all over again.

Entrepreneurs should build a prototype or a working model of their product, to determine whether their innovation will actually work and deliver what it promises. This provides them with an opportunity to make improvements before going into full production. You can test the product on a limited number of potential customers, to gather client feedback and refine the product before going into full implementation. If this process proves satisfactory, then you can implement your production plan with measurable targets and milestones. Working to a strict timeline and budget will help the entrepreneur achieve business objectives.

Smart entrepreneurs adjust their products and services in response to changing market demands and conditions. They are ahead of the competition, and are able to define the next key market changes. This means staying on top of market conditions by constantly gathering good information. Attending industry events, such as trade shows, exhibitions, conferences and seminars gives you first-hand knowledge on what your competitors are doing. You also gain valuable insights from experts about new developments that you can profitably apply to your business.

In addition, keep in touch with the research that is going on in universities and government establishments, and in innovation minded companies. This will help you to be aware of pertinent developments that you can adapt as appropriate to your business. Competition is now global, and customers are always seeking better products and solutions and superior value for money.

Entrepreneurs need to be confident and energetic and be knowledgeable about the business they are about to enter. They need to have a well-developed business plan and have social contacts, combined with an ability to spot and exploit opportunities. Entrepreneurs are motivated by the prospect of the success of their business. The entrepreneur must demonstrate strong leadership skills by shaping business strategy and motivating their employees through example.

His vision should inspire followers and be communicated across the organisation. Initiative, problem solving and creativity should be encouraged in employees to enhance intrinsic motivation. The entrepreneur can encourage creativity by facilitating a participative work environment, where creative individuals and groups prosper. High employee engagement has been linked with many business benefits, including revenue growth, cost containment and enhanced productivity. Creativity may be easier to encourage within a small firm where flexibility is a key factor in exploiting business opportunities.

> "I firmly believe that all human beings have access to extraordinary energies and powers. Judging from accounts of mystical experience, heightened creativity, or exceptional performance by athletes and artists, we harbour a greater life than we know."
>
> Jean Houston

Summary of Chapter 6

The traits of creative people can be recalled by the acronym PRINCE. This stands for playfulness, resilience, imagination, novelty, curiosity and energy. Many famous creative people show symptoms of extreme personality disorders such as schizoid, histrionic, narcissistic and manic depressive.

The DISC Personal Profile System attempts to measure a creativity quotient in people under dominance, influence, steadiness and conscientiousness. It claims to be the oldest, most validated personal assessment tool for creativity. Thinking style preferences include the inventive style and the evaluating style. Optimistic and confident people think more positively, flexibly and creatively. Men and women are equally creative.

Creativity is the ability that develops over the course of the human lifespan. This is despite the fact that some people might consider themselves too old to be creative. In all walks of life people can be creative into old age including scientists, artists, politicians, entertainers and writers.

The diffusion of innovation curve is a predictive tool used in marketing suggesting how fast different types of consumers adopt a new product. The types of customers are called innovators, early adopters, early majority, late majority and laggards. The range is from those people who take up innovations quickly to those who adopt a wait and see strategy.

Education lays a good foundation for creativity. An individual must have knowledge of a specific field of study to engage in problem solving related to that field, and make a creative contribution to that domain. As well as having plenty of initiative entrepreneurs must have knowledge and experience in their chosen business endeavours if they want to be successful.

References and Bibliography

Alder, Harry. (2002). *CQ Boost Your Creative Intelligence*. Kogan Page, London.

Allen, Frederick E. (2012). 'The Zen at the Heart of Steve Jobs' Genius'. Forbes.com. 20/3/2012. P53.

Amabile, Teresa M. (1998). 'How To Kill Creativity'. *Harvard Business Review*. Sept-Oct 1998.

Amabile, Teresa M. (2008). 'Creativity and the Role of The Leader'. *Harvard Business Review*. Vo. 86. Issue 10. P100-109.

Anderson, Joseph V. (1992). 'Weirder than fiction: the reality and myths of creativity'. *Academy of Management Executive*. Vol. 6. No. 4.

Andriopoulos, Constantine. (2001). 'Determinants of organisational creativity: a literature review'. *Management Decision*. Vol.39. Issue 10. Pp834-841

Appleyard, Bryan. (2011). 'End of the genius era'. *New Statesman*. 31/10/2011. Vol.140. Issue 5077. P22-25.

Baer, Markus. (2012). 'Putting Creativity To Work: The Implementation Of Creative Ideas In Organisations'. *Academy of Management Journal*. Vol.55. No 5.

Baker, Diane F. (2012). 'To "Catch the Sparkling Glow:" A Canvas for Creativity in the Management Classroom'. *Academy of Management Learning & Education*. Vol. 11. No.4. pp704-721

Bankert, Michelle. (2013). 'Problem Solved'. *Quality*. January 2013.

Barnes, Russ. (2003). 'Creativity Delivers Growth in the Aging Brain: A new medical model'. *Focus*. Vol. 15. No. 1. Jan-Feb 2003.

Barrett, Sam. (2006). 'Think Inside The Box'. *Employee Benefits*. February 2006.

Berkun, Scott. (2010). *The Myths of Innovation*. O'Reilly Media Inc. Sebastopol.

Bluestein, Adam. (2013). 'You're Not That Innovative (And That's Okay)'. Inc. Sept. 2013. Vol. 35. Issue 7. P109-114.

Borowsky, George. (1994). 'What colour is your hat?' *Executive Report*. Sept. 94. Vol.13. Issue 1. P6.

Bower, Bruce. (2005). 'Possible Worlds'. *Science News*. 26/3/2005. Vol. 167. Issue 13. P200-202

Breen, Bill. (2004). 'The 6 Myths of Creativity'. *Fast Company*. Issue 89. P75-78.

Bronson, Po. (2010). 'The Creativity Crises'. *Newsweek*. Vol. 156. Issue 3. P44-49. 19/7/2010

Business Wire. (2012). 'Study Reveals Global Creativity Gap'. 23 April 2012

Carroll, Jim. (2009). 'Keep those ideas coming'. *CAmagazine*, March 2009.

Ceserani, Jonne. (2009). 'An innovator's toolkit'. *Training Journal*. November 2009.

Cetindamar, Dilek & Gunsel, Ayse. (2012). 'Measuring the Creativity of a City: A Proposal and an Application'. *European Planning Studies*, Vol. 20. No. 8. August 2012.

Cohen, Gene (2000). 'Creativity and Aging'. *GIA Reader*. Vol. 11. No 2. (Fall 2000)

Cox, David. (2013). *Creative Thinking for Dummies*. Wiley, Chichester.

Coyne, Kevin P, Clifford. Patricia Gorman & Dye, Renee. (2007). 'Breakthrough Thinking from Inside the Box'. *Harvard Business Review*. December 2007.

Clark, Regina M. (2012). 'Innovate or Perish'. *Business NM Magazine*. May 2012.

Crail, Mark. (2006). 'Fresh Ideas From The Floor'. *Personnel Today*. 20/6/2006. P30-31.

Csikszentmihalyi, Mihaly. (1997). 'Happiness and creativity, Going with the flow'. *Futurist*. 9/1/1997. Vol. 31. Issue 5. P8.

David, Nicola. (2014). 'Bionic ears: let's hear for cochlear implants…' *Observer*, Sunday, 16 March 2014.

De Bono, Edward. (1985). *Six Thinking Hats*. Penguin Books. London.

Denison, Daniel; Ko, Ia; Kotrba, Lindsey & Nieminen, Levi. (2013). 'Drive an Innovative Culture'. *Chief Learning Officer*. June 2013.

Desrochers, Pierre & Leppala, Samule. (2011). 'Creative Cities and Regions: The Case for Local Economic Diversity'. *Creativity & Innovation Management*. Vol. 20. No. 1.

Deutschman, Alan. (2004). 'The Fabric of Creativity'. *Fast Company*. Issue 89. P54-62. 12/1/2004.

Dickey, Christopher. (2013). 'Let's Talk About Sleep'. *Daily Beast*. 13/9/2013

Edelson, Sharon. (2014). 'Drexler Sounds Off On Creativity'. *WWD Women's Wear Daily*. 29/1/2014. Vol. 207. Issue 19. P1.

Falooni, John G. (2008). 'Absurd or genius?' *Mechanical Engineering*. March 2008. Vol. 130. Issue 3. P4

Fey, Victor & Rivin, Eugene. (1996). 'TRIZ: A New Approach to Innovative Engineering & Problem Solving'. *Target*. Vol. 12. No. 4. Pp7-13.

Fobes, Richard. (1996). 'Creative Problem Solving. A way to forecast and create a better future'. *The Futurist*. Jan-Feb 1996.

Fora, Carlin. (2009). 'Everyday Creativity'. Psychology Today. Nov/Dec 2009.

Foster, Jack. (1996). *How To Get Ideas*. Berrett-Koehler Publishers. San Francisco.

Fillis, Ian. (2010). 'The Role Of Creativity In Entrepreneurship'. *Journal of Enterprising Culture*. Vol. 18. No 1. March 2010.

Finn, Bridget. (2005). 'Brainstorming for Better Brainstorming'. *Business 2.0*. April 2005. Vol. 6. Issue 3. P109-114.

Firestien, Roger L & Kumiega, Kenneth J. (1994). 'Using a Formula for Creativity to Yield Organisational Quality Improvement'. *National Productivity Review* Autumn 1994.

Fisher, James R. (2000). 'The Need For Lateral Thinking In The New Century'. *National Productivity Review*. Spring 2000.

Fisher, Richard. (2012). 'Dream a little dream'. *New Scientist*. 16/6/2012. Vol. 214. Issue 2869. P34-37.

Florida, Richard & Goodnight, Jim. (2005). 'Managing for Creativity'. *Harvard Business Review*. July-August 2005.

Florida, Richard. (2004). 'America's Looming Creativity Crisis'. *Harvard Business Review*. October 2004.

Freedman, Michael. (2010). 'Nature is the Model Factory'. *Newsweek* (Atlantic Edition). 6/7/2010. Vol. 155. Issue 23. P7.

Freundlich, August L & Shively, John A. (2006). 'Creativity and the exceptional aging artist'. *Clinical Interventions in Aging* 2006: 1(2) 197-200.

Freyne, Patrick. (2014). 'Design for life'. *The Irish Times Magazine*, June 21, 2014

Friedman, Ron. (2013). 'Motivation is Contagious'. *Psychology Today*. March/April 2013. Vol.46. Issue 2. P50-51.

Furnham, Adrian. (2000). 'The Brainstorming Myth'. *Business Strategy Review*. Vol. 11. Issue 4. Pp21-28.

Gagliardi, Mary. (2008). 'Working smarter – your innovation planning checklist'. *Canadian Plastics*. Sept 2008.

Galenson, David W. (2007) 'Wisdom and Creativity in Old Age: Lessons from the impressionists'. *National Bureau of Economic Research*, Cambridge, MA. NBER Working Paper Series 13190.

Gallos, Joan V. (2009). 'Creativity forums: learning from the lives of extraordinary leaders'. *Organisation Management Journal*. Vol. 6. P 76-88.

Gamez. George. (1996). *Creativity. How to Catch Lightning in a Bottle*. Peak Publications, Los Angeles.

Glausiusz, Josie. 'Devoted to Distraction'. *Psychology Today*. March/April 2009

Goleman, D & Kaufmann, P (1992). 'The art of creativity'. *Psychology Today*. March 1992, Vol. 25. Issue 2. P40.

Greenwald, John (2003). 'Scientists Gather Inspiration from Nature'. *NJBIZ* 15 August 2005.

Gregory, Annie. (2012). 'The ideas factory'. *Works Management*. April 2012.

Gryskiewicz, Stanley S. (2000). 'Cashing in on creativity at work'. *Psychology Today*. 9/1/2000. Vol. 33. Issue 5. P62.

Groth, John C & Peters, John. (1999). 'What Blocks Creativity? A Managerial Perspective'. *Creativity and Innovation Management*. Vol. 8. No. 3. Sept. 1999.

Hadazy, Adam. (2013). 'Flapping Airplane Wings'. *Discover*. March 2013. Vol. 34. Issue 2. P16.

Hagel, Jack. (2013). 'Five Skills That Distinguish Innovators'. *Journal of Accountancy*. July 2013. Vol. 216. Issue 1. P22-23.

Hare, Jenny. (2011). *Unlock Your Creativity*. Hodder Education, London.

Hesline. Peter A. (2009) 'Better than brainstorming? Potential contextual boundary conditions to brainwriting for idea generation in organisations'. *Journal of Occupational and Organisational Psychology*. Vol. 82. P129-145.

Hiam, Alexander. (1998). '9 obstacles to creativity-and how you can remove them'. *Futurist*. 1/10/1998. Vol. 32. Issue 7. P30.

Hill, Bernd. (2005). 'Goal Setting Through Contradiction Analysis in the Bionics-Oriented Construction Process'. *Creativity and Innovation Management*. Vol. 14. No. 1. March 2005

Honigsbaum, Mark. (2013). 'The future of robotics: in a transhuman world, the disabled will be the ones without prosthetic limbs...' *Observer*, Sunday 18 June 2013.

Hughes, David G. (2003). 'Add Creativity to Your Decision Processes'. *The Journal for Quality & Participation*. Summer 2003.

Huppke, Rex. (2013). 'A relaxed mind good for us'. *McClatchy-Tribune Collection*. 26/10/2013

Isaacson, Andy. (2008). 'Engineering by Nature'. *Popular Mechanics*. Oct 2008. Vol. 185. Issue 10. P46-49.

Isaksen, Scott. (2013). 'Put Creativity in Concrete'. *Credit Union Management*. August 2013.

Isen, Alice M. (2006). 'Happily Ever After'. *Money*. June 2006. Vol. 35. Issue 6. P28.

Jakobson, Leo. (2012). 'Looking for the Big Picture'. *Successful Meetings*. Nov 2012. Vol.61. Issue 11. P38-41.

Johansson, Frans. (2013). 'How to Seize Opportunity'. *Management Today*. February 2013.

Kaufman, Scott Barry. (2013. 'The Real Neuroscience of Creativity'. *Scientific American*. 19 August 2013.

Kelley, Tom & Kelley, David (2012). 'Reclaim Your Creative Confidence'. *Harvard Business Review*. December 2012. Vol. 90. Issue 12. P115-118.

Kelley, Tom & Kelly, David. (2013). *Creative Confidence. Unleasing The Creative Potential Within Us All*. William Collins, London.

Khandwalla, Pradip N. (2006). 'Tools for Enhancing Innovativeness in Enterprises'. *The Journal of Decision Makers*. Vol. 31. No.1. January – March 2006.

Kotz, Deborah. (2012). 'How to Unleash Your Genius'. *US News Digital Weekly*. 17/2/2012. Vol. 4. Issue 7. P23.

LeBoeuf, Michael. (1980). *Creative Thinking. How to generate ideas and turn them into successful reality.* Piatkus, London.

Lehrer, Jonah. (2008). 'The Eureka Hunt'. *The New Yorker*. 28 July 2008.

Lehrer, Jonah. (2012). *Imagine How Creativity Works*. Canongate, Edinburgh.

Lemley, Mark. 'The Myth Of The Sole Inventor'. *Michigan Law Review*. March 2012. Vol.110: 709

Lehrer, Jonah. (2012). 'How To Be Creative'. *The Wall Street Journal*. 12 March 2012.

Leslie, Ian. (2014). *Curious. The Desire to Know & Why Your Future Depends on it*. Quercus Editions Ltd. London.

Lewis, Gareth. (2012). *Outstanding Creativity*. Hodder Education, London.

Lizotte, Ken. (1998). 'A Creative State of Mind'. *Management Review*. May 1998.

Lodato, Franco. (2005). 'The Nature of Design'. *Design Management Review*. Winter 2005.

Lovewell, Debbie. (2003). 'Recipe For Success'. *Employee Benefits*. October 2003.

Lucey. John Dr. (2009). 'Staff Suggestion Schemes'. *Management Services*, Winter 2009.

Lumsdaine, Edward; & Lumsdaine, Monika. (1995). 'Creative Problem Solving. Thinking Skills For A Changing World'. *McGraw-Hill International Edition*. Singapore.

Malechki, Edward J. (2010). 'Global Knowledge and Creativity: New Challenges for Firms and Regions'. *Regional Studies*. Vol. 44.8. pp1033-1052

Mann, Darrell. (2001). 'An Introduction to TRIZ: The Theory of Inventive Problem Solving'. *Creativity and Innovation Management*. Vol.10. No.2. June 2001.

McFadzean, Elspeth. (2001). 'Critical factor for enhancing creativity'. *Strategic Change*. August 2001.

Meikle, James. (2014). 'Man gets bionic hand with sense of touch nine years after accident'. *Guardian*, Wednesday, 5 February 2014.

Meinert, Dori (2012). 'Social Rejection May Fuel Creativity'. *HR Magazine*, October 2012.

Michalko, Michael. (2003). 'From Bright Idea to Right Ideas. Capturing the Creative Spark'. *The Futurist*. September-October 2003.

Milman, Oliver. (2013). 'Bionic eye promises vision for the blind'. *The Guardian*, Friday, 7 June 2013.

Morris, Michael W. & Leung, Kwok. (2010). 'Creativity East and West: Perspectives and Parallels'. *Management and Organisation Review*. 6:3. P313-327.

Morris, Steven. (2009). 'Sport-loving student took minutes to adapt to bionic hand'. *The Guardian*, Monday, 19 January 2009.

Moukheiber, Zina. (2005). 'Genius for Hire'. *Forbes*. 25/4/2005. Vol. 175. Issue 9. P74-77.

Nissing, Nick. (2007). 'Would You Buy A Purple Orange'. *Research Technology Management*. May - June 2007.

O'Dwyer, David. (2014). 'Google puts technology at the wheel'. *Irish Times*, 31/4/2014

Oliverio, Alberto. (2008). 'Brain and Creativity'. *Progress of Theoretical Physics* Supplement. No 173.

Parv, Valerie. (1995). *The Idea Factory. A guide to more creative thinking and writing*. Allen & Unwin, St Leonards, NSW.

Patterson, Fiona & Zibarras, Lara. (2009). 'Creative problem-solving at work'. *General Practice Update*. June 2009. Vol. 2. Issue 8. P48-51

Paul, Anne Murphy. (2011). 'The Uses And Abuses Of Optimism (and Pessimism)'. *Psychology Today*. Vol. 44. Issue 6. P56-63.

Phillips, Helen. (2004). 'The genius machine'. *New Scientist*. Vol. 182. Issue, 2441. P30-33.

Pink, Daniel. (2008). 'Do the Right Thing'. *People Management*. 4/3/2008. Vol. 14. Issue 7. P34-38

Pollack, Ted. (1995). 'Mind your own business'. *Supervision*. Jan 1995. Vol. 56. Issue 1. P21.

Puccio, Gerard J; Firestien, Roger L; Coyle, Christina & Masucci, Cristina. (2006). 'A Review of the Effectiveness of CPS Training: A Focus on Workplace Issues'. *Creativity and Innovation Management*. Vol.15. No. 1.

Puccio, Gerard & Grivas, Chris. (2009). 'Examining the Relationship between Personality Traits and Creativity Styles'. *Creativity and Innovation Management*. Vol. 18. No.4.

Rowe, Alan J. (2004). *Creative Intelligence. Discovering the Innovative Potential in Ourselves and Others*. Pearson Prentice Hall, New Jersey.

Saltzman, Joel. (2005). '12 Tips to Creative Problem Solving'. *Small Meetings Guide.*

Sample, Ian. (2013). 'Soldier controls bionic arm using power of thought'. *The Guardian*. Wednesday, 11 December 2013.

Schnitzer, Erika. (2010). 'Natural inspiration'. *Multi-Housing News*. Vol. 45. Issue 3. P38-39.

Schweizer, Tanja Sophie. (2006). 'The Psychology of Novelty-Seeking, Creativity and Innovation: Neurocognitive Aspects

Within a Work-Psychological Perspective'. *Creativity and Innovation Management*. Vol. 15. No. 2.

Seelig, Tina. (2012). *Ingenius. A Crash Course on Creativity*. Hay House, New York.

Sexton, John. (2012). 'A Measure Of The Creativity Of A Nation Is How Well It Works With Those Beyond Its Borders'. *Scientific American*. Oct 2012. Vol. 307. Issue 4. P36-40.

Shalley, Christina E & Gilson, Lucy L. (2004). 'What leaders need to know: a review of social and contextual factors that can foster or hinder creativity'. *The Leadership Quarterly* 15. Pp33-53.

Shalley, Christina E; Zhou, Jing & Oldham, Greg R. (2004). 'The Effects of Personal and Contextual Characteristics on Creativity: Where Should We Go from Here?' *Journal of Management*. 30(6). Pp933-958.

Simonton, Dean Keith & Ting, Shing-Shiang. (2010). 'Creativity in Eastern and Western Civilizations: The Lessons of Historiometry'. *Management and Organisation Review*. 6:3, 329-350.

Springen, Karen & Seibert, Sam. (2005). 'Artful Aging'. *Newsweek*. Vol. 145. Issue. 6. P45-48.

Spector, Bertram I. (1996). 'Metaphor of International Negotiation'. *International Negotiation* 1: 1-9.

Sprigman, Christopher; Rausiala, Kal; Beilock, Sian; Gray, Peter (2013). 'The Enemies of Invention'. *Psychology Today*. June 2013. Vol. 46. Issue 3. P78-86

Srinivasan, Shiva Kumar. (2007). 'Drucker: On Learning (to Learn) Management'. *The Journal of Decision Makers*. Volume 32. No 4. December 2007

Steele, John & Murray, Mike. (2004). 'Creating, supporting and sustaining a culture of innovation'. *Engineering, Construction and Architectural Management*. Vol. 11. Issue 5. Pp 316-322.

Sternberg, Robert J; O'Hara, Linda A; & Lubart, Todd I. (1997). 'Creativity as Investment'. *California Management Review*. Vol. 40. No. 1. Fall 1997

Stickgold, Robert. (2009). 'The Simplest Way to Reboot Your Brain'. *Harvard Business Review*. Oct 2009. Vol. 87. Issue 10. P36

Taylor, Ross. (2013). *Creativity At Work. Supercharge your brain and make your ideas stick.* Kogan Page, London.

Thompson, Leigh. (2003). 'Improving the creativity of organisational work groups'. *Academy of Management Executive*. Vol. 17. No. 1.

Underwood, Anne. (2005). 'Nature's Design Workshop'. *Newsweek*. 26/9/2/2005. Vol. 146. Issue 13. P55.

Underwood, Ryan. (2014). 'Science of the Creative Mind'. *INC*. February 2014

Valenzuela, Peter. (2012). 'Apply Creativity to Health Care: Learning from Innovative Companies'. *Physician Executive Journal*. September/October 2012.

Vella, Matt. (2008). 'Using Nature as a Design Guide'. *Business Week Online*. 2/12/2008. P14.

Vygotsky, Lev Semenovich (2004). 'Imagination and Creativity in Childhood'. *Journal of Russian and East European Psychology*. Vol. 42. No 1. Jan-Feb 2004. pp7-97

Wade, Jamie. (2008). 'Cash for cost-saving ideas'. *Australian Mining*. Vol. 100/3. March 2008.

Walker, David. (2004). 'Five ways to kill a great idea'. *EBF* Issue 18. Summer 2004.

Wallendorf, Melanie. (1997). 'Breaking Out of Boxes, Creativity, Community, and Culture'. *Advances in Consumer Research*. Vol. 24.

Walton, Andre P. (2003). 'The impact of interpersonal factors on creativity'. *International Journal of Entrepreneurial Behaviour & Research*. Vol. 9. Issue 4. Pp146-162.

Watters, Ethan. (2007). 'Product Design, Nature's Way'. *Business 2.0*. June 2007. Vol.8, Issue 5. P86-92.

Weiss, W. H. (2002). 'Demonstrating Creativity and Innovation'. *The American Salesman*. February 2002.

Whitlock, Gary. (2011). *Nurturing Creativity Through Cognitive Design Therapy*. The Design Management Institute.

Wolff, Jurgen. (2012). *Creativity Now. Get inspired, create ideas and make them happen!* Pearson Education Ltd, Harlow.

Wright, Howard. (2012). *100 Great Innovation Ideas from leading companies around the world*. Marshall Cavendish Business. London

Web sites:

www.mindtools.com/pages/article/newCT_92.htm

http://en.wikipedia.org/wiki/TRIZ

http://www.neiu.edu/~ourgift/Archives/SallyReis/Creativityand Womenarticle2.htm 'Towards a Theory of Creativity in Diverse Creative Women' by Sally M. Reis, University of Connecticut.

http://personal.ashland.edu/~jpiirto/why_are_there_so_few.htm 'Why Are There So Few? (Creative Women: Visual Artists, Mathematicians, Scientists, Musicians)' By Jane Piirto 2000.

INDEX